The Romantic Prison

Moritz von Schwind,
"The Prisoner's Dream" (1836).
Munich Schackgalerie

THE
ROMANTIC
PRISON
The French Tradition

VICTOR BROMBERT

PRINCETON UNIVERSITY PRESS
Princeton, New Jersey

ALSO BY VICTOR BROMBERT

The Criticism of T.S. Eliot
Stendhal et la voie oblique
The Intellectual Hero
The Novels of Flaubert
Stendhal: Fiction and the Themes of Freedom
Flaubert par lui-même

NOTE: Originally published as *La Prison romantique*, Paris: José Corti, 1975.
English text by the author.
Some sections of this book appeared in an earlier form in *Revue des Sciences
Humaines*, January-March 1965; *Yale French Studies*, 38, 1967; *Novel*, 1969;
Symposium, XXIII, 1969; *Revue d'Histoire Littéraire de la France*, March-April
1971; *L'Arc*, 57, 1974; *Critique*, November 1974.

To Beth
To Henri Peyre

Contents

I. Perspectives

‖ I ‖

Introduction:
The Prison Dream

The prisoner is a great dreamer.—Dostoevsky

*. . . this eternal image of the cell, always recurring in the
poets' songs . . .* —Albert Béguin

Prison haunts our civilization. Object of fear, it is also a subject of poetic reverie. The prison wish does exist. The image
of immurement is essentially ambivalent in the Western tradition. Prison walls confine the "culprit," victimize the innocent, affirm the power of society.[1] But they also, it would
seem, protect poetic meditation and religious fervor. The
prisoner's cell and the monastic cell look strangely alike.

Poets in particular, as Albert Béguin remarked, are taken
with the prison image. Is this because they have been frequent
inmates of jails, ever since jails have existed? Béguin suggests
a deeper reason: the poet sings of freedom. Between his vocation and the prisoner's fate there appears to be "a natural and
substantial bond, a significant affinity."[2] For the freedom in
question is of the mind; it can be attained only through withdrawal into the self. It is the turbulence of life that the poet—a
"spiritual anarchist"—comes to view as exile or captivity.

Romanticism, especially in France, has endowed the prison
symbol with unusual prestige. This is not to deny that grim
jails—real and metaphoric—served to bring out themes of terror and oppression; that images of labyrinths, undergrounds,
traps, buried secrets, crushing covers, and asphyxiating encir-
clements provided the symbolic décor for a tragic awareness.
The motif of the gloomy prison became insistent toward the
end of the 18th century, in large part for political and ideological reasons. The symbolic value attributed to the Bastille and
other state prisons viewed as tyrannical constructs, the

nightmarish architectural perspectives in the famous "Prigioni" etchings of Piranesi, the cruel fantasies of the Marquis de Sade conceived in prison and projected into further enclosed spaces, the setting of Gothic novels in dungeons, vaults, and oubliettes—all this can tell us a great deal about the structures of the Romantic imagination, and the favored dialectical tensions between oppression and the dream of freedom, between fate and revolt, between the awareness of the finite and the longing for infinity.

The link between enclosure and inner freedom is at the heart of the Romantic sensibility. The title of Stendhal's novel, *La Chartreuse de Parme*, has puzzled many a reader, not merely because Parma is without a charterhouse, but because not even a fictional charterhouse appears in the novel's field of vision. It is clear, however, that the charterhouse in question is really none other than the Farnese Tower—in other words, the prison-fortress. The title thus proposes the central metaphor, as well as the parable of a fear translated into a blessing. The link between enclosure and spirituality is unmistakable. Paul Jacob, one of the strangest figures of the period, noted in his preface to Saintine's *Picciola*—the story of a disbeliever who regains his faith while in jail—that the prisoner in his dungeon and the monk in his cell are "eternal sources of reverie and meditation."[3]

Fictional metaphors and social problems overlap. The monastic model is explicitly brought to bear on utopian penology. Prison reform, very much debated since the end of the 18th century, became a burning issue under the Restoration. The controversy, which was to reach fever pitch under the July Monarchy, centered on the question of the cellular prison régime. Was the cell a redemptive punishment? Tocqueville and Beaumont travelled to the United States to observe and compare the model penitentiaries in Philadelphia and Auburn. Which was preferable, the cenobitic or the anchoritic system? One thing was clear: the monastic model seemed the pattern for the future. In 1838, Léon Faucher (*De la Réforme des prisons*, p. 180) came to the conclusion that the original inspiration for prison punishment (hence the word

"penitentiary"!) was monastic existence, "voluntary penitence." In 1847, the International Penitentiary Congress pronounced itself in favor of solitary confinement.[4] Isolation in
the cell was to be redemptive, regenerative. Salvation and re-
habilitation were increasingly viewed as dependent on the
privacy of the cell. *Punitur ne pecatur*: a prison historian
somewhat ironically recalls this formula, after reminding his
readers that it was the French Revolution, destroyer of the
Bastille, which elevated prison to the dignity of rational
punishment.[5]

The monastic prison image is reflected in the popular imagination. Prison inmates themselves seem aware of the
metaphor. A recent survey by the politically activist GIP
(Groupe d'Information sur les Prisons) quotes a prisoner in
the "model" prison of Fleury Mérogis: "No complaints about
the cells. They're not very big, but they're clean. They're a
little like a monk's cell" (*ça fait un peu cellule de moine*).[6] The
underlying shuttle or reversibility of images is profoundly re-
vealed in a book that has left its imprint on generations of
readers. Dantès, the hero-prisoner of *Le Comte de Monte-
Cristo*, is fated to be reborn and liberated in the cell occupied
by the monastic figure of Father Faria. The prisoner-monk
and the monk-prisoner: the two images converge in
Alexandre Dumas' novel.

The place of enclosure and suffering is also conceived of as
the protected and protective space, the locus of reverie and
freedom. Our tradition is rich in tales that transmute sequestration into a symbol of security. *Securum carcer facit*. The
motto is developed in lines that go back to the 17th century:

> *Celui qui le premier m'osta la liberté*
> *Me mit en sureté:*
> *De sa grace je suis hors de prise et de crainte.*

> (He who first took away my freedom
> Put me in safety:
> Thanks to him, I am beyond reach and fear.)[7]

But, even earlier, folklore, legends, fairy tales, the tradition of

romance, provide variations on the theme of protective custody. The motif occurs repeatedly in Renaissance epics. The
magician Atlantes builds an enchanted castle to lock up his
favorite hero Rogero, the better to shield him from danger.
Merlin renders similar service in the Arthurian legend. Psychoanalysis has since confirmed the yearning for the enclosed
space, the latent fear of the threatening outside. Agoraphobia
is a recognizable symptom. Constriction is not necessarily a
feared condition. Bertram D. Lewin, in *The Psychoanalysis of
Elation*, suggests that the idea of the closed space corresponds
not to an anxiety phantasm but to a phantasm of safety.

But with the safety dream goes the dream of freedom
through transcendence. The spirit wills itself stronger than
prison bars.

> Stone Walls do not a Prison make,
> Nor Iron bars a Cage . . .

writes the poet Richard Lovelace, who sings of the victory of
the prisoner's mind over suffering:

> Tryumph in your Bonds and Paines,
> And daunce to th' Musick of your Chaines.

It is in the same spirit that Byron conjures up the figure of the
poet-prisoner Tasso to extol the tragic liberation through
confinement. The "wings" of the mind make it possible to
soar beyond oppressive walls:

> For I have battled with mine agony,
> And made me wings wherewith to overfly
> The narrow surface of my dungeon wall.

Heine's famous epigram is apposite: "The love of freedom is a
prison flower" (*Die Freiheitsliebe ist eine Kerkerblume*). In this
perspective, the characteristic Romantic figure of the
convict—the *forçat*—acquires a special meaning. Larger even
than the figure of revolt (Balzac's convict Vautrin) looms the
figure of salvation (Hugo's convict Jean Valjean). For, in its
mythic dimension, the carceral imagery implies the presence
of a threshhold, the possibility of a passage, an initiation—a

passage from the inside to the beyond, from isolation to communion, from punishment and suffering to redemption, from sadness to that profound and mysterious joy which poets such as Hugo associate with the eternal secret of human bondage.

The prison fear and the prison dream have been powerful literary themes. But never, it would seem, have they so persistently pressed themselves on the writer's imagination as during the 19th century. History and politics are no doubt largely responsible. The arbitrary arrests (*lettres de cachet*) and the state prisons of the Ancien Régime, the symbolism of the Bastille and of its epic fall, the revolutionary jails, the political detentions throughout Metternich's Europe, the shadow of the Spielberg, where Silvio Pellico and other victims languished, the police repressions of popular uprisings—all conspired to dramatize and poetize the prison image. This pervasive prison concern explains in part why the 19th-century sensibility was incapable of separating moral indignation from poetic vision. The ambivalence was to be vividly illustrated, toward the end of the century, in the fictional biography of the revolutionary socialist Louis Auguste Blanqui. Gustave Geffroy's *L'Enfermé* (*The Captive*) is a documentary novel on the strange destiny of this political activist whose prison vocation made him live out his own fiction. For Blanqui, the *enfermé*, viewed himself as determined by literary models: the Mont-Saint-Michel fortress, where he and other inmates became fascinated with the prison fate of Silvio Pellico, is repeatedly referred to as the "French Spielberg"; his "cup of bitterness" makes of him, in his own eyes, a "Job" and a victim of "Dante's hell"; the spiritual "freedom" discovered in jail becomes so precious to him that, having returned to "free life," he reconstructs his own cell. "Prison followed the man, reconstituted itself around him by his own volition, no matter where he was."[8]

The Romantic imagination exploits the dramatic potential of sequestration and exile. But the importance of the carceral

themes is clearly prefigured in the literature of the 18th century. The nightmarish locales of the Gothic novel indicate a
yearning for the irrationality of depths and labyrinthine constriction. Their oneiric structures are graphically confirmed in
Piranesi's imaginary prisons, his *carceri d'invenzione*.[9] These
dizzying descents to the underground, these crushing stone
constructs, appear again in many a Romantic text. But it is
not fortuitous if the taste for Piranesi and for Sade's rape
scenes (always in situations of confinement) corresponds historically to the growing dream of political freedom and individual dignity.[10] The 18th century is known to be the age of
"reason"; but it is also—especially as the century comes to a
close—an age that delighted in horror, and was fascinated by
all the manifestations of coercion. The obsession with walls,
crypts, forced religious vocations, inquisistional procedures,
parallels the beginnings of a revolt against arbitrariness.

Imaginary plight and real plight reflect each other. Events
were to confirm the latent sense of anguish. Many families, at
this turning point of history, underwent the harrowing experience of imprisonment. It was in prison that André Chénier
composed some of his most powerful poems. The new century added further distress. For the young Hugo, as for the
young Vigny, the word "prison" was to retain a grim resonance. The fall of Napoleon plunged Europe into a renewed
fear of political detentions. If the image of the Bastille, after
1815, continued to function as a symbol, this is because it had
come to mean more than itself. This Bastille metaphor was
clearly understood as a meaningful anachronism: the prisons
of post-Napoleonic, reactionary Europe were being denounced obliquely. Michelet, for whom the Bastille myth
was a lasting inspiration, diagnosed the anachronism. He
knew full well that, from the Spielberg to Siberia, Europe
was covered with prisons more terrible than the destroyed
Bastille. Casanova, who had been detained in the infamous
Piombi of Venice, knew it too: "I have seen at the Spielberg,
in Moravia, prisons far more gruesome. . . ."[11] It is against
this political background that one must assess the prestige of

Casanova, Cellini, Sade, Baron von der Trenck, Latude, Linguet, Pellico, Andryane, as well as many other prison heroes past and present.

Certain favorite themes might also explain the intense interest of Romantic writers in the prison image: tragic beauty of solitude, glorification of the individual and concern for the problem of identity, existential anguish (Freud was later to insist on the relation between *Angst* and *angustiae*), spatio-temporal motifs (*arrested* prison time viewed as an utopian atemporality), exaltation of the rebellious outlaw who indicts society as a prison and himself becomes the hero of a double drama of fall and redemption, pride in any punishment under the dual aegis of Prometheus-Lucifer.

The *topoi*, or commonplaces, of prison literature can also be listed: the sordid cell and the hospitable cell, the cruelty of jailors (but also the presence of the "good" jailor), glimpses of the landscape and of the sky, the contrast between the ugliness of the "inside" and the supposed splendor of the surrounding scenery, prisons within the prison (the image of the iron mask), the insanity of the captive, the inscriptions in the stone, the symbolism of the wall as an invitation to transcendence. If even the most atrocious jail can be transformed into a mediating space where consciousness learns to love despair and takes full possession of itself, it is no doubt because —as Gaston Bachelard put it—man is a "great dreamer of locks."[12] Even man's consolatory prison activities, as repeatedly presented in Romantic literature, betray the urge to exploit creatively the possibilities of concentration and expansion. On the one hand, mental prowess and experimentation (geometric progressions formulated without help of paper, imaginary chess games); on the other hand, an outward reach, love at a distance (often for the jailor's daughter), conversations with the beloved (in fairy tales the beloved may be changed into a bird!), a movement of the mind toward the *outside* which makes the prisoner reinvent communication. For the "other" remains a presence. Hence the obsession with writing, secret alphabets, tappings on the walls, underground communications.

Two opposing and simultaneous movements can here be followed: the one toward an inner center (a search for identity, knowledge, the operations of memory); the other toward a transcending outside which corresponds to the joys of the imagination and the *ecstasy* of spiritual escape. Intimacy with the elusive self is the aim of the first movement, the quest within. Essentially unheroic, the movement toward the internal cell of meditation corresponds to a nocturnal lyricism, to a quest for authenticity which, at its extreme point, tolerates no histrionics, leaves no room for any pose. Novalis speaks of the mysterious road that leads to this interior region. The most diverse texts, in our literary tradition, confirm this association of the prisoner's descent into the self with the quest for a personal truth, the quest for an original identity. Robinson Crusoe is an exemplary figure: on his prison-island, he is quick to create further limits within limits; he builds a fortification, he erects walls, not merely to ward off danger, but to *surround himself*, to confine himself—and thus to *define* himself. Rousseau, on another island, dreams of living for the rest of his life as a happy prisoner. In one of the basic texts for an understanding of Romanticism—the fifth "Promenade" in the *Rêveries* (where the Bastille image occurs in association with the very notion of reverie)—Rousseau describes his happy stay on the island of Saint Pierre, and expresses the desire to see the island refuge become for him a "prison perpetuelle." The key words (*circonscrite, enfermé, asile, confiné*) all suggest an interiorization of the prison image which corresponds to the sense of almost God-like self-sufficiency (this state in which *"on se suffit à soi-même comme Dieu"*), and points to the central metaphor of Rousseauistic solipsism: *". . . ce séjour isolé où je m'étais enlacé de moi-même . . ."* (this isolated abode where I did entwine with myself . . .).

But as Albert Béguin observed—precisely in talking about Novalis—the inward movement implies a glance toward what lies beyond, an ascent, an expansion.[13] Neither the island nor the narrowest of cells represents an obstacle, in metaphoric terms, to the dynamics of escape. A wall asks to be scaled. The eye seeks the chink, measures the distance. The mind is carried through space. Nothing appears more constant than the notion of freedom associated with the cell—freedom, as it were, from the imperatives of time and space. Poets repeatedly sing of this *utopia* and of this *atemporality*.

> There were no stars, no earth, no time

writes Byron in the admirable ninth stanza of *The Prisoner of Chillon*, entirely based on a series of negative constructions. To which Tristan Corbière, in a poem ironically entitled *Libertà—A la Cellule IV bis (prison royale de Gênes)*, seems to provide an echo:

> *Plus de jours, plus de nuits. . . .*

What is involved is an affirmation of tragic elation and dauntlessness. In Schiller's *Die Raüber*, not exactly the setting of a happy imprisonment, it is in the darkest dungeon that the dream of freedom penetrates "like lightning in the night" (. . . *wie ein Blitz in der Nacht*).

It is of course perfectly logical that the dynamics of escape (and escapism) should affirm themselves most powerfully within the context of captivity. Balzac evokes the *art* of convicts who know how to conceive and execute masterful schemes. Escape becomes a challenge to human ingeniousness. Nineteenth-century readers were likely to appreciate Benvenuto Cellini's defiant advice to his jailors ("*guardatemi bene*"—"lock me up well"), for he promised that he would do all he could to escape. (Pope Paul III, ex-virtuoso of prison escape, had spoken of Cellini's feat admiringly as a "*maravigliosa cosa.*") The 19th century rediscovers Cellini. And Romantic literature is crowded with its own virtuoso jail-breakers: in the works of Stendhal, Alexandre Dumas, and above all Victor Hugo, who describes with relish the "muscle science" of convicts and the "incredible art" of rising perpendicularly.

Hugo, as we shall see, does not merely praise the unusual skill in fabricating escape instruments of precision ("There are Benvenuto Cellinis in the penitentiary"); he sees in any man fired by the frightful thirst for liberty an "inspired" dreamer struggling toward the "sublime."[14]

The darkest dream of freedom, in the Gothic novel particularly, carries an otherworldly intentionality. Clare, in *The Monk*, evokes with rapture the "glorious sunbeams." But this spiritualized yearning for escape also appears in works far removed from the Gothic, or even Romantic, tradition. Jack London, in a prison novel entitled *Star Rover*, partly a documented denunciation of torture and human degradation in California penitentiaries, invents a prisoner-hero who, through a process of mental concentration and self-hypnosis, attains a temporal and spiritual freedom that allows him, at will, to "leave" not only his cell, but his era and the limits of this world. The levitation-ascent leads to a walk "among the stars." The confrontation with anguish and nothingness in a prison setting, the tête-à-tête with ultimate fear, are of course recurrent motifs fully exploited in the Existentialist tradition. Leonid Andreyev, in *The Seven Who Were Hanged*, pungently conveys the sense of absurdity as the prisoner, awaiting execution, views the most ordinary objects and gestures with a feeling of terror and incongruity. Yet even Andreyev's protagonist, from within the cellular limits symbolizing the limits of his existence, experiences the "divine spectacle" of walls that vanish, of time and space that are destroyed, leaving him with the impression that he is in the presence of a "supreme being."

The link between visible loss and secret victory underlies the prison theme. It is not unrelated to the Christian notion of lost paradise and *felix culpa*. Robinson Crusoe, very much in favor with the Romantics, is once again exemplary, as he declares never to have been happier than in his "forsaken solitary condition," and gives thanks to God for having there opened his eyes and provided cause "to praise Him for dungeons and prisons."[15] Simone Weil, in our time, has given the

Christian paradox its deeper resonance, stressing the dialectics of *absence* and *presence* ("One must therefore love that which does not exist") and suggesting that the relation of man to God is dependent on a barrier. The knocking against the wall becomes a metaphysical symbol. "Every separation is a bond."[16] This religious thematization of the prison image confirms its metaphysical power. *The Imitation of Christ* teaches indeed that he who will cherish his cell will find peace. Western literature provides countless illustrations of the salvational virtue of the prison cell. Mary Stuart, in Schiller's play, comes to consider her prison as fitting for the visit of the celestial messenger who will show her the way to eternal freedom. Dimitri, in *The Brothers Karamazov*, declares that one cannot exist in prison without God. He discovers that a "new man" has risen up in him as he confronts the peeling walls that enclose him.

A wide range of mediating and stereotyped images links the dream-prisoner to what lies beyond the symbolic walls: windows, hills, clouds, birds—even water. The image of the bird seems favored, perhaps because it lends itself to a fundamental ambiguity. For the bird, in its free flight, brings to mind the cage from which it might have escaped, the cage that awaits it, the cage that it perhaps regrets. If indeed the quest for spiritual freedom and the redemptive thrust carry toward an elsewhere, a reverse impulse tends toward the still center, toward another form of release, a deliverance from the causal world of phenomena. It is at this still center, this still point of the turning world, that the hidden secret, the ineffable treasure, the perception of the *numen*, are to be found. Enclosure becomes the warrant of perfect fulfillment. It allows the constricted spirit to leave behind what Villiers de L'Isle-Adam calls the "*geôle du monde*," the worldly jail, and to escape from the world of Becoming.[17]

The dream of the happy prison defies the worldly jail. How else is one to interpret King Lear's elation, toward the end of the play, at the thought of imprisonment together with Cordelia? "Come, let's away to prison"—he seems almost impatient to be locked up. How is one to explain this impatience and hint of joy? Is it battle fatigue (he has indeed incurred the worst!); is it mental derangement; is it despair? All is lost, to be sure—but Cordelia has been found. In twelve intensely suggestive lines, Shakespeare indicates the reason for this unexpected delight. For father and daughter, so Lear hopes, prison will be an enchanted cage. Indeed like "birds i'the cage" they will be able to sing their poem of love, forgiveness and innocence:

> So we'll live,
> And pray, and sing, and tell old tales, and laugh
> At gilded butterflies.

In this cage they will feel freed from life's snares and servitudes; they will—so the old king dreams—be endowed with superior vision and glimpse the mystery of things "as if [they] were God's spies."

The idea that prison can be the locus of spiritual freedom and revelation is not merely a dream of mad, sinned-against kings. A similar notion determines Benvenuto Cellini, in his *Vita*, to write a chapter in praise of incarceration (*In Lode di detta prigione*) and to insist—he the fiery adventurer-artist—on the spiritual initiation he underwent in jail.

> *Chi vuol saper quant'è il valor de dio,*
> *e quant' un uomo a quel ben si assomiglia,*
> *convien che stie'n prigione, al parer mio.*

Similar effusions inspire the famous *Le Mie Prigioni* by Silvio Pellico, the Milanese liberal who experienced years of "hard prison" (*carcere duro*) in Metternich's political prison, the Spielberg. There were those who loudly deplored his Christian lyricism, discovered in jail, as a weakness. But the unusual success of Pellico's book (in France alone there were five translations during the first year after publication in 1833) suggests that its tone and message had immense appeal. Pellico insists on the rediscovered light; he copies with deep emotion the edifying graffiti on his prison walls (*Benedico la prigone*); he glorifies suffering. A century and a half later, his name is still revered by another famous political prisoner, Solzhenitsyn. The author of *The Gulag Archipelago* indeed sums up the prison theme: "It has been known for many centuries that prison causes the profound rebirth of a human being. The examples are innumerable—such as that of Silvio Pellico." And Solzhenitsyn adds, as his own testament to the future: ". . . I turn back to the years of my imprisonment and say, sometimes to the astonishment of those about me: '*Bless you, prison!*' "[18]

The rebirth in question implies the redemptive powers of imagination. Repressed freedom and poetic inventiveness are intimately related. This would explain the specific prestige of the sequestered artist. Tasso in jail continues to be a subject of inspiration for other poets. The enclosed space is also the locus of artistic creativity.

We return to the figure of the writer. If indeed poets experience an affinity for the world of walls, bars, and locks, it is because it reflects the image of their own condition. Leopardi, in the imaginary dialogue between Tasso and his own *genio familiare* exalts sequestration because it rejuvenates the soul (*ringiovanisce l'animo*) and galvanizes the imagination—the *virtu di favellare*.[19] Gérard de Nerval imagines the jailor as eternally jealous of the prisoner's dreams. Tristan Corbière is more explicit still; in his poem on liberty-in-jail, he proclaims the lyric joy of the prisoner-poet singing about the inspiration of (and to) his happy cage:

> —*Moi: jamais je n'ai chanté*
> *Que pour toi, dans ta cage,*
> *Cage de la gaité.*[20]

The joyous confinement is here clearly associated with the creative act. It is also viewed as a sanctuary.

> *Prison, sûre conquête*
> *Où le poète est roi!*

Metaphor implies reversibility and the negation of literal meaning. The abhorred prison becomes a holy place. "A prison is a sacred asylum," affirms one of the characters in Pétrus Borel's *Madame Putiphar*. And Byron, whose *Prisoner of Chillon* explains in the final stanza that "These heavy walls to [him] have grown/ A hermitage," writes even more directly in the *Sonnet on Chillon* (referring to "the eternal spirit of the chainless mind"):

> Chillon! thy prison is a holy place,
> And thy sad floor an altar. . . .

But the figurative sense is also convertible. Poetry *becomes* prison, just as the mind (more specifically the skull) becomes the substitute for the abstract notion of closed space. Hugo provides rich examples of this interiorization of enclosure. The *noir cerveau* of Piranesi in the poem *Les Mages* prepares for the metaphor of the brain–jail (*crâne-cachot*) where the spider suspends its web. What the brain of the poet holds locked up preciously is nothing less than the infinite dimension of poetry and the secret of the world. "Un poète est un monde enfermé dans un homme" (A poet is a world locked up in a human being).

This internalized prison space is not merely the trope for the writer; it is the metaphor of the textual space. What is involved is the question of spatial form, and specifically the challenge of formal contraction as well as the fecund struggle with the limits of language. It is surely not a coincidence that Wordsworth, in his defense of the sonnet form, strings together a series of monastic and cellular images:

> Nuns fret not at their convent's narrow room;
> And hermits are contented with their cells . . .

and that Baudelaire, also celebrating the sonnet, develops the notion that constricting forms give a deeper sense of infinity.

But beyond strictly formal problems, beyond the *circumscription of space* (as Edgar Allan Poe put it), there is the emblem of the writer's vocation. Enclosure conjures up the image of the writer-at-work: Balzac's *mansarde féconde*, the "fertile garret"; Vigny and the ivory tower; Stendhal and the *prison de soie*, the "silken prison"; Flaubert and his study with its shutters closed, the Croisset cell where he gets drunk "on ink" (". . . I live like a monk"); Huysmans and the decadent retreat, the *thébaïde raffinée*; Kafka and the life-prison converted into a pleasure castle, a *Lustschloss*; Sartre for whom writing *is* sequestration ("I envied the famous prisoners . . ."). The list is far from complete.

The textual space and the prison space of salvation ultimately merge. Proust, for whom the shuttle operation between reading and writing required the intimacy of the secluded room (the darkened room offering the *spectacle total de l'été*), proposes an image that might well serve as epigraph for this study. This image strikingly telescopes a metaphor of enclosure and a metaphor of survival: the invalid's room transformed into a diluvial ark. "I understood then that Noah never saw the world so clearly as from inside the ark, though it was closed and there was darkness on the earth."[21]

Salvation through enclosure, insight into darkness—the paradox is rooted in the age-old symbol of the captive soul, in the religious notion of a happy captivity. The importance of this paradox for the Romantic imagination will perhaps be better grasped if it is first set in the context of a tradition that Pascal extends and illustrates with his famous image of the prisoner's cell—the *cachot*.

‖ 2 ‖

Pascal's Dungeon

servitude heureuse . . . —Cardinal de Bérulle

THIS PRISON CALLED LIFE

"The natural fate of man is neither to be chained nor to be slaughtered. . . ." Voltaire's indignation is well-known: he despised the sublime misanthropy of Pascal and felt revulsion at the thought of a cosmic dungeon where man-the-sinner awaits his execution. "To consider the universe as a prison, and all men as criminals to be executed, is the idea of a fanatic." The vehement objection to the prisoner status, a corollary of the execration of conventual life, reveals a deep-seated inability to accept resignation. Voltaire held that man was created for action. "Man is made for action, as fire moves upwards and a stone falls."[1] In this respect, the author of *Candide* was a congenital optimist.

The entire "philosophic" movement of the 18th century was of course hostile to monastic values. Diderot's monk, in the *Supplément au Voyage de Bougainville*, admits to the vice of parasitism ("What do you do?"—"Nothing").[2] The sterility and repressiveness of convents and monasteries were to become key themes in Revolutionary literature. Marie Joseph Chénier summed up these reprobations in *Fénelon, ou les Religieuses de Cambrai* (IV/3)

> *Dieu créa les mortels pour s'aimer, pour s'unir:*
> *Ces cloîtres, ces cachots ne sont point son ouvrage;*
> *Dieu fit la liberté, l'homme a fait l'esclavage.*[3]

But Voltaire's anti-Pascalian sallies cannot be dismissed as a blunt rejection of monastic values or as a simple expression of social consciousness. They go to the heart of Pascal's theological and poetic vision.

Cachot is one of Pascal's favorite expressions. It is precisely

this image that he conjures up when he situates man in relation to infinity: "*Ce petit cachot où il se trouve logé, j'entends
l'univers . . .*" (This little cell where he is lodged, I mean the
universe—72).[4] Pascal may have been reminded of Montaigne's image in the *Apologie de Raimond Sebond* ("*Tu ne vois
que l'ordre et la police de ce petit caveau où tu es logé*"), but his uses
of the image, and the metaphysical implications, belong to
another tradition. Montaigne's *caveau* is that of ignorance; the
cachot of Pascal symbolizes man's fall. It connotes tragic
blindness, but also exile and expiation. In one of his characteristic telescopings of concrete and spiritual realities, Pascal
insists on the horror of any confinement and on the notion of
punishment associated with it: ". . . hence prison is such a
horrible torture . . ." (139). And when it comes to summing
up the terror and hopelessness of man's condition, Pascal's
imagination quite naturally projects a concentration-camp
image: "Imagine a number of men in chains, and all of them
condemned to death . . ." (199). A death sentence indeed
hangs over humanity. Pascal's prison image is inseparable
from capital punishment, inseparable from the essence of
man's anguish—mortality.

The *pensée* which follows in the Brunschvicg edition il-
lumines this hallucinatory tableau of a penal colony where all
of mankind awaits in terror the fatal moment. "A man in a
cell, not knowing if his sentence has been pronounced, having
but one hour to find out. . . ." In the face of this imminent
death of the body, it is *contre nature* not to worry about the
survival of the soul. Yet such is the case; and the "supernatural" irresponsibility of man, capable under these circum-
stances of indulging in the frivolities of a card game, is no less
a sign of the hand of God than is his confinement to Death
Row. The word *cachot* becomes for Pascal a shortcut to the
crucial question of salvation or perdition. Pensée 218, which
carries the elliptic title *Cachot*, immediately jumps to the conclusion that there is only one truly important issue in life: "It
is vitally important to know if the soul is mortal or immor-
tal." And nothing better confirms the centrality of the prison

metaphor than the letter to Madame Périer dated April 1,
1648. After referring to fallen man's sense of loss and to his
present "captivity," Pascal asserts that we must consider ourselves as "criminals in a prison filled with the images of our
liberator," but that we are unable to perceive or decipher the
images without Divine help. Blindness in this Jansenist jail is
like a prison within a prison.

Images of enclosure, stated or implicit, give further support, on almost every page, to the central prison metaphor.
Man occupies a "tiny space" in time and in the infinite vast-
ness of the unseen whole. He is *here*, but not there; he is *now*,
and not before or after (205). He is bounded (*borné*) in knowledge, size, and duration (208). He will die alone, immured in
his helpless self (211). The long section 194 presents one of the
densest developments of the detention trope in relation to
temporal and spatial anxiety. The *effroyables espaces* lock man
in; he is tied (*attaché*) to a remote "corner" (*coin*) of the universe; he has been assigned to a tiny spot (*point*) in eternity; all
around him infinity interns him: "*Je ne vois que des infinités de
toutes parts, qui m'enferment comme un atome et comme une ombre.
. . . .*" This imprisonment within space prefigures Hugo's
pest-houses of the infinite: in *Dieu*, the visionary poet has the
experience of being thrown into space and at the same time
into jail (*dans l'espace et pourtant au cachot*). Hugo's impalpable
space prison is filled with Pascalian echoes. But for Hugo,
man becomes the navigator of the twin seas of time and space,
a prowler along the outskirts of heaven: he escapes to freedom. No such liberation occurs in Pascal; no human imagination, no Icarian or Promethean venture, can ever abolish
prison. Just as the soul is thrown (*jetée*) into the body (233), so
man remains in chains; only Divine grace can deliver him.
"*Jésus-Christ n'a fait autre chose qu'apprendre aux hommes . . .
qu'ils étaient esclaves, aveugles. . . ; qu'il fallait qu'il les délivrât
. . .*" (545). In the meantime, man is subject to the fear and
trembling that comes with feeling "abandoned" to himself,
lost in a hidden corner (*recoin*), not knowing who "placed"
him there, and discovering daily that he has awakened on a

"terrifying and deserted island" without the means or the hope of setting himself free (693).

Bossuet also speaks of being relegated to the very far end of the universe (theme of exile) and of the tiny spot we occupy (theme of humility): "How small is the space we occupy in this world!" The blind soul, pent up in the body, moreover seems to love its confinement![5] But how far we are with Bossuet from the terror inspired by Pascal's hidden God, the *Deus absconditus*. For Pascal's is not a banal lesson in submission. His images are forceful because his thought is vehement and perturbing. Between his rhetoric and his perception there is hardly ever a gap. The authentic ring of Pascal's art, in his best fragments, has much to do with this tight correlation. The island metaphor, for instance, is not a mere rhetorical device involving a time-tested symbol of exile; it acquires poetic and psychological concreteness because of the *awakening* to a sense of total deprivation and total disorientation. More lost than a lost child, man is here seen as totally bereft of his bearings. Georges Poulet may stretch analogies somewhat in establishing a parallel between Pascal's *égarement* and Proust's first moment of elemental consciousness upon awakening.[6] But certainly the island image, just as the image of the bed at the beginning of *Combray*, suggests the physical awareness of ignorance: the inability to *situate oneself*. Only Proustian memory, unlike Jansenist grace, comes to the rescue almost immediately.

The high charge of Pascal's prison metaphors accounts for their lasting impact. Malraux certainly had fragment 199 echoing in his mind ("Imagine a number of men in chains . . .") when he described, in *La Condition humaine*, how Kyo and Katov, together with hundreds of other wounded prisoners, wait for torture and for death, to the sinister accompaniment of a locomotive whistle. Even the title of Malraux's novel must be read against Pascal's conclusion to that fragment: "*C'est l'image de la condition des hommes.*" But the real heir to Pascal's carceral vision is not Malraux, whose revolutionary heroes discover that to die is easy if one does not die alone. Pascal's message is radically different: "One will die alone" (211). A truer descendant is Vigny, who was clearly haunted by Pascal's tragic dungeon: "In this prison called life from which we depart one after the other. . . ." This ante-chamber of death is without flowers, without hope. Some of the images are strikingly similar, though transposed in a romantic key. Vigny also conceives of a group of men who *wake up* in jail and who are, inexplicably, taken away forever. Even the association of metaphysical blindness with the term *cachot* can be found in his *Journal d'un poète*.[7] As for the specific terror of the death sentence bound up with the topos of the cell, a long list of more recent writers could also be invoked. With Andreyev and with Sartre this terror, and the accom-panying sense of the "absurd," take on a visceral quality.

But in drawing a writer such as Pascal toward our own concerns, there is the risk of losing sight of the specific tradi-tion within which he conceived his *apologia*. The image of servitude is a classic image of the corrupt and sinful condition of man, and as such a specific symbol in the drama of Chris-tian salvation. (*Est tractus de carcere corporis iste*—is an example of hagiographic style for the act of dying.)[8] The soul, prisoner of the body and of the world: a glance at other 17th-century writers confirms the contemporary vitality of the image. Pas-cal might have found it in the writings of Saint-Cyran, who considered the world as "a true prison with regard to our souls."[9] Bossuet also describes the human soul as utterly cap-tive, led "from captivity to captivity, captive of itself, captive of its body," and all the while ashamed of its servitude. In his famous sermon on death, the soul appears as languishing in-side the body into which it has been "cast." And resurrection is evoked in terms of a freeing from jail: "It is the Prince who opens the prison doors for the miserable captives."[10] Cardinal de Bérulle had earlier developed the basic metaphor in even greater detail. Beyond the usual reference to life as "ser-vitude," he insists on Jesus' own willful "captivity" (in his in-carnation), and on the "honor" He thus bestows on man by assuming his prisoner-condition. The cross, symbol of this chosen suffering, thus functions as the symbol of a specific

human powerlessness as well as of the divine attribute of
Jesus: the power to transmute slavery into freedom.[11]

The prison image serves in fact as a soteriological symbol
well before the Christian era. The Pythagorean word-play on
soma and *sema* (body and tomb) expresses the concept of a
dualistic rift between flesh and spirit which was later to be
elaborated in the Platonic and neo-Platonic traditions. Pierre
Courcelle, in his study of the Platonic and Christian traditions, points out that Tertullian attributed the body-prison
doctrine specifically to Plato.[12] Plato's cave, in Book VII of
The Republic, where chained men see only shadows of reality,
represents spiritual blindness to the deeper truths, and human
propensity for error. Man's imprisonment in a world of
senses, and his longed-for journey upward to the world of
light, constitute a myth that feeds Christian lore. And although Saint Augustine himself rejected the Platonic notion
of the soul's imprisonment in the body (*De Vera religione*,
XXXVI), the main Christian tradition, from Saint Paul and the
Church Fathers down to the theologians of the 17th century,
stresses the servitude of sin and the incarceration of the *anima*.
Saint Paul expressly referred to the soul as pent up in the
body, as brought into captivity "to the law of sin" ("who
shall deliver me from the body of this death?"—Romans VII:
23-25). Origen viewed the soul's union with the body as a
downfall, the body being a "prison" where the soul expiates
unknown sins while waiting for "deliverance."[13] The image
of spiritual incarceration was to become so habitual in Western thought that an important tradition of love poetry, often
inverting or perverting religious values, came to exploit conventional relationships between the unhappy soul and the corrupt body. Tristan l'Hermite, in Pascal's time, writing about
his "incomparable Sylvie," sings of the physical allurement of
her "*belle prison.*"

HAPPY SERVITUDE

The image of the *cachot* could not possibly surprise Pascal's
contemporaries. What, then, is his originality in elaborating

the basic metaphor of incarceration? The answer may well be found in his dialectical bent of mind. Pascal's letter to his sister of April 1648 contains a statement which deserves to be quoted in full. It follows the Pauline idea of sins that "hold us shrouded amidst corporeal and terrestrial things," and the suggestion that this bondage might be benificent:

> Thus we must consider ourselves as criminals in a prison filled with images of their liberator and with the necessary instructions for coming out of bondage. But it must be admitted that one cannot perceive these holy characters without supernatural light. For as all things speak of God to those who know Him, and reveal Him to all those who love Him, so these same things hide Him to those who do not know Him.[14]

The underlying thought is doubly involved. On the one hand, the life prison is seen as a place of retribution. But it is also a potentially blissful place, filled with the precious signs of a Divine presence. Yet it is a hidden presence, which further stresses man's blindness and impotence without his Saviour. Punishment and redemption are thus intimately wedded in the prison metaphor. The image of the *cachot* serves the Pascalian theme of duplicity.

This duplicity finds its expression in two radically opposed yet complementary views of solitude. For solitude is a form of torture. Prison is a horrible *supplice* and aloneness an unbearable condition. Pascal goes so far as to affirm that the pleasure of solitude is "incomprehensible" (139). But solitude is also salutary: in fact, a means of salvation. ("*O solitudo sola beatitudo,*" in the words of Saint Bernard.) The prison cell is easily converted into a monastic cell. Theologically this elating imprisonment refers back to the concept of the *felix culpa*, the happy fall.

In psychological terms, the fear of immobility is linked to the yearning for repose. Some of Pascal's sharpest observations on human nature deal with this basic contradiction. "Nothing is so unbearable to man as to be completely at rest"

(131). The *plein repos* is terrifying: it brings out man's forlorn-
ness, his emptiness, his nothingness. In fact, total repose is the
negation of life. "Our nature is in movement; full repose is
death" (129). That is why man finds it so difficult to remain
alone in his room. Baudelaire was to speak in very similar
terms of the "*grande maladie de l'horreur du domicile.*"[15] The
important section 139 takes on its full meaning once this
fidgetiness of man is set against the potential happiness to be
found in confinement: ". . . all the unhappiness of man comes
from one thing: his not being able to remain quietly in a
room." The unhappiness (*malheur*) in question is both negative and positive: negative, because man is miserable in solitude; positive, because stasis could mean access to forgotten
joys.

Forgotten indeed, or rather dimly recalled and secretly
yearned for. The image of perfect repose is an image not only
of death but of paradisiacal bliss. The obverse of claustral terror is the felicity of enclosure. Immobility is here linked with
intimations of man's state before the fall, with vestigial
memories of the greatness of man's *première nature*. It is an involuntary reminder as well as a prefiguration of eternity. The
two apparently irreconcilable "urges" (Pascal says "in-
stincts") are admirably brought into interplay in fragment
139:

> They have a secret urge that drives them to seek distrac-
> tion and occupation on the outside, which comes from
> resentment against their continuous misery. Yet they
> have another secret urge, a vestige of the greatness of our
> original state, which teaches them that happiness can in
> fact only be found in repose, not in agitation. And out of
> these two contrary urges there arises in them a vague
> project, hidden to their own view deep in their soul,
> which induces them to seek repose through agitation . . .

This vague project (*projet confus*), almost subconsciously
formed within man, points toward his secret intuition of immortality. Léon Brunschvicg very acutely points out, in his

chapter on Pascal's solitude, that aloneness is for Pascal the discovery of *reality* in the context of eternity.[16] Life, for the true Christian, should be a preparation for death. One will die alone. Hence one should live "as though one were alone . . ." (*Il faut faire comme si on était seul . . .* —211).

Pascal's *cachot* is thus, paradoxically, a happy prison. Man is in fetters, no doubt; and he has only one hour left before he will learn of the irrevocable judgment. But he does have this one hour to obtain its repeal (*pour le faire révoquer*—200). The place of internment, provided the signs on the wall are deciphered, becomes the place of hope and salvation. A world of meaning separates voluntary from involuntary submission and enchainment. What difference, asks Pascal, is there between a soldier's obedience and the obedience of a Carthusian monk? Both are "subordinate." But the soldier, who always hopes to command someday, deludes himself; even captains and princes are slaves. The monk, on the other hand, attains quietude and release through the very vow of obedience (539).

The monastic reference is not fortuitous. It points to the good use of life—that is, of suffering—for penance and prayer. The *Prière pour demander à Dieu le bon usage des maladies* is surely one of Pascal's most revealing texts. Thanking God for his "salutary suffering," Pascal states the wish to make of his life a "continuous penitence." Illness—is not life itself a disease?—foreshadows death and thus teaches man how to detach himself from life in order to be *alone* with God.[17]

Western literature is partial to the theme of imprisonment as spiritual rebirth. Benvenuto Cellini, locked up in the Castel Sant'Angelo, writes poetry in praise of incarceration. Silvio Pellico conceives his prison memoirs *Le Mie Prigioni* as a "high testimonial to the boundless charity of the Lord."[18] As for Dostoevsky, he repeatedly blesses purgatorial imprisonment. The variations on this theme, before and after Pascal, are endless. Pascal's originality is that he most sharply related it to a dialectical tension fundamental both to Christian theology and to human nature as he understood it. Faced with the alternative of seeking happiness in ourselves (as the Stoic tradition recommends) or seeking it outside us, Pascal answers with characteristic ambiguity: "Happiness is neither outside us nor in us; it is in God, outside and inside us" (465).

Inside *and* outside. Lucien Goldmann suggests that Pascal situates man at an equal distance from extremes, while demanding their merger: an "unbearable and tragic" situation, since this immobility means not equilibrium but the permanent tension of a *mobilité immobile*. Fortunat Strowski had already noted that for Pascal *inquiétude* and *tranquillité* implied a dialectical tension, that "on the same subjects, *yes* and *no* are both true."[19] It is hardly necessary to invoke Hegel. Sound Christian doctrine fully accounts for the paradox of a dynamic immobility, just as it accounts for the even more crucial paradox of a separation which is in fact a spiritual reunion. Cardinal de Bérulle once again sheds helpful light. His argument, in the *Elévation sur Sainte Madeleine*, runs about as follows. Just as God's holiness separates Him from all that is outside Him, no matter how perfect, so all "rare and holy souls" achieve a state of *separation* in relation to everything that is not God, the better to "adhere" to Him. This separation, a kind of death-in-life, marks in fact a true accession to the life-giving state of grace (*la grâce excellente qui donne la vie à ces âmes*). Solitude is here viewed as a Divine attribute, and the vocation of reclusion as a release from spiritual exile. The paradox sums up the theme of happy captivity. The blessed souls penetrate into a *solitude intérieure et divine* which imitates the solitude and *singularity* of God.[20]

This plenitude of emptiness corresponds to the wall-less nature of the Pascalian *cachot*. Georges Poulet speaks of the horror of the unpalpable, of the terror which this spaceless jail inspires.[21] Terror and horror there are, to be sure; and so are disarray and metaphysical dizziness. But the absence of walls signifies the omnipresence of God. Infinity may lock man in (. . . *ces effroyables espaces de l'univers qui m'enferment*—194); but this metaphysical walling-in is less a devalorization of the finite than a glorification of infinity. A prisoner of space—that is indeed Pascal's predicament and ultimate comfort: "*Je ne vois que des infinités de toutes parts, qui m'enferment comme un atome . . .*" (194). The obverse of the prison terror is the top-ophilic and geometric reassurance that any point in space is always infinitely distant from either infinity or nothingness. *Pensée* 232 ("Infinite movement, the point that fills everything . . .") must be set against the pages of "De l'esprit géome-trique." Pascal never ceased believing that the two infinites between which man is situated are necessarily related to each other (*relatifs l'un à l'autre.*)[22] Gaston Bachelard's observation in *La Poétique de l'espace* applies excellently to Pascal: "Im-mensity is the movement of immobile man."[23] Too much has been made of Pascal's empyreal panic. The fright and the ob-session are real enough. But confinement in space implies a reassuring cosmic order.

Such reassurance is achieved at the cost of a steady, almost unbearable, tension. The Pascalian "consolation" is devoid of personal guarantees. The power of Pascal's *cachot* metaphor is that it imposes a metaphysical urgency that offers no respite and little assurance of reprieve: ". . . having but one hour left . . ." (200). Its ultimate efficacy is that it suggests Divine pres-ence almost exclusively in terms of a felt *absence*. Pascal's God—the severe and lonely "God of Abraham"—is also the Hidden God.

A comparative study of these themes of solitude and ab-sence at different periods might help bring out the singular features of "classical" tensions, in particular the conflicting exigencies of metaphysical and worldly concerns. Pascal's tragic prison imagery is founded on the psychological as-sumption that solitude is unbearable to man (". . . *le plaisir de la solitude est une chose incompréhensible*"—139). But Mon-taigne, for instance, would not have accepted the premise. For him the pleasures of solitude were not only "comprehensi-ble"; they were highly desirable. His freedom he sought in his own *arrière-boutique*. Yet precisely because he felt that man was endowed with a *natural* gift for self-sufficiency (*une large faculté à nous entretenir à part*), he experienced no specific ten-sion.[24] All in Montaigne tends toward reconciliation rather than tragic discordance. In the essay "Des Trois commerces," the equilibrium is made explicit. "I find that it is in no way more bearable always to be alone than never to be so."

Romanticism was to bestow a special value on solitude. J. G. Zimmerman's much-read and much-translated *Solitude* seems to echo Pascal: rare is the person who knows how "to retire to his own room." But the moral and psychological context is altogether different. Isolation in meditative retirement is presented by Zimmerman as valuable only insofar as it is ultimately beneficial to mankind. The "inactivity" of monastic solitude is denounced as a "sterile tranquility." Social usefulness is seen as the foremost criterion. In fact, the reader is repeatedly warned against the dangerous excesses of retirement. Zimmerman, a true son of the 18th century, preaches a "wise and active solitude." He moreover recommends sharing this idyllic solitude with an "amiable female."[25] As for Rousseau, his solipsistic joys are such that all tension resolves itself into mystic harmony. Far from dreaming of an escape from his island, he imagines instead, as we have seen, a happy life imprisonment that would detach him from worldly cares. The Bastille is specifically evoked as the ideal setting for reverie. Nothing, in fact, could be more alien to the Pascalian vision than this island immobility in which all movement comes from within us, in which man becomes sufficient to himself, like God. Nothing could be more removed from the classical sense of tragedy than this surrender to a "sufficient, perfect and full happiness" which leaves in the soul no void to be filled.[26]

The image of the Bastille is not fortuitous. Various social, political, and cultural factors, at the dawn of the Romantic era, confirm the figurative value of the prison fortress. The metaphor revives old fears and old dreams. The myth of the Bastille, as we shall see in the next chapter, implies a perspective different from, and complementary to, Pascal's metaphysical *cachot*. The two images, taken together, allow us better to grasp the Romantic dialectics of the prison theme.

‖ 3 ‖
The Myth of
the Bastille

. . . la Bastille archétype *est éternelle, ses copies seules
ont des époques.*—Apologie de la Bastille

*Vaincre à Austerlitz, c'est grand; prendre la Bastille,
c'est immense.*—Victor Hugo

THE PRESTIGE OF WALLS

The taking of the Bastille, according to Alexandre Dumas, was an "act of faith." For Pétrus Borel, the exploit was a holy rebellion. "When a people rebels against its divinities, its first act is to break their images. . . ."[1] In the popular iconography, the Bastille continues to represent the tyranny of the Ancien Régime. Its seizure by the Parisian populace, celebrated yearly by street dancing, fireworks, and three days of festivities, conjures up the image of political freedom. French schools, the political parties, bourgeois ideology itself, all carefully cultivated this image and this symbol. Michelet, France's most fervent historian, has consecrated the glory of the fourteenth of July: "Let this great day remain one of the eternal celebrations of mankind." For him, the event had an apocalyptic meaning; it was a last judgment *(jugement dernier)* of the past. Michelet read the event as the chief symbol of the Revolution. In his introduction to the *Histoire de la Révolution Française*, he devotes a special section to the Bastille. He goes further still, placing the entire work under the sign of the fortress. He sees the epic of the rue Saint-Antoine as his rhapsodic inspiration: "All of Europe went delirious with the taking of the Bastille. . . . Unforgettable days! Who am I to have narrated them? I do not know, I shall never know how I was able to reproduce them. . . . My heart was enlarged with heroic joy, my paper seemed inebriated with tears."[2]

All of Europe went delirious. The reputation of the fortress had long been established: *Die Hölle der Lebendigen*, the living hell, according to the title of a text on the Bastille published in 1719. The European repercussions of the taking of the Bastille were immediate. The Italian poet Alfieri, not usually given to francophilic outbursts, hailed the "great people" of Paris in his ode *Parigi sbastigliato*, and imagined that the revolutionary action took place under the direct supervision of the "beautiful and terrible goddess Liberty." In Russia—"this monstrous Bastille between Europe and Asia"—there were street manifestations, according to quoted witnesses.[3] As for England, Camille Desmoulins reported in the first installment of the chronicle-pamphlet *Révolutions de France et de Brabant* that the taking of the Bastille, in the form of a play, was being constantly re-enacted in London, with the enthusiastic public giving support to the actors in the most dramatic scenes, and then drinking gallons of French wine to the health of the citizens of France.

The Bastille was not only, in the words of André Chénier (who, ironically, came to know revolutionary jails, and later the guillotine), a "tomb of holy liberty"; it represented more specifically the oppression and repression of thought itself. Dumas, who amply documented himself on the traditions and legends of the Bastille, concludes as follows: ". . . during the last hundred years, it was not merely inert matter that was being locked up in the royal fortress, it was thought. Thought exploded the Bastille. . . ."[4] He of course repeated a commonplace. Michelet, paying tribute to the "holy Revolution," explained that the Bastille had been a *"prison de la pensée"*—a prison of intellect.[5] And Michelet was also echoing others, some of whom, like Voltaire, had known the fortress of the Faubourg Saint-Antoine—this "palace of vengeance"—from the inside, and dreamed of its demolition. Many writers had indeed sojourned there, conferring to its walls a quite special prestige. The figure of the marquis de Sade appeared to some as exemplary: his destiny and his somber fictions remain associated with the king's fortress.

Michelet's expression *"la sainte Révolution"* casts light on the mystique of the fourteenth of July. Not that Michelet was responsible for the sacralization. Camille Desmoulins already dreamed of building a "temple of liberty" on the exact place where the Bastille had stood.[6] And before Desmoulins, the popular imagination had conferred a double value on the site and the exploit. A revealing document stresses the solemn, religious associations. The *drame sacré* or *hiérodrame*, entitled *La Prise de la Bastille*, provides as its subtitle: *"Hiérodrame tiré des Livres saints suivi du cantique, en Actions de grace, 'Te Deum Laudamus.'* " A Latin translation faces the French text. A choir sings to the accompaniment of a tocsin, while the siege is going on. The piece comes to a climax as a "total explosion" of the orchestra suggests the storming of the drawbridge.

The Bastille had in fact become archetypal long before novelists, historians, and authors of apocryphal documents metaphorically seized its walls. The ironic *Apologie de la Bastille*, published in 1784 to serve as an answer to Linguet's *Mémoires*, states it explicitly with the bitter remark that the Bastille *is* by divine right: ". . . the archetypal Bastille is eternal; only its copies belong to periods."[7] One of the documents that most powerfully contributed to the creation of a legend, *Mémoires Historiques et Authentiques sur la Bastille*, makes the same point, without irony: the "deadly cells" *(cachots mortifères)* are the symbol of the lasting servitude *(éternel asservissement)* of the French people; the royal prison contains the "symbol of [its] slavery."[8] This symbol, however, transcends national boundaries. The adjective *universel* is no less frequent than *éternel*. Historians and novelists were quick to formulate what was present in the collective consciousness. Dumas felt that it was perfectly useless to describe the Bastille. "It lives as an eternal image. . . ." And Pétrus Borel, the author of *Madame Putiphar*, inspired by Latude in particular, speaks of the Bastille as the "most manifest symbol" of age-old tyranny. But it is once again Michelet who came up with the most striking formulas. He knew that if the Bastille was indeed an archetype, its "copies" could be more atrocious than the model; that the destruction of the model would not abolish the bitter political reality. Hence a tragic awareness of anachronism: "Alas! why spend so much time on demolished prisons. . . ? The world is covered with prisons, from the Spielberg to Siberia, from Spandau to the Mont-Saint-Michel. The world is a prison."[9]

A FIRST-CLASS HOTEL?

The anachronism plays in two directions. Frantz Funck-Brentano, who set out in *Légendes et Archives de la Bastille* to debunk the melodramatic images associated with the royal prison, suggested that it had been a relic of the past long before 1789, that its days were numbered. Were there not projects to demolish it and to raise, on its former site, a monument to the glory of Louis XVI? As early as 1784, the architect Corbet had drafted a *Projet d'une Place Publique à la gloire de Louis XVI*; and in June 1789, M. Davy, counsellor to the king, presented to the Royal Academy of Architecture the project of a column with the king's statue to be erected where the Bastille stood.[10] The idea of demolishing the "monument of despotism" was indeed in the air before the Revolution. There exist curious engravings of that period representing the king with one hand graciously pointing to the high towers of the fortress which workers are in the process of demolishing.[11]

One such print serves as frontispiece to the famous *Mémoires* of Linguet, and represents a statue of Louis XVI standing in the midst of a half-destroyed castle—no doubt a symbolic representation of the Bastille destined to be demolished. The king extends his hand to the liberated prisoners, whose poses express gratitude. A half-line from Voltaire's *Alzire* ("*Soyez libres: vivez*") appears below the print, and on the pedestal of the statue one can read the following inscription: *"A LOUIS XVI—Sur l'Emplacement de la Bas-tille."* In the background there is the famous clock, described by Linguet, with its two enchained figures. The dial is here cracked by a bolt of lightning. In other words, it is an image of a symbolic Bastille destroyed—by the Ancien Régime![12]

The efforts to debunk the horror stories are interesting in themselves. Funck-Brentano and Victorien Sardou (the latter wrote the preface to *Légendes et Archives de la Bastille*) set out to discredit Michelet and Louis Blanc, insisted that the Bastille inflicted a minimum of discomfort, that its prisoners were treated with utmost consideration behind "harmless walls," and that, far from being "martyrs of intellect," men of letters—these "spoiled children of the 18th century" —were only too glad to be imprisoned there in order to medi-tate and write in peace and comfort. The famous iron mask was really a velvet mask! And of the seven prisoners liberated on the fourteenth of July, two were madmen, one a sadist, and four were counterfeiters. Sardou's demystifying verve feeds on paradoxes. In order to cast discredit on the melo-dramatic Bastille invented by the "rancorous" Linguet and the "sharper" Latude, he talks at length of the amusing games indulged in by the prisoner-guests of this *hôtel des gens de lettres* (XVI). As for Funck-Brentano, he sees the *lettre de cachet*— symbol of the king's arbitrary power to incarcerate—as primarily serving the "tranquility of families" by protecting them against profligate children.[13] He also cites the example of Madame de Staal, who claimed that her stay at the Bastille had been the best time of her life. Were there not endless love intrigues! The Bastille, he asseverates, was the gentlest *(la plus douce)* prison of France. Almost a luxury hotel, it would seem—or better, a pleasure castle.

Funck-Brentano and Victorien Sardou have "authorities" to support their assertions. These include not only polemicists such as J. Dussaulx, so provoked by the "fraudulent" *Mémoires* of Linguet that he makes fun of the so-called "cemeteries of human life" and praises the pleasantness and humaneness of the castle,[14] but established historians as well.

François Ravaisson, who discovered in 1840 the Bastille archives hidden at the Arsenal library, plays down the prisoners' complaints ("Renneville's complaints have no credibility"), and insists on the good food, the good care, and the distractions enjoyed by the inmates. In his introduction to the *Archives de la Bastille*, one already finds the image of a resort-Bastille, of a "hotel or first-class bourgeois pension."[15] These deflating commentaries go beyond polemics or objective scholarship. They are evidence of widely spread notions, true and false, that have attained the proportions of a myth.

A LEGEND—A PUBLIC

The abundance of texts about the Bastille published during the last two decades of the 18th century cannot be attributed exclusively to measurable political events. At face value, these publications—some of them historical studies, some of them pamphlets, some both—claim to be "useful." Two collections are exemplary: the already mentioned *Mémoires Historiques et Authentiques sur la Bastille* published in two volumes, in London, and the three volumes entitled *La Bastille Dévoilée ou Recueil de pièces authentiques pour servir à son histoire*. Both collections purport to be historical documents, and both indulge in Revolutionary rhetoric. The *Mémoires Historiques* list almost three hundred prisoners since 1475, with reason (or lack of reason) and duration of their imprisonment, including the unavoidable man of mystery with the iron mask. The thirty-two-year-long incarceration of Count de Lorges is stressed. And the taking of the Bastille is told with details that reappear in numerous later narratives, including novels—a clear proof that the *Mémoires Historiques* had many readers. As for *La Bastille Dévoilée*, its tone is perhaps less dramatic, but equally sentimental. The proceeds of the sales of each installment were destined "to the widows and orphans of the citizens who died as the result of their patriotic zeal"— presumably the families of the victims of July 14. *La Bastille Dévoilée* also lists prisoners (though only since 1663), proclaims the emergence of a new "moral" era ("Thus one could already call our period the twentieth century"—II, 1); and in its description of the taking of the Bastille also comes up with details which are later echoed, with variants, in other studies and in fictional accounts such as Alexandre Dumas' *Ange Pitou*. The editor prides himself on what he claims is a document of unimpeachable historical value, and deprecates other publications on the same subject, such as the *Mémoires Historiques et Authentiques sur la Bastille*, as being of "no interest" and "no usefulness" (VI, 3-4).

There is ample evidence that this rash of texts on the Bastille corresponded to the curiosity of the public, to its taste for revelations and sensationalism. A tradition did in fact already exist: a corpus of prison texts. (Personified prisons at times engage in dialogue, as in the *Dialogue entre le Donjon de Vincennes et la Bastille*.) This tradition implies a rich system of references and allusions. Thus *La Bastille Dévoilée* refers to the famous prisoner Latude, *"le Trenck françois."* (Baron von der Trenck was himself another famous prisoner whose escape from the prison of Glatz, and subsequent sufferings in the prison of Magdeburg, are classics in prison literature.) As for the *Mémoires Historiques et Authentiques*, beside the inevitable reference to the iron mask, they include an important section of Latude's *Mémoires*, as well as Linguet's well-known *Mémoires sur la Bastille*, and Mirabeau's indictment of the Ancien Régime's arbitrariness, *Des Lettres de cachet et des Prisons d'état*, composed some ten years before the Revolution.

The Bastille had indeed become a subject as well as an object of literary "consumption." The expectations of the public, whose appetites are being whetted, are referred to explicitly. In the preface to *La Bastille au Diable* (1790), whose imprecatory epigraph is a parody of lines from *Horace*, the author congratulates himself on his narrative gifts capable of gratifying "the reader avid for details on this horrible vale of all human miseries."[16] This *Bastille au Diable* refers to Voltaire and Diderot, provides a fictional version of the fourteenth of July, repeats the legendary story of the insane old man who was a victim of Madame de Pompadour, indulges

metaphorically in Dante's episode of Ugolino. Despite its
documentary pretense, it is a text inscribed into an already
existent literary tradition. There is nothing surprising, therefore, if the *Mémoires Historiques et Authentiques*, as well as the
texts by Linguet and Latude, lead directly to the novels of
Pétrus Borel, Alexandre Dumas, and Clémence Robert,
whose *Les Martyrs vengés* in fact fictionalizes both Latude and
Linguet.

One can speak of a fashion, even a rhetoric, almost a literary genre. The Bibliothèque Nationale in Paris as well as the
more specialized Bibliothèque Historique de la Ville de Paris
are mines of collections, tracts, pamphlets, dialogues, tales,
poems related to the infamous fortress. Some are facetious
writings, such as the *Anecdote rare et piquante sur la Bastille,
Trouvée parmi les chiffons de la rue Saint-Antoine, avec le titre:
RESPECTEZ LES TROUS*. Others are simply jolly poems
or songs based on well-known airs such as *"l'air de Henri IV"*
or *"l'air des Matelots."*[18] But the majority are serious, fervent
texts. A few are solemn, even pompous, such as *Arx Parisiensis expugnata et Deleta* ("Carmen" in Latin verse!). Many seek
to combine documentation and dramatic effects. Such is the
case of the *Langage des Murs ou des Cachots de la Bastille dévoilant leur secret* and the *Oubliettes retrouvées dans les souterrains de
la Bastille*. Some occurrences or exploits not explicitly situated
in the Bastille are nonetheless derived from the same tradition. *Le Cachot de Beauvais*, given as a "historic fact" in one
act and in prose, carries the spectator to the "realm of the
dead," where citizen Beauvais utters words that point to the
political sacralization of jail: "I swear by my cell, abode of my
glory. . . ."[19]

This literature is heavily loaded, emotionally and historically. A legend implies a temporal dimension. Already in the
17th century, the Bastille casts a threatening shadow. The
playful stanzas of Claude Le Petit (he was burned at the stake,
on the Place de Grève) seek in vain to exorcise the terror
spread by the eight heavy towers of the castle:

> *Il tâche à servir de prison,*
> *S'il ne sert pas de forteresse . . .*

As a literary corpus, the Bastille legend is particularly indebted to two texts of the early 18th century. The escape adventure of the abbé de Bucquoy, which later so delighted Gérard de Nerval, is told by Madame Du Noyer, the author of the *Lettres de deux Dames au sujet de l'abbé de Bucquoy* (1719). The other, more influential, text carries a partially polemical title: *L'Inquisition Françoise ou l'Histoire de la Bastille* by one Constantin de Renneville, who was imprisoned as a spy and claims to describe in detail his eleven years in the Bastille.[20] Renneville's five volumes are of great interest not only because of their aggressive realism (the rot, the toads' slime, the loss of teeth, scurvy and scabies, the tortures, the cruelty of the jailers) but because of their inscription into a whole system of literary and mythological references: Polyphemus' cave, Hades, the Acheron, Pluto, Theseus, Ixion, the Harpies, Orpheus.

The Bastille legend, as Renneville's text makes clear, rests on identifiable symbolic and mythopoetic categories: personification of the edifice ("I held in my bosom famous heroes . . ."); hieratic animal figures (Phalaris' bull); mythological geography ("Tartarus"); symbolism of the Clock introducing into life the eternity of death. At the legend's core there is the reign of secret. In a bitter understatement, Vigny calls the Bastille the "temple of discretion." But it is Renneville who, much earlier, imposed the image, describing the "masked mass" attended by all the prisoners covered with a double or triple veil. (The verb "unveil" recurs insistently in the texts on the Bastille.) The prison doctors, it would seem, had instructions to refer to their patients only by the name of the tower and the floor (for instance: "The top of Basinière spat blood"). More interestingly still, this reign of mystery and silence itself tends to be expressed through archetypal images: ". . . all the JONASES it [the Bastille] regurgitates are compelled to SWEAR that they will never reveal anything. . . ."[21]

Muffled by secrecy are the horrors. Here the legend turns out to be particularly inventive. Beyond the trite brutalities (beatings, floggings, pulling of teeth) and the more refined atrocities described or suggested (traps, turning wheels equipped with razor blades), a nameless zone leaves the worst atrocities to the imagination. Thus Louis Blanc, in a serious historic work, continues to write about the fallen fortress: ". . . horrible trophies were brought back . . . strangely shaped, frightening weapons; devices whose use no one could guess." A legendary history of French kings is pressed into service, in particular of Louis XI, who allegedly conceived the iron cages with enormous chains known as "Fillettes du Roi," and who listened with relish to "the sighs of his victims."[22]

The most striking feature in this elaboration of a legend is, however, the referential and mediational role played by the "belles lettres." Virgil, Plutarch, Seneca, Dante serve to inscribe texts that pretend to be documentary into a cultural system that poetizes and de-realizes them. Mirabeau quotes the famous line from the *Inferno* (*"Lasciate ogni speranza . . ."*) and denounces prison houses by a reference to the *cachot de la faim*—an obvious allusion to the 33rd Canto. He explains in a note: "See the frightening story of count Ugolino. . . ."[23] These mythopoetic tendencies determine rhetorical and stylistic devices. The "national poem" entitled *Prise de la Bastille*, in addition to the inevitable allusions to Dante and to Latude as a "figure out of Plutarch," contains a summary of the legend written in epic alexandrines.

> *On dit . . . mais en tremblant de rompre le silence,*
> *Car soudain d'un endroit un espion s'élance . . .*
> *On dit que ses cachots se perdent sous le sol,*
> *Que la chauve-souris les heurte de son vol,*
> *Que le hideux reptile y séjourne sans cesse,*
> *Que le trépas y glane au sein de la jeunesse,*
> *Que les parois des murs suintent de sang humain,*
> *Que les gémissements y résonnent en vain. . . .*[24]

BEST SELLERS

Ideological themes contribute to the formation of a legend. Long before the days of revolutionary fervor, the prison image functions in the social and political cause. Hatred for inquisitional methods is a key motif in 18th-century literature. At times, the denunciation of injustice covers up a more "subversive" intention. It is not fortuitous that Voltaire, in *Questions sur l'Encyclopédie*, gave credence to the story that the man with the iron mask was none other than the son of Mazarin and Anne d'Autriche, and consequently a compromising elder brother of Louis XIV. The political consequences of this account cast doubt on the legitimacy of the last of the Bourbons.

In another register, the widely read *Dei Delitti e delle pene* (*Essay on Crimes and Punishments*, 1766) by the Italian jurist and economist Cesare Beccaria did much to draw attention to jails and to the acute problems of penology. The name of Beccaria soon became synonymous with indignation and demands for reform. His ideas, which influenced Jeremy Bentham and the Utilitarians, stressed the interdependence of individual liberties. He expressed outrage at the cold-blooded cruelty (*fredda atrocità*) of incarceration. Prison transforms a human being into an object. The secrecy it imposes is a political weapon of despotism ("*il più forte scudo della tirannia*").[25] Beccaria maintained that a prison sentence could be more terrible than death. The tortures of the imagination, greater than physical discomfort, make of imprisonment, without liberation in sight, the worldly equivalent of damnation. Victor Hugo throughout his writings quotes Beccaria's name with veneration.

Mirabeau, inveterate reader and paraphraser of Beccaria, denounces more specifically the arbitrariness of the French state prisons of which he had a taste in Vincennes (for dissoluteness, to be sure, and on his father's legal request!). His own "odious jail" incited him to unveil the internal tyranny of these "houses of suffering." But it is the polemical rather than the autobiographical element that predominates, although the polemical note is constantly heightened by dramatic details and evocations of anguish. Mirabeau's aim is to underline man's "inalienable right" to liberty. He provides a historical survey of carceral cruelty and of the tradition of "sacerdotal despotism." His most telling pages are, however, directly inspired by Beccaria's *Dei Delitti e delle pene*: on the corrupting influence of jails, suffering in cellular solitude, endless exposure to tortures of the imagination, the temporal anguish that comes with the prisoner's ignorance of his fate. Prison is seen as a "mutilation of existence." The bloodlessness of the horror only increases the intensity. Mirabeau's most striking passages exploit a language and an imagery that have already served. M. de Rougemont becomes a symbol of all the jailers (*enfermeurs d'hommes*). As for the turnkey, he is described through lines from Gresset and explicit reference to a literary tradition.

> *Payé pour être terrible,*
> *Et muni d'un coeur de Huron,*
> *Réunit dans son caractère*
> *La triple rigueur de Cerbère,*
> *Et l'âme avare de Caron.*

Even Shakespeare ("the slings and arrows of outrageous fortune") is enlisted.[26]

But the most influential spreaders of clichés are Linguet and Latude. These two "braggards" (*hâbleurs*), as they were characterized by a hostile critic, are almost singly responsible for a series of *topoi*. Latude in particular, accused of being a "conniver" and "charlatan," is also taken to task for having produced a "web of lies."[27] The word "web" could not be better chosen, and acquires here its full metaphoric force. The *Mémoires*, in view of their texture, must be considered as fiction.

Linguet's *Mémoires sur la Bastille et sur la détention de l'auteur* are more specifically an autobiographic prison document. With eloquence, but also with verbosity and pathos (he compares himself with Job), this opportunistic man of letters— lawyer, journalist, pamphleteer—surveys all manner of prisons from antiquity to his own days, only to conclude that nothing more cruel than the Bastille ever existed. This text was influential, no doubt, but less so than Latude's more picturesque revelations, *Le Despotisme dévoilé ou Mémoires de Henri Masers de Latude*, dedicated to Lafayette. Latude recounts the thirty-five years of his imprisonment in various state prisons (but mostly in the Bastille), his epic escapes, his pitiful recaptures, his own hatred as he hopelessly waited for Madame de Pompadour's—the "proud prostitute's"—hatred to relent. These memoirs appeared in several editions; the one published in Amsterdam in 1787, the language of which was more colorful, at times even scatological, was later repudiated by the author. But no matter what the edition, Latude's account of his sufferings and exploits did have something of the appeal of a best seller, and left its mark on the popular imagination. What remained with readers, next to the horror of dark *cachots* and heavy chains, was the pride of working out sensational escapes against overwhelming odds. Latude speaks of the courage and ingeniousness (*génie*) that comes with despair. Together with the accounts by Casanova and Cellini, Latude's text was to become a model for glorious literary escapes.[28]

Latude's literary gifts were less those of imagination than of amplification. He (or his "collaborator" Thiéry) had, however, a sense for the dramatic detail. He vividly describes the "frisking" ceremony upon entrance to the Bastille (known as *"faire l'entrée du prisonnier"*), the secret prison vocabulary (cable drum = Anubis; hole in the floor = Polyphemus; ladder = Jacob), the consoling friendship with pigeons and rats, the patient construction of the escape ladder, the perilous climb through the chimney, the escape and recaptures, the brutality of guards who made him eat by force, the ingenious fabrication of paper and ink. These descriptions are handled with a touch of the novelist, ranging from suspense to pathos, from sentimentality to horror. Recurrent themes are sketched out. Socrates' stature in persecution is seen as a symbol of freedom in the face of any tyranny. And when the prisoner conceives a project for the creation of public granaries to forestall the possibility of famine, it is impossible not to conjure up the archetypal Joseph, brought forth from jail to advise the Pharoah to store food against the catastrophic years ahead. The parallel takes on increased meaning since the king's mistress, Madame de Pompadour, assumes throughout the *Mémoires* the vengeful stance of a Putiphar. It is hardly a coincidence that when Pétrus Borel, half a century later, wrote his novel about the prison sufferings of an innocent young man who refused the advances of Madame de Pompadour—a novel clearly influenced by Camille Desmoulins and by Latude—he entitled it *Madame Putiphar*.

Stendhal, in some curious pages called *"Les gens dont on parle,"* claims that in 1788 Linguet was as much talked about as Voltaire.[29] The impact of his writings must have been considerable, to judge by the violent reaction to his book from hostile quarters. As for Latude, the devoted interest Madame Legros had taken in his fate made his incarceration an emotional issue and a prime subject of conversation. Latude himself, after his liberation, willingly assumed the role of Revolutionary hero. The salon of 1789 displayed his portrait by Vestier with the following inscription:

> *Instruit par ses malheurs et sa captivité*
> *A vaincre des tyrans les efforts et la rage,*
> *Il apprit aux Français comment le vrai courage*
> *Peut conquérir la liberté.*

The sufferings described in these memoirs were indeed proposed as a moral lesson in classrooms. The *Mercure de France* exhorted parents to read the text to their progeny and to use this "sublime work" to teach them how to read.[30] It would seem that copies were officially sent out to all the *départements* of France, together with an edifying miniature model of the Bastille. By 1793, some twenty editions were already out of print. The impact was to be lasting. When Father Faria, in *Le Comte de Monte-Cristo*, lists all the famous escapes, the name of Latude is the only one associated with the Bastille.[31] Latude finally entered the world of myth. The visitors at the 1889 Paris Exposition, which commemorated the taking of the

Bastille, could glimpse in a dark corner of the mini-model of the fortress a bearded old man lying on damp straw, who mumbled incoherent words. The guide explained that it was Latude!

A RESERVOIR OF IMAGES

Pétrus Borel, *enfant terrible* of Romanticism, evokes the Bastille in the following terms:

> At the far end of an old boulevard that once upon a time protected the city, and, gradually surrounded by it, became effeminate in its bosom (in the bosom of the queen of the world) just as happened long ago to Hercules at the feet of Lybia's queen (and much like Hercules stripped of his mass and lion's skin by Omphale);—at the far end of this old boulevard, today very much like a woman singing a lullaby in the sun while spinning her distaff, there was a huge prison of stone. . . .[32]

One may not appreciate the logic of these images, as well as the syntax that almost defies translation; yet the mythic vocabulary is revealing. The literary exploitation of the Bastille goes beyond polemics and ideology. Deeper needs are at work. Mythical over-determination characterizes the Romantic imagination. The referential role of writing, especially since the beginning of the 18th century, is related to proliferating mythological references. Renneville thus assimilates his personal experience to an archetypal experience, with occasional recourse to pictorial models. Captain des Portes, of the Bastille, appears in such a mediated perspective: "He was a horrible man, in the manner Rubens depicted his hangmen when he wanted to give a violent idea [*sanglante idée*] of Christ's Passion. . . ."[33]

This carceral tradition, mythifying the edifice (the evil monster, the devouring bull—Dumas compares the greenish bulk to "fabulous monsters of antiquity covered with scales")[34] ultimately confers on the prison image an uncanny, *sacred* quality. The Bastille, in a dialogue with the Dungeon of

Vincennes, prides itself on having enfolded in its bosom "personages . . . descended from a divine ancestry." The Dungeon in turn speaks of "profanation," of underground cells that must remain inaccessible to daylight, whose fearful abyss must not be measured by "human eyes."[35] This sense of mystery finds support in various mythic categories: history (Caligula, Tiberius, Phalaris, the Inquisition), the biblical tradition (Job, Jericho, Jonas), an underworld topography (Tartarus, the Abyss, caves, Acheron), a full repertory of personages (Ixion, Sisyphus, Hercules, Pluto, Polyphemus, the Harpies, Orpheus, Charon, the Titans), as well as in the specific descents to Hades in Homer and Virgil. *"Facilis descensus Averni"* is the inscription on a frontispiece on which are depicted devils and monsters flying over the Bastille, spitting fire and sulphur. The Virgilian quotation appears side by side with the names of Beelzebub and Astaroth.[36]

Neo-classicism "mythologizes" all too eagerly. The Revolutionary rhetoric at times borders on caricature. Yet the mythic diction and vocabulary associated with the Bastille were to survive neo-classical taste. Beyond the historic event, the Bastille trope remained wedded to a permanent prison theme. On the one hand, as Michelet sadly observed, the world continued to be "covered with jails." But, more important, the carceral images provided a lasting reservoir of metaphors and symbols on which the Romantic imagination could draw with fervor because this objective correlative was perceived within a political context. Source hunters may demonstrate that Pétrus Borel carefully perused certain Bastille texts. But whether he was struck by the contrast between the prisoner's litter and the courtesan's voluptuous sofa upon reading the *Mémoires Historiques et Authentiques sur la Bastille*, whether he owed the idea of the Pompadour-Putiphar to Latude, or found his inspiration for the mad old man in *La Bastille au Diable*—these are but trivial aspects of the question. More far-reaching is the evidence that from the destroyed Bastille, and other jails of the Ancien Régime, there arises a modern prison obsession that mirrors and challenges a society bent on coercing and oppressing.[37]

II. Prison and the Romantic Imagination

‖ 4 ‖

Pétrus Borel:
Prison and the Gothic Tradition

THE VIGOR OF MATURIN

Pétrus Borel, according to Baudelaire, was one of the stars of the "dark romantic sky." Yet in 1859, the year of his death, he was at best remembered as the most eccentric among the eccentric Bousingots.[1] A member of the *petit cénacle* to which Théophile Gautier and Gérard de Nerval also belonged, he was a colorful exponent of "frenetic" literature. He liked to call himself the *lycanthrope*—the wolf-man. *Champavert* (1833) subtitled "*Contes immoraux,*" established him as a specialist in gory tales at a time when charnel-house writing was in fashion. Some of Flaubert's early exercises in literary violence were heavily influenced by these texts. Even as late as 1861, when he was writing *Salammbô*, he had Pétrus Borel in mind as he himself described tortures and disembowelments.[2] Rape and child murder are among the more innocent subjects of Borel.

The *lycanthrope* was half forgotten when Baudelaire wrote his article. One text, however, deserves to be better known. *Madame Putiphar*—Borel's only full-length fiction—appears at first glance less outrageous than *Champavert*. The title itself points in the direction of allegory and myth. It is meant to evoke, not a biblical setting, but that aspect of the Joseph story which deals with temptation, purity, and injustice. The "Madame" in question is Madame de Pompadour, and her Joseph a handsome young Irishman, in political exile, whom she has jailed for life when he dares reject her lascivious advances. This climate of sexual aggression is confirmed in the parallel plot: Deborah, the hero's wife, is raped, first by the husband's colonel, then by "Pharaoh" himself—that is, Louis

XV—who spends lavish sums on his gynaeceum. Sexual aggressiveness, linked to the modalities of political power, appears from the outset over-determined by the symbolism of confinement. The king's gynaeceum brings to Deborah's mind images of state prisons and of convents (I, 249).[3] Eros is a trap. The assault on Patrick's virtue is evoked in terms of "ambush," "snares," "nets," "traps," "noose" (I, 218). The correspondence between libido and tyranny connects the erotically determined first part of the novel and the rest of the book, which is given over to the horrors of jail. An internal logic, not merely the taste for lurid images, requires that desolation and despair be set in the prisoners' underground dungeon.

The story opens with a prefatory poem, an allegorical prologue in which the soul is assailed by three temptations: the world, the cloistered existence, the seduction of Death. In part, this moralistic beginning is a concession to the taste of the time. "Philosophical" considerations frequently surrounded the flimsiest fictional productions, and the theme of metaphysical temptations was popular. Borel's preliminary poem about surrender to life, withdrawal from worldly involvement, and attraction to non-being contains some powerful lines. It has the feverish tone and pungency of some of Baudelaire's finest poetry. And who knows if Flaubert did not find an inspiration for the metaphysical *satyriasis* of his saint Antony in the section of the poem devoted to the obsessive temptations of the cloister (*cloître suborneur*)?

> *Au cloître, écoute moi, tu n'est pas plus idoine*
> *Qu'au monde; crains ses airs de repos mensongers;*
> *Crains les satyriasis affreux de saint Antoine:*
> *Crains les tentations, les remords, les dangers,*
> *Les Assauts de la chair et les chutes de l'âme.*
> *Sous le vent du désert tes désirs flamberont . . .*

Lines such as these would be perfectly at home in *Les Fleurs du Mal*. Baudelaire, in fact, admired this "strange poem" for its intensity and "glittering sonorousness."[4] But there is more to this preliminary poem than sheer virtuosity.[5] It is indeed a thematic overture centering on the antitheses involvement-withdrawal, freedom-oppression, movement-immobility. The cloister, later transmuted into jail, is here a central symbol—both as a positive and negative value, as an expression of fear and of yearning. Cloister and anti-cloister in the prologue point to prison and anti-prison in the novel itself.

Baudelaire was probably more concerned with the dynamics of Borel's imagery than with its thematic significance. Yet in stressing the epic grandeur of some of the scenes—especially the description of "dungeon horrors and tortures" which, he felt, matched the "vigor of Maturin"[6]— he situated Borel's work in a historical and cultural context. The allusion to the Reverend Mr. R. C. Maturin, author of *Melmoth the Wanderer* (1820), suggests that *Madame Putiphar* belongs to the tradition of the Gothic novel. Structurally, there can be no doubt about the central nature of the incarceration theme. Just as the novel deals with a double attempt at seduction in a confined atmosphere (Madame Putiphar vainly provokes the sexual desire of Patrick amidst the snares of her boudoir, Pharaoh-Louis XV succeeds in raping Deborah), so the protagonists, because of their virtue, are arbitrarily jailed, the one in the relatively "happy jail" of Sainte-Marguerite, the other in the fort of Vincennes and later in the Bastille. This prison motif is further stressed by other parallel developments: family and city are viewed as places of captivity (parental tyranny, urban airlessness); Patrick is joined in prison by his friend Fitz-Harris; two separate jails are their places of martyrdom (the repetition suggests the hopelessness of their situation); within their prison they move from a gloomy cell to an even more atrocious cesspool-dungeon, where they are spared neither cloacal horrors nor the tortures of hunger. The vertical descent symbolizes the downward movement toward despair.

This acrid book reads like a compendium of Romantic horrors. The cynical vehemence hides a genuine attraction to pain. Some passages are explicit: ". . . there is in pain a mysterious pleasure [*volupté mystérieuse*] . . . suffering is as savoury as happiness" (II, 180). Shades of the marquis de

Sade? Not only is Patrick, after the storming of the Bastille, interned in Charenton (where Sade died), but there is explicit mention of the marquis as one of the glories of France (ii, 217). Certain gratuitous cruelties (the turnkey dashing out the brains of the prisoners' dog and besmearing Fitz-Harris with his blood) could be taken as a parody of a literary fashion. Evil affirms itself through destructive lechery, social inequities, vengeance, pleasure in human degradation, slow tortures leading to raving madness. Yet the text cannot be reduced to facile parody. We are far from Jules Janin's tongue-in-cheek violence in *L'Ane mort et la Femme guillotinée* (1829), where debauchery, prostitution, murder, macabre elements, sadism and voyeurism in jail, hints of hideous copulations, remain part of a literary game. It is not surprising that Jules Janin, who himself indulged in sensationalism, should have been scandalized by *Madame Putiphar*.[7] The reason is simple: Pétrus Borel was *serious* about the horrors he described. Irony is offset by indignation. "There is not an outrage I represented that did not incense me with genuine anger . . ." (ii, 187).

A DOUBLE TRADITION

Baudelaire's mention of Maturin is indeed apt. It points to a "Gothic" world filled with castles, tyrannical fathers proud of their lineage, dungeons, vaults, pits, cells, underground passages and cloistered anguish, toads, reptiles, haunted locales and violent eroticism. This Gothic tradition has come to be considered a predominantly English specialty. Thus Eino Railo gave *The Haunted Castle* the subtitle "A Study of the Elements of English Romanticism."[8] But the tradition is not limited to England. What is involved is not only a "sub-baroque" for popular consumption, but a collective myth with architectonic fixations, as Maurice Lévy's masterful study amply demonstrates.[9] Illustrations can be adduced from all over Western Europe. Von Gerstenberg and E.T.A. Hoffmann in Germany, Balzac and Victor Hugo in France—to mention but a few—also wrote in this "dark" vein.

The chief exemplars of the Gothic tradition are clearly relevant to a study of Pétrus Borel's novel. Horace Walpole's *The Castle of Otranto* (1764) characteristically centers on a crime that has been committed and not yet avenged. A father-despot, a symbolic race to the bottom of the stairs, the terror of isolation in a "labyrinth of darkness," the grating of rusty door hinges, the theme of treachery—all these acquire archetypal status in Walpole's influential text. Mathew G. Lewis' *The Monk* had perhaps even greater impact, though it tends to empty the Gothic tradition of supernatural elements, stressing the cruel and the macabre. Forced religious vocations, repressive actions, hideous immurements, a sacrilegious rape in a crypt, decomposing bodies, make of this a particularly gruesome work. Some of these elements seem to prefigure the tone and subject of *Madame Putiphar*: the charnel-house material with its repulsive objects, the images of putrefaction, the pestilential air, the atrocities in solitary confinement, the vengeance by a mob. It is quite likely that the poem "Inscription in an Hermitage"

> Let me, O Lord! from life retire
> Unknown each guilty worldly fire,
> Remorseful throb, or loose desire . . .

is echoed in Borel's preliminary lines on the dangerous monastic temptations.

As for Maturin's *Melmoth the Wanderer*, a true "noctuary" of terror and of brainwashing, it points forward directly to the lightless, airless, and timeless world of *Madame Putiphar* ("Terror has no diary"). Especially the second part, "The Tale of the Spaniard"—the account of the immured lovers left to die of hunger, with variations on asphyxiating confinement—shows many affinities with Borel's fiction. Maturin also insists that it is quite possible to become "amateurs in suffering," that even the most delicate of women can feast on "groans and agonies." His characters cross the novel like "pioneers of darkness"; they roam near the "frontiers of hell." The abode of stone ("I awoke *in the darkness of day*" sums up this death-in-life) is here also a setting that suggests

Dantesque suffering. The Ugolino motif is in fact exploited in the story of the lovers ultimately driven to feed on each other's flesh. *"Here is no hope,"* according to the author, should be the inscription on the prison gate.[10]

These allusions to Dante are not fortuitous. The episode of Ugolino, starved to death with his sons and grandsons (*Inferno*, XXXIII), haunts the Romantic imagination. Even the social reformers of the latter part of the 18th century frequently refer to it when challenging current penology. Mirabeau, in discussing Beccaria, quotes Dante and mentions specifically Ugolino's "hunger cell."[11] In that same light, von Gerstenberg's play *Ugolino* (1763) illustrates the often neglected interconnection between myths and psycho-ethical problems in the Gothic tradition: the high tower, Job's trial, Saturn devouring himself, the dream of cellular bliss. "We would have been a world of joy for each other," recalls King Lear's dream of a happy cage. It also speaks of the mystery of innocence profaned.

This interconnection becomes more complex in works such as E.T.A. Hoffmann's fantasy-novel *Die Elixiere des Teufels* (1815-1816) and Victor Hugo's *Notre-Dame de Paris* (1831). Hoffmann's monk Medardus is a spiritual brother of Lewis' monk Ambrosio: his mental *camera obscura*, the duality of his being, the experience of alienation and the loss of identity, solitary confinement leading to madness—all dramatize the duplicity of human nature, the obsessive tête-à-tête with the self as it tries in vain to break out of solipsistic constriction. The affinities of Hugo's Claude Frollo with Lewis' monk are equally striking. Cloistered, "walled in with his books," the evil archdeacon inhabits a cell at the top of the tower. Gothic architecture, grotesque elements, and images of violence underscore the demonic tensions of the novel. Hugo's work, less oneiric than some more typically "gothic" texts, is more powerfully structured in terms of symbols and themes. Human and architectural figures are linked in a common metaphoric network. Quasimodo assumes the shape of his shell, the cathedral: "a strange, symmetrical, unmediated, almost co-substantial coupling of a human being and an edifice." This prison imagery is internalized. Caught in the jail of ugliness, deafness and materiality, Quasimodo's "chained psyche" is doomed to a dark existence "like the prisoners of the Piombi in Venice. . . ."[12]

But no matter how much *Madame Putiphar* may have in common with this Gothic tradition, in particular with the complex valorization of seclusion and labyrinthine passage-ways, it also stands apart in some essential aspects. Pétrus Borel indulges very little in anti-clericalism, and not at all in satanism and the supernatural. Sin, in the theological sense, does not concern him. Nor does the splitting of the personality and the loss of identity. Horror is de-spiritualized; the "haunted castle" has vanished. The reason for these dissimilarities is that two traditions are simultaneously at work in *Madame Putiphar*, and that they have come to merge: on the one hand, the conventions of the *roman noir* and the devices of melodrama; on the other, the themes of a "Revolutionary" literature and the myth of the Bastille. These diverse elements are in fact related more than appears at first glance. Not only are there points of contact between anti-monasticism and the Bastille myth, but it is clear that some of the Gothic novels were directly animated by Revolutionary themes. Thus Lewis probably found the basic inspiration for *The Monk* in the Parisian theater of the Revolution (he was in Paris in 1791), and in particular in Monvel's *Les Victimes cloîtrées*, with its archetypal figure of the lustful, malevolent monk. The Revolutionary theater was rich in oppressive conventual and prison settings. Marie-Joseph Chénier's *Fénelon ou les Religieuses de Cambrai* and Charles Pougens' *Julie, ou la Religieuse de Nismes*—the titles themselves declare the theme of claustration—are characteristic of this fashion. These plays are filled with the harsh noise of heavy keys and ominous locks.[13] The liberation of the victimized nuns parallels the political emancipation from the Ancien Régime of which the Bastille was the oppressive symbol.

The myth of the Bastille is altogether central to *Madame Putiphar*. The novel leads up to a theme of political expiation: the People, glorified as a divinely inspired force (*verge de la*

vertu de Dieu—II, 299), is destined to avenge all the crimes of
the Ancien Régime. Borel's indignation and apocalyptic hope
animates the text. "No! the villains shall not triumph on this
earth!" (II, 252.) The storm of Revolution will sweep away
the abominations of the past. "Patience! The workman will
receive his wages. After the insult comes the vengeance" (II,
107). Yet Pétrus Borel does not exploit the Revolutionary
mystique; political fervor never was his chief inspiration.[14]
The silhouette of the Bastille projects more than a political
shadow. Borel certainly read the memoirs of Latude and Linguet, as well as Camille Desmoulins' *Révolutions de France et de
Brabant*. His Bastille typically also assumes "mythic" charac-
teristics. One penetrates into the "body of the monster," or
more precisely into "the belly of this stone bull" comparable
to the monstrous bull of Phalaris into which victims were
thrown alive (I, 157; II, 275). The king's fortress is compared
to the Laconian cape and cavern, Tenarus, close by the gates
of hell (II, 267). During the siege of the Bastille, the crowd—
the redemptive "people"—is compared to David as he faced
the giant.

The echoes of the Bastille literature are unmistakable.
Deborah, at Sainte-Marguerite, visits the cell of the famous
prisoner with the Iron Mask. The names of important state
prisoners—all inscribed in the conventional prison mar-
tyrology—are mentioned: Count de Thunn, Lenglet-
Dufresnoy, Crébillon, Diderot, Mirabeau, and of course
Latude, who had also been in jail for thirty-five years, a victim of Madame de Pompadour-Putiphar. Borel denounces
her "whorishness" (*putanisme*—II, 8) in terms that closely recall Latude's invectives. And when Patrick explains to his fellow prisoner Fitz-Harris that tyrants expose one to death, but
do not kill (II, 144), he is in fact paraphrasing Mirabeau, who
himself paraphrased Beccaria.[15]

THE SACRED ASYLUM

A prison, one of the victims of the novel explains, is a tomb,
but also a sanctuary, an *asyle sacré* (II, 103)—though not in the

sense of a happy captivity, of which there are many examples in Western literature. We are far here from the prison King Lear extols with the courage of despair, where he hopes, singingly, to glimpse the "mystery of things"; far indeed also from Pomfret Castle, where Richard II, poet of solitude, intends to "people this little world." To be sure, there are lyric elements in *Madame Putiphar*. Deborah's detention in the Mediterranean fortress of Sainte-Marguerite functions as a spiritual retreat. She enjoys a "grandiose" panorama. The governor, a benevolent gentleman of the old school, tells her that she can live "in calm, quiet, and comfort," that she can consider herself "as free as the birds" who build their nests in the walls of the fortress (II, 15). All the *topoi* of the happy jail appear. There is even an allusion to Walpole, according to whom all sensible people would gladly be put away *en sûreté* in Bedlam (II, 15-16).

This idyllic, parallel captivity serves to bring out the horrors of the "real" prison. *Madame Putiphar* hardly belongs to the same tradition as Saintine's *Picciola*, where the prisoner, thanks to the double mediation of a flower and of a woman, accedes to a spiritual realm. Prisons, for Borel, remain atrocious; their reality is not transmuted into beauty. The overwhelming impressions are those of injustice, abjection, and horror. The sepulchral atmosphere of death-in-life, the poetry of bars, locks, and bolts, the gloomy poetry of hostile silence—all these Borel evokes with deliberate "realism." He describes in detail his cell, with its muddy soil, its oozing walls, its latrine hole. He insists on the *pathology* of the prisoner (stiff legs, emaciation, edemas), as well as on the rotting corpses and smell of decomposition. Truth stinks—this seems to be Borel's predominant idea. "When truth is made of mud and blood, when it offends the sense of smell, I say that it is made of mud and blood, I let it stink. . . !" (II, 146.) This proclamation of realistic intent also points to one of the permanent features of literary realism: its underlying moral fervor.

The moral foundation of realism, often unformulated or semi-conscious, is here related to the basic prison image, which traditionally lends itself to the exploring of moral and metaphysical categories. For it is not enough to explain the prevalence of carceral images in 19th-century literature by referring to the political realities (the Ancien Régime, the Revolution, the Restoration), to social problems (penology, the question of capital punishment), or to the combined influence of Piranesi, the Gothic novel and the marquis de Sade. All these factors are no doubt relevant; but they also correspond to fundamental Romantic concerns and obsessions. The dialectical tensions between the finite and infinity, between fate and revolt, between oppression and the dream of freedom, between victimization and vengeance, are repeatedly given a symbolic setting in the context of solitary confinement. Deborah, who gives birth in prison to a son called Vengeance, formulates the essential aspirations of the *homo romanticus*: ". . . free or captive, in mourning or in joy, his soul is always agitated by yearnings for inexplicable infinity and the unknown" (II, 41).

Free or captive? *Madame Putiphar* is in a sense, from beginning to end, a novel of tyranny. The opening signals point to oppression. The father, Lord Cockermouth, is a despot who not only talks of locking up his daughter in a "house of correction" (I, 22), but who inflicts physical violence on his entire family. It is not enough that he throws a dish at Deborah; he has her almost murdered. The tyrannical father, forcing his daughter into exile, is also a tyrannical husband whose brutal laughter sounds like the "onomatopoeic rendering of a prison lock in a melodrama" (I, 62). Borel's comparison may seem a trifle grotesque, but it is revealing of the thematic unity of the book. For passion also is seen as a despotic force—a "puissance qui nous possède" (I, 30). And what is true of love is true of eroticism and of character. What applies to the individual also applies to a collective reality: French libertine society, the political oppressions of a "cowardly and dark tyranny" (II, 300-301), the moral dissolution of a period undermined by its own sense of inequity. It is not by coincidence that the two heroes-in-exile are Irish. The country that persecutes them is itself oppressed by England. Borel glorifies local dialects as a form of resistance to an invader's tyranny, and pities poor Ireland "crushed by the most inhuman persecutions," while every attempt to break this bondage only further burdens the country with chains (I, 88-89). Here again Borel remains faithful to his basic theme. When Deborah is freed by a group of Irish sailors, they all express in solemn song their love for their enslaved homeland (*"Irlande, notre mère, tu souffres, l'Anglois t'a chargée de chaînes. . . !"*—II, 91).

In a broader perspective, it is Fate that appears as the real tyrant, depriving man of choice and dignity. Here too, Pétrus Borel states his theme from the outset: ". . . there are fatal destinies . . . there are individuals destined to misfortune . . ." (I, 9). Baudelaire called this *le guignon* (congenital hard luck) and felt that Borel was irremediably afflicted with it.[16] Moral defeatism accompanies such a view; it is useless to argue with one's destiny. Hence the paradox: *guignon* seems to be the apanage of truly superior beings; yet it is also that which prevents them from establishing their superiority. With bitter pride, Borel stresses man's weakness. If jail seems unavoidable within the plot of the novel, it is because it is a symbol of the human condition. Pascal's dungeon continues to cast its shadow.

With cruel insistence, Borel lays bare human infirmity. The "human animal" has no choice; he is like a beetle pinned alive against a wall; he is the victim of pervasive whoredom; there is no use hoping . . . (I, 10, 12; II, 108, 234). The tone is at times strident, as the author indulges in a rhetoric of bitterness. It would have been preferable, we are told, for one marked by fate to have been choked to death in his mother's womb (I, 12). Yet hopelessness does not imply resignation. True, Borel paints the world black. Ironically and haughtily, he proclaims that the decent must suffer. The jailor's motto—"You are here to suffer"—amounts to a metaphysical declaration (II, 121). But a revolting condition such as this can only foster the dream of revolt. In his determination to overstate the horror of existence, to compete with the stripping nature of life, Borel also affirms a will. His vehement misanthropy and the acrimony of his tone ultimately sound like an appeal. The novel logically ends with the outburst of the Revolution.

The clash of will and despair results in a glorification of escape. Deborah, whose name has a symbolic ring, is "possessed by the demon of liberty," and liberty itself is seen as an "inexorable need" (II, 87, 101). The paradox is double: in the "sacred asylum," the most "sacred duty" of the captive is to break his chains (II, 103, 87). In the dialectical scheme of the novel, Deborah represents the pole of *will*. She writes to Patrick: "My mind is dumbfounded when I think of all that which an invincible will can achieve . . ." (I, 65). The tone becomes dithyrambic on the subject of will and emancipation: "The trumpets at whose sound the walls of Jericho came tumbling down are the telling symbols of the will. Sound them, and the thickest walls will crumble" (I, 65). The image of the walls suggests confinement, and confinement in turn is the specific figure of hopelessness. After Deborah witnesses the wounding and supposed death of Patrick:

> Through a natural movement of despair, she struck her forehead as though to break it and to let escape the horrible thoughts. . . . She kept beating her breasts as a prisoner strikes the wall of his cell, in order to break it and open up a passage for his captive soul which rebels against the body that forces it to live. . . . (I, 230)

The metaphorical prison once again precedes literal imprisonment, which in turn becomes metaphor. As for the opposition fate-will, it is further exploited through the specific absence of light and perspective in Patrick's dungeon, in contrast with the airy room and panoramic view which the "willful" Deborah enjoys at Sainte-Marguerite, where she plans and successfully carries out her escape.

The antithetical construction of the novel is confirmed in other registers and through other motifs. But, in every instance, the antithesis is intimately related to the theme of incarceration. Eroticism and chastity clash, yet they complement each other. The gynaeceum (the degraded convent) and the boudoir-trap represent the privileged enclosures of vice, as well as the oppression of virtue. Deborah's sequestration, which ends in rape, is in the image of Sade's apologia of cruelly voluptuous incarcerations of women for the purpose of sexual humiliation. (Bandole, in *La Nouvelle Justine*, explains why Asian despots lock up their women: "A woman is a delight to fuck only when she hates you cordially. . . .")[17] Conversely, it is because of their chastity that the two central characters are imprisoned.

This antinomy of innocence and perversity is paralleled by the opposition of country and city. The early chapters evoke the Irish landscape. What is interesting is not the hackneyed Romantic preference for the "grand spectacles of nature" (I, 216), but the fact that, in this respect also, the antithesis is conceived in terms of the basic prison image. Life in cities is seen as "confining"; houses are "boxes" or "cages" where one must wilt as in a prison (*on s'étiole emprisonné*); the soul is compressed as though by a straitjacket, the mind is "restricted" between four walls, and compelled to retire into the cell of the self (. . . *nous nous amoindrissons, nous nous raccornissons*—I, 216).

This diagnosis implies an affirmation. Thought itself seems to depend on constricting forms. A novel so centered on a recurrent metaphor involves a metaphorical inversion. The dream of a location must also be read as the location of the dream. There is no better illustration of this reversal than the prisoner's hallucination. Fitz-Harris, as he approaches the point of madness, conceives of a "breach" in the wall. Sick and feverish, he imagines that he sees through the dungeon walls, that he glimpses the immensity of space (II, 172). Freud, in his analysis of Schwind's "Prisoner's Dream," was to explain that the liberation dream results directly from the "dominant situation."[18] Such is the case in *Madame Putiphar*. The prisoner's ravings, illustrating Bachelard's "poetics of space," locate in prison the possibility of dreams.

|| 5 ||

Stendhal:
The Happy Prison

. . . nous sommes obligés de laisser Fabrice dans sa prison,
tout au faîte de la citadelle de Parme; on le garde bien, et
nous l'y retrouverons peut-être un peu changé.
        —La Chartreuse de Parme, *chap.* XVI

Cette laide bête ne veut plus manger, elle a besoin de
grimper et de faire sa prison de soie.
        —Souvenirs d'Egotisme, *chap.* IX

FEAR OR ENCHANTMENT?

Prisoners, in the world of *La Chartreuse de Parme*, are locked up with care. Duchess Sanseverina tries in vain to bribe Fabrice's jailor. Stendhal comments ironically that the only kind of business that is carried out to perfection in a petty, despotic regime is the custody of political prisoners (II, 307).[1] This authorial intervention reaches beyond the horizon of the court of Parma. It is a judgment on reactionary, post-Napoleonic Europe. Parma, with its operetta court, is also a "land of secret measures" (II, 338), a symbol of any regime founded on fear and police control.

Stendhal's intrusion is ironic in more ways than one. The fortress which now holds the Duchess's beloved nephew is indeed associated with a delightful memory: an excursion on a hot summer day to the tower of the famous citadel. On that occasion, she experienced a strange sense of elation. The foreshadowing is bitter: the citadel will later cause her most intense suffering. As for the legend surrounding the construction of the Farnese Tower, erected especially for a prince who was the lover of his own stepmother, it clearly points forward to the aunt's forbidden love for her nephew. More cruelly still, her delight on top of the Tower prefigures Fabrice's future enchantment, as he experiences, at the Duchess's expense, the joy of solitude and the joy of love for another woman.

The most suggestive irony is in fact of a thematic nature. What causes the Duchess's pleasure during that summer excursion corresponds to the symbolic values later associated with jail: the twice-stated sense of altitude (*là-haut*, *position élevée*) opposed to the flatness of nearby Parma; the oppressive (*accablante*) atmosphere of the town; the liberating sensation provided by the *air frais*; the exaltation of a discovery (II, 131). Even the desire to prolong the stay, to remain in prison, is here suggested, long before Fabrice will wish to settle in a prison happiness, freed from the imperatives of time and action.

The episode relates to a basic paradox. On the one hand, Stendhal evokes the shadow of political prisons, the threatening images of repression and captivity: deportation to the subterranean caves of the Bocche di Cattaro, men rotting in the chains of the *carcere duro*, cruel confinement in the Spielberg fortress, where Silvio Pellico and his friends experienced the rigors of the Metternich regime. Yet the novel also exploits the metaphor of the happy prison: . . . *notre héros se laissait charmer par les douceurs de la prison*. Fabrice is the first to be surprised by his own "charmed" state. There is nothing, after all, this dreamer of action feared more than incarceration. "But is this really a prison? Is this what I have dreaded so very much?" (II, 311.)

Can political realism and the privacy of joy be reconciled? Perhaps the secret of *La Chartreuse*, and of much of Stendhal's work, lies in this thematic counterpoint. Surely Stendhal cannot be charged with moral or political indifference. No one has diagnosed more acutely the modern threat of ideologies, the dangers of the police state. All his writings, in one way or another, denounce the faces of tyranny. Even Stendhal's famous irony makes place for unmasked indignation when confronted with degrading images of fetters and punitive walls.

When all the prisoners in the Farnese citadel, even those chained up in airless dungeons, order a *Te Deum* to be sung at their expense to celebrate the recovery of their governor, Stendhal intervenes with vehemence: "May that man who blames them be led by his destiny to spend a year in a cell three feet high, with eight ounces of bread per day, and *fasting* on Fridays!" (II, 378-379.) It is nonetheless this same prison that so "charmed" the young hero that he escapes against his will, cultivating in the exile of so-called "free" life the lasting nostalgia for his prison happiness! The text could not be more explicit: ". . . he was in despair at being out of prison" (II, 390).

The final sentence of the novel, which grants the prison motif a privileged status, echoes and prolongs this ambivalence:

> The prisons of Parma were empty, the Count was immensely rich, and Ernest V adored by his subjects, who compared his rule to that of the Grand Dukes of Tuscany.

At first glance, this sentence conveys the elegant serenity of the historian. Events seem integrated into a larger order. The rhythm and superficial meaning of the sentence also suggest the "happy ending" of a tale (the word "happy" indeed appears immediately after, in the postscript dedication of the novel "To the Happy Few"). The freeing of the prisoners, the wealth of Mosca, the popularity of the sovereign—all seem to proclaim felicity. Yet all take on another meaning if one reads backwards. The adjective "empty" points to vacuity. The unoccupied cells are the negative emblems of a vanished bliss: the two prisoners of love, Fabrice and Clelia, no longer are. As for Mosca's immense fortune, what for? He who has never valued money can know only abundance of bitterness, now that he has lost the only thing he valued: Gina. And it is surely not fortuitously that, in the preceding sentence, Gina's own life is described in terms of outward appearances of happiness: ". . . *les apparences du bonheur.*" Ironic "appearances" indeed, in the light of which the entire last sentence must be re-read.

For who can take the adoration of Ernest V's subjects seriously? What emerges, behind the superficial stylization of syntax and language, is the sadness of a world emptied of a beauty that could exist nowhere but in the book itself.

ARCHITECTURES

The ambivalence of the prison image operates from the start. Fabrice's childhood is shadowed by the "formidable castle" built by the most bellicose of his ancestors. This 15th-century prison-castle, with its drawbridges and deep moats, with its walls eighty feet in height and six in breadth, is a symbol of paternal tyranny. As he flees this family oppression, other images or forebodings suggest that his destiny will lead him to jail. As soon as he joins Napoleon's army, he finds himself locked up for over a month because of his suspicious foreign accent. The jailor's wife who helps him escape (feminine help is a key to all his escapes) provides him with the uniform and marching orders of a hussar who died in prison. The superstitious hero interprets this as a sign: "Beware of prisons! . . . The omen is clear, I shall have much to suffer from prisons!" And a little later: "All this is of the most sinister augury; my fate will lead me into prison" (II, 55, 82). These premonitions are soon confirmed by the abbé Blanès, his spiritual father, whose vague predictions also introduce the notion of prison happiness. Blanès does indeed stress the "rare happiness" (*rare bonheur*) of his first imprisonment which serves to prepare his soul (*ton âme peut se préparer . . .*) for a prison far more severe: ". . . *une autre prison bien autrement dure, bien plus terrible*" (II, 171). This "terrible" prison is of course the citadel that casts its mythic shadow over the entire landscape of *La Chartreuse*. Architecture and ominous legends (*on raconte des choses horribles*) combine to make of the Farnese Tower an even more threatening counterpart of the paternal walls. Visible from a long way off, the prison is the "queen" through fear (*reine, de par la peur*) of the wide plain that stretches from Milan to Bologna (II, 113).

Early signals in the text suggest, however, that the prison

image—whether masculine or feminine—will not necessarily be negative. The old black walls of the paternal castle in Grianta are associated in Fabrice's mind with the beauty of the landscape. The castle is an antechamber of death; but it stands in a position that is "possibly unique in the world," overlooking the *lac sublime* of Como (I, 30). A sentence in the second chapter hints at a very special function of imprisonment: protection and salvation. Fabrice's mother resigns herself to his mad project to join Napoleon when she realizes that nothing "except the walls of a prison" would prevent him from leaving (II, 51). What is conjured up, though negatively, is the motif of the hero's protective custody in the tradition of the chivalrous epic: thus Ruggiero in Ariosto's *Orlando furioso* is kept away from dangerous actions by a magician who sequesters him in an enchanted castle. The Como landscape has in fact only a few pages earlier been linked with the names of Tasso and Ariosto.

Soon the prison image becomes more engaging still. The first encounter with Clelia takes place under the sign of imprisonment. Clelia and her father, General Conti, are surrounded by gendarmes. This first meeting prepares for the second meeting, when the roles will be reversed. But the secret wish is formulated prophetically from that initial moment: "She would be a charming prison companion . . ." (*Ce serait une charmante compagne de prison* . . . [II, 99]). It is a dream of love (. . . *elle saurait aimer*); it is also a dream of emancipation and rebirth. The anguished marchesa fears for her son: "Fabrice will be arrested, she sobbed, and once he is in prison, God knows when he will get out! His father will disown him" (II, 102-103). But that too is a secret wish: the disowning of the son by the father, or better of the putative father by the son! Prison, whether inside or outside the paternal house, thus connotes a father-rejection, and a liberating impulse. Prison birth or prison rebirth? Twice Stendhal stresses the *nine months* of Fabrice's incarceration in the Farnese Tower; and each time it is to remark that he has emerged a new being: *Fabrice était entièrement changé.* . . .

This shift from oppressive to liberating connotations leads

to the paradox of the happy prison. Fabrice, as soon as he is locked up in his cell, discovers an unexpected sense of liberation. How else is one to interpret his uncontrollable laughter? (. . . *il riait comme jamais peut être on n'a ri dans une prison* [II, 311].) The awareness of well-being is soon translated into explicit statement, as he discovers the ability to love: "In all my life I have never been so happy! . . . Isn't it amusing to find that happiness should have been awaiting me in a prison?" (II, 336.) The next stage follows logically: the unwillingness to escape, the full recognition of prison as the *locus amoenus*. "Did anyone ever escape from a place where he was at the height of happiness? . . ." (II, 355.)

The paradox of a refused freedom must not be construed as mere flight into fantasy, or as a perverse refusal to take politics seriously. The key to this conversion of fear into happiness is provided by Father Blanès during Fabrice's secret visit to this substitute "father." The old priest offers a double prediction. On the one hand, he warns Fabrice that his "soul" must prepare to suffer in jail; yet at the same time, he promises a serene ending: ". . . you will die, my son, sitting on a wooden seat, far removed from all luxury, and with no illusions about it" (II, 172). Clearly the two predictions coincide. The prison experience and the monastic experience merge.

It is here that the title becomes supremely important. A charterhouse is announced, which in fact never appears in the field of vision of the novel. Yet, retrospectively, the visible citadel and the invisible monastery combine into one. The metonymic nature of the text provides a gradual substitution, and ultimately an identity between Fabrice's detention in the Farnese Tower and his withdrawal to a Carthusian cell. The tower answers the title, and stands as the central metaphor. The unreal charterhouse, barely mentioned in the last pages, was somehow present from the very start, as though to warn the reader that behind the petty court intrigues, beyond the tensions of politics and the games of lifesmanship, there existed a privileged and almost inaccessible region: the world of withdrawal, of renunciation, of hidden spirituality.

This metaphoric prison-charterhouse presents interesting

architectural features. It is a "pentagonal edifice" with an "immense round tower," on the platform of which stands the governor's residence. Stendhal himself explains that the tower was built on the model of Hadrian's tomb in Rome. The fictional Farnese citadel does indeed bear an uncanny resemblance to the Castello Sant'Angelo, a monument factually linked with the destiny of the Farnese family.[2] It is from this prison-fortress that Benvenuto Cellini succeeded in his acrobatic escape, a feat already accomplished by the young Alexander Farnese, who later became Pope Paul III—the very Pope who had Cellini imprisoned. A multiple irony thus presides over the ominous citadel. Moreover, in Stendhal's mind, the Castello Sant'Angelo is associated, many years before the conception of *La Chartreuse*, with images of freedom and elation. In *Promenades dans Rome* (II, 141-143), he evokes the Carbonari prisoners who enjoy there a soaring perspective on the eternal city. Such a magnificent view, he imagines, transmutes sadness into *douce mélancolie* and serene contemplation. Even the Duchess's pleasure excursion is prefigured: the Roman tourists, on top of the Castello Sant'Angelo, are caressed by a cooling breeze, the *venticello ponentino*, while ices are being served.

On closer inspection, the history and architecture of the Farnese Tower present mythic and symbolic peculiarities. This tower on top of a tower, erected in honor of a new Hippolytus who did not repel the advances of a young stepmother, suffers from a verbal interdiction: any reference to it is forbidden. Yet it can be seen from everywhere. More significant: the tower, massive and ugly on the outside, appears on the inside as the privileged habitat of graceful and delicate beings. To reach his lofty cell, Fabrice must climb up a small, very light, openwork iron staircase (*construit en filigrane*) which, however, quivers under the weight of the jailors (II, 309). It would seem that it is the jailors, not the prisoner, who are strangers in this world of elegant fragility. Similarly, the gout-ridden body of the governor can hardly make it up the little wooden staircase that leads to Clelia's prison refuge, the aviary (II, 325). Only the spirit of youth and dreams seems to be at home in this tower, whose oppressive mass casts an almost Kafkaesque shadow on the smiling Emilian plain.

The significance of the prison's architecture corresponds to its importance in the architecture of the novel. The two meetings between Clelia and Fabrice, under the sign of the erotic "arrest," imply dynamics of contempt. Already once, the presence of vulgar gendarmes served to bring out the gentleness and beauty of Clelia. Under the Farnese Tower, at the moment of incarceration, the contrast is more powerful still. This time, it is Fabrice who is surrounded by coarse gendarmes, and Clelia who is launched on a prison dream. She hears the uproar of the loud burst of laughter in the guardroom; she sees the ugly clerk Barbone still blood-bespattered from Fabrice's blow. She cannot repress a cry of horror: "never had she seen at such close range so atrocious an expression on anyone's face." It is at this precise moment that Fabrice is allowed to make his theatrical entrance, "escorted by three gendarmes." Nowhere in Stendhal's work does ugliness serve more clearly the perception of beauty: ". . . Fabrice was superb amidst these gendarmes." The dynamics of contempt are furthermore thematized: the "smile of disdain" that hovers on Fabrice's lips is explicitly contrasted (*un charmant contraste*) with the gross appearance of the gendarmes who surround him. Profoundly struck by the emblematic value of the scene, having in her heart of hearts decided to follow her father's prisoner ("I will go with you"—*Je vous suivrai*, she automatically says to her father, but obviously thinks of another), Clelia continues to rehearse in her mind all the iconographic contrasts of the ritual she witnessed. "How noble he looks amongst those coarse fellows!" And on the following page: "What nobility! What serenity! How like a hero he looked, surrounded by his vile enemies." As for Fabrice, seen but also seeing, he translates the contrast into a revelation. "Who would have thought that I would find such sweet eyes in such a place! [. . .] Heaven appeared to me in the midst of those vile creatures" (II, 268-270, 319-320).

The episode in abbé Blanès' tower confirms the structural importance of the prison motif. Not only does the old abbé predict the hero's prisoner vocation, but many details, during this pious consultation, announce the stay in the threatening tower: the cage of planks that forms the observatory, the *vue sublime*, the sight of the birds, the sound of bells, the two holes which he makes in the scraps of old linen in order to see without being seen. Father Blanès' routine warning at the moment of departure ("Take care not to fall; that would be a terrible omen") points in fact forward to the perilous prison escape.[3]

Even the Waterloo episode, though in the epic or mock-epic register, prepares for the cellular lyricism of the second part of the novel. The war scenes are framed by two seclusions: the thirty-three days in jail, the therapeutic claustration when Fabrice is wounded. Gilbert Durand has shown, in *Le Décor Mythique de La Chartreuse de Parme* (J. Corti, 1961), how sequestration and claustrophilia cancel the epic project. In reality, the war scenes themselves undermine the epic structure: they call for the protection of a private world, while stressing the incompatibility of dreams and action. Stendhal's vocabulary points to deconstruction: "He undid [*il défaisait*] one by one all his fine dreams of sublime and knightly friendship, like that of the heroes of *La Gerusalemme liberata*" (II, 69). Fabrice does not know, of course, that he will later retrieve his two favorite poets, Tasso and Ariosto, but in a lyric, not martial, mode. Yet once again, the evolution is foreshadowed: Fabrice's aunt, the future Duchess Sanseverina, early in the novel looks forward to the somber reclusion in the family castle by promising herself specific literary delights: "Among these hills so admirably shaped [. . .], I can preserve all the illusions of Tasso's and Ariosto's descriptions" (II, 45).

The structural cohesion of the novel, depending in large part on the interplay of epic and lyric modes, is stressed by repetitions and parallelisms. After the battle of Waterloo: ". . . Fabrice became another man . . ." (II, 93). At the time of his escape from the citadel: "How different I am . . . from the fickle, libertine Fabrice who entered this place nine months ago!" (II, 382.) The gestation time underscores the notion of renewal. The escape episode, when set against the debacle of the epic dreams, does in fact propose significant elements of mythic reconstruction. Fabrice describes his own exploits as ceremonial acts (". . . *j'accomplissais une cérémonie*" [II, 382]). The ritualistic gesture is part of a solemn, oneiric performance. The counterpoint of vagueness and precision, of lucidity and near automatism ("*Il agissait mécaniquement . . .*") serves to transform the narration of an exploit into a metaphor of transformation. Even the fainting spell relates to the rebirth symbolism. It is followed by a transfiguring awakening. "Fabrice was entirely changed. From the first moments of his awakening out of the lethargic sleep which followed his escape, the Duchess became aware that something out of the ordinary was going on inside him" (II, 390). Significantly, the idea of the "nine months" spent in prison is repeated on the following page.

THE "SECRET JOY"

All points to prison as a place of initiation. A special autumnal light seems to bring into sharp relief the walls of the Farnese Tower, suggesting the illusory suspense of time. Hence the hero's surprise: this "arrested" time signifies a change in rhythm. Fabrice's inner joy in his *solitude aérienne* has much to do with a sense of liberation. Spiritual elation seems to come naturally in this citadel, where the governor's daughter already enjoys the *liberté du couvent*, close to her birds. Fabrice himself will listen with Franciscan rapture to the warblings with which "his neighbors the birds" (*ses voisins les oiseaux*) greet the day. The theme of the happy bird is of course prepared by the pretty cages (happy cages within the larger Farnese cage) in front of Clelia's windows.

Liberation also comes from intimacy with the self. Fabrice, who feared that love was just another illusion, discovers love in jail. But the notion of amorous *intimacy* (the words *intime* and *intimité* are repeatedly linked to the secret sign language between Fabrice and Clelia) is protected by the very distance that separates the couple, protected so to speak by the impossible realization which interiorizes experience. One explicit reason for dreading a return to freedom is the thought of surrendering the joys of this private language. "How could he recapture the perfect intimacy he now enjoyed for several hours every day? What would be the drawing-room conversation compared with that they were carrying on by means of alphabets?" (II, 344.)

Nothing in fact could be more chaste than the allusion to the first experience of physical contact. The love scene, in the prison cell, barely fills a few lines:

> *Elle était si belle, à demi vêtue et dans cet état d'extrême passion, que Fabrice ne put résister à un mouvement presque involontaire. Aucune résistance ne fut opposée* (II, 437).

The physical act is translated into stylized gesture; rhythm replaces description or analysis. The embrace in the cell (Mme de Rênal's and Julien's most fervent moments are also protected by prison walls) confirms and symbolizes the theme of unrealized love. The dungeon walls suggest the enchantment of constriction, the prestige of the forbidden, the poetry of the inaccessible. It would seem that the test of love is a denial or fundamental refusal. "What more touching proof of love could a young man give? After seven long months in prison, which had seriously affected his health, he refused to regain his freedom" (II, 345-346).

A double notion of exile informs *La Chartreuse*. It is in fact Parma—that is, any locus of social and political life—that turns out to be the place of banishment. Fabrice is explicit: ". . . *et vous voulez que je fasse la duperie de m'exiler à Parme, ou peut-être à Bologne, ou même à Florence!*" (II, 345). This ambivalence of exile is further complicated by the powerful suggestion of inner exile. Stendhal's prisons do indeed restore the privileged individual to his true self. Or, rather, they allow him to dis-

cover, and even create, that self. Jail thus assumes both a protective and dynamic function: it liberates, but also reveals. Julien Sorel, in *Le Rouge et le Noir*, also attains freedom and
lucidity in his cell. His only complaint is that, in prison, a
door cannot be locked from the inside! To die dreaming
(*mourir en rêvant*), that seems to be Julien's vocation in the *pays
des idées* called prison. For him also the prisoner's dreams and
insights are related to the experience of altitude and vast
panoramas.[4] Isolation and topographic elevation correspond
in Stendhal's world to poetic fervor and exalted privacy.

To this privacy, love itself is subservient. True, it is in the
Besançon jail that Julien and Mme de Rênal experience their
most ineffable moments. These moments make concrete, as it
were, the playful and slightly precious metaphor at the end of
part I of *Le Rouge et le Noir*, when Julien, hiding in Mme de
Rênal's room, is called "her prisoner" (I, 429). Yet what
counts, as in *La Chartreuse de Parme*, is the protagonist's descent into himself. The joy of confinement has much to do
with *de-fining* the self. Julien experiences an uncanny security:
"*Son âme était calme.*" The title of one of the central prison-
chapters is indeed *La Tranquillité*. And this newly discovered
serenity is coupled with a lucidity that tolerates no pose. "Julien felt strong and resolute like a man who sees clearly into
his soul" (. . . *qui voit clair dans son âme* [I, 693]).

The pistol shot, the immediate cause for Julien's arrest, also
marks the end of a trance, the "return" to the self. The banal
expression *revenir à soi* (twice at the beginning of chapter 36:
"*Quand il revint un peu à lui*"; ". . . *tout est fini, dit-il tout haut en
revenant à lui* . . .") refers to the end of Julien's quasi–hypnotic
state, but also takes on a deeper meaning. After the vanity of
action comes the stasis of plenitude. Is that not the real significance of the double ending of *Le Rouge et le Noir*? At the end
of chapter 34, having obtained recognition from the marquis
de La Mole, as well as an officer's commission, Julien says to
himself: ". . . *mon roman est fini*." Another fiction can now begin. Its setting is the prison cell.

This retreat from ambition, this return to the self, also

means a temporal shift: the discovery of the *present*. Tired of
the demands made by his energy, freed from the constraints
of sham, Julien can finally devote himself to immediacy. Liberated from time, he can now value the privileged moment.
All becomes present, even the past: ". . . he could give himself up entirely to the memory of the happy days he had spent
in Verrières and in Vergy" (I, 664). He no longer feels judged
by the glance of others. Out of time, yet in full possession of
his being—that is the enviable prisoner fate. Such integrity
can, however, be achieved only at the end of an itinerary. Julien understands that his life has been but a *longue préparation
au malheur*. But *malheur* is transmuted into a positive value.
During his first day in jail, he realizes that he no longer has
any business on this earth (*je n'ai plus rien à faire sur la terre*).
Whereupon he falls asleep. But this observation, followed by
a symbolic slumber, does not betray resignation or sadness; it
conveys the intuition of transcendence.

Sleep, prefigurative of death, corresponds to the descent
into the less conscious regions where the privileged moment
(Julien calls it *"l'art de jouir de la vie"* [I, 667]) can be fully experienced. This non-erosive temporality recalls Rousseau. Indeed Stendhal's sharpest formulation of the mystique of the
privileged moment occurs in *Vie de Henry Brulard* at the point
of intensest evocation of *La Nouvelle Héloïse*: *"Pour un tel moment il vaut la peine d'avoir vécu."*[5] Such epiphanies, however,
belong neither to the irretrievable past, nor to the transitory
present. No Stendhalian hero is ever tempted by the sinful
wish denounced in Goethe's *Faust*: *"Verweile doch, du bist so
schön!"* Invulnerable to smugness, protected by their author
against the corruption of time, Stendhal's heroes learn how to
transpose the past event into the present. This having been
achieved, death prevents retrospective joy from degenerating
into banal satisfaction. The abrupt endings of Stendhal's two
great novels thus find their poetic justification.

The fear of lapsing into routine existence would also explain Fabrice's wish, communicated by secret signals to the
Duchess: *"I do not wish to escape; I wish to die here!"* After he

does escape, the text is explicit: ". . . he was in despair at being out of prison" (II, 390). He will find solace only when he can once again occupy his old cell in the citadel. This yearned-for withdrawal must not be confused with the hedonistic *retraite* Mosca and the Duchess anticipate in a Neapolitan setting. Fabrice's retreat is to be understood radically, as a withdrawal from lived life. Such a withdrawal opens unto the charterhouse—and soon after, unto death.

A TRADITION OF HAPPINESS

Stendhal's prison theme belongs to a multiple tradition: the contemplative seclusion, the escape exploit, the austere hermitage, the prison of love. Model texts can be identified. Benvenuto Cellini's *Vita*, which for the Romantics came to illustrate Renaissance energy and individualism, was one of Stendhal's favorites. As early as in the Introduction to *Histoire de la peinture en Italie*, he praised this "candid book" (*livre naïf*) which reminded him of Rousseau's *Les Confessions*. Many details of Cellini's prison escape found their way into the escape episode of *La Chartreuse de Parme*: both exploits are achieved by means of ropes, on a night of festivities; in both narratives, there is the proximity of sentinels, a fall, an injury, a fainting fit. Cellini provided Stendhal with something more fundamental still: a fully articulated theme of cellular elation. Much could be said about metaphoric inversions in the *Vita*: life is compared to a prison (*carcer mondano* [I, 116]); the dungeon becomes the place of a spiritual discovery, where the artist-adventurer learns to meditate on human frailty and reads the Bible with fervor. Love of God, confirmed by jail, provides legitimacy to an irrational jubilation. The words *lieto, letizia, dolcezza* stud accounts of dark moments converted into spiritual celebrations (*festeggiai con Dio*), such as in the passage describing him on his knees, in adoration of a fresco he improvised on his prison wall with a piece of charcoal (I, 120). Even more telling is the long poem in praise of jail ("*In lode di detta prigione*") which concludes the first book of the *Vita*.

Another influential text, this one by a contemporary, is Silvio Pellico's *Le Mie Prigioni*, relating the author's long stay in the Spielberg fortress. The pious resignation of this book disappointed his former liberal friends, but it proved to have immense appeal and contributed to the catholic revival. Stendhal read it with perhaps even greater interest than the famous prison accounts by Casanova, Latude, and Andryane. Certain images and episodes made a lasting impression: the cruel regime of the *carcere duro*; the heavy chains; the oppressiveness of cellular confinement; the urge to write, to make contact; the secret signals; the fancies of the imagination; the prisoner's walk; the relations with the jailor's daughter. The name of the Moravian fortress does indeed echo throughout *La Chartreuse de Parme*. Count Mosca thus ironically refers to the Spielberg as a "pleasant abode" (*lieu de plaisance*) where one's legs risk gangrene: an obvious allusion to Pellico's friend Maroncelli, whose leg had to be amputated.

As for the "prison of love," Stephen Gilman has convincingly shown how this tradition, going back indirectly to Boccacio's *Fiammetta* and typified by Diego de San Pedro's *Carcel de Amor*, has contributed to the genesis of *La Chartreuse de Parme*.[6] A novel published only a few years earlier must be mentioned: Saintine's *Picciola*. This novel, whose notoriety testifies to the importance of the prison theme throughout the 19th century (32 editions between 1838 and 1895), belongs as much to the tradition of famous prisoners (Silvio Pellico's influence is clearly felt) as to that of the emblematic tower of love. Its hero, Count de Charney, is held in the fortress of Fenestrelles for having conspired against Napoleon. In his jail, he discovers love through the double image of a flower and of Teresa, the daughter of a fellow inmate. It is the flower, first, which converts the blasé scholar-conspirator to simple faith and love. Prison, despite all its rigors, thus provides a therapy for Charney's *ennui* and sense of sterility. From his cell, he enjoys a panorama very similar to the one that delights Fabrice: the chain of the Alps, a view of the sky "*dans un cadre de pierres.*"[7] More relevant still are the communication motifs (autobiographical scribblings on the wall, ingenious fabrication of ink and paper) as well as the special signals. Inspired by "tender exaltation," the prisoner of Fenestrelles transmits by means of a strip of cloth a *"vibration affectueuse"* (155-156).

The cure of rationalism holds a particular interest in a Stendhalian perspective. Saintine's hero, a conspirator out of boredom, suffers from an icy intellect, a *cerveau de glace*. Sapped by skepticism, he is the prisoner victim of his own mind, his *démon fatal*. Picciola, the symbolic prison flower that provides the title for the novel, humbles this intellectual pride and succeeds in "opening up" (*élargir*) his mental prison house. The caring for the fragile flower, the botanical preoccupations (shades of Rousseau!), harmonize with the prison idyll: the flowering of love within the tragic prison walls. Anticipating Fabrice's lyric immobilism in the Farnese Tower, Saintine's Count de Charney, in order to remain near Teresa, would willingly "give up freedom, fortune, worldly concerns . . ." (277).

This tradition of idyllic imprisonment can easily degenerate into affectation. Alexandre Dumas' *La Tulipe noire* tells of a prisoner's double love for a flower and for a jailor's daughter who, like Clelia, takes the prisoner's side against her father. Here, too, the view through the barred windows opens unto an "immense horizon," nests are filled with cooing pigeons, and the prisoner's greatest wish is to remain near his Rosa in his prison home (*le domicile de la prison* [149]). But when the prisoner, speaking to Rosa, calls the tulip *"l'enfant de notre amour,"* Dumas' novel falls into irredeemable pathos.

No such pathos in Stendhal: the tired topos is vivified by personal themes and obsessions.

A PRIVATE THEME

Stendhal's claustrophilia answers the deeper needs of "Beylisme"—a name Henri Beyle-Stendhal himself gave to a semi-tender, semi-ironic way of watching himself cultivate his sensibility, as well as to the art of masking it. From the start, young Beyle conceives of the solitary tower as a privileged place. Writing to his sister from Richmond, where he spent several weeks in "deepest solitude," he asks: "Don't you think that Gil Blas, in the Segovia tower, enjoyed very sweet mental pleasures?" (*Corr.*, III, 117-118.) The tower is quite spontaneously associated with a literary reference and an intellectual satisfaction. That solitude should appear to the young man as propitious to spontaneity ("When I am alone, I laugh and cry over a trifle . . ." [*Corr.*, IV, 143]), such a commonplace can hardly surprise. More significant is the bond between *solitude aérienne* and the act of writing. The *quatrième étage* is for him the symbolic locus of poetic meditation. Or better still, the garret: "*Le vrai métier de l'animal est d'écrire un roman dans un grenier*" (*Corr.*, IX, 186).[8]

All his heroes, even those who at first think themselves committed to action, share a longing for enclosure. Octave de Malivert, at the beginning of *Armance*, feels an acute nostalgia for his *petite cellule* of the Ecole Polytechnique which offered him the "image of retreat and tranquillity in a monastery" (I, 32). He later observes that his "unique pleasure" comes from living in isolation, with no one having the right to talk to him (I, 34). Julien, long before his prison experience, values precious moments of lofty solitude. As for Fabrice, is not all of his brief career a preparation for withdrawal and claustration? The mediocrity of his battlefield companions, the betrayal of epic and lyric illusions nurtured by Tasso and Ariosto, the loss of blood which cures him of his fervor for war: the mock heroic mode stresses the inadequacy of all action.

This basic option for retreat and privacy has its risks. Not only do all of Stendhal's protagonists (and he himself) learn Julien's lesson that "difference engenders hatred"; they discover that solipsism is a cause of blindness. The young Henri Beyle observes: "I am too busy looking at myself to see others" (*Pensées-Filosofia Nova*, I, 137). But can he in fact see himself clearly at such proximity? To his sister Pauline, he writes: ". . . one must enjoy oneself in solitude" (the French is stronger: "*jouir de soi-même*" [*Corr.*, II, 240]). The same idea, only the tone is somewhat sharper, reappears in a letter to de Mareste: ". . . the only worthwhile thing in this world is the *self*" (*Corr.*, v, 107). For retreat and self-enclosure are the necessary conditions of creative self-observation. From adolescence on, Stendhal indulges in cryptic note-taking, diaries, discussions and dialogues with himself, analyses of his defects and qualities, clinical self-consultations. The scribbling mania leads to amusing extremes. Yet even the scribblings on his clothes—those coded jottings, similar to a prisoner's secret messages, on his cuffs, his belts, his suspenders—betray the need to see himself both as object and subject.

Such privacy extends to moral values and to moral judgments. Duchess Sanseverina needs to be alone with herself to assess her own actions. Her great quality, we are told, is that she knows how to be "honest with herself" (*de bonne foi avec elle-même* [II, 120]). Fabrice, exercising self-arrogated prerogatives of self-judgment, occasionally indulges in self-clemency ("I forgive myself my fright" [II, 179]). Julien locks himself up in his room to become his severest judge. Needless to say, this private tribunal or private stage does not help solve the mystery of personality. The eye cannot see itself. That is Stendhal's anguished conclusion in his autobiographic *Vie de Henry Brulard* (126). "What kind of man am I?"—this self-addressed question on the first page of *Souvenirs d'Egotisme* haunted him all his life. But where is one to find the answer? Certainly not in the self: "I do not know myself; and that is what distresses me, when I think of it sometimes at night" (*Souvenirs d'Egotisme*, 1394). Lucidity is a deception. The trouble is that not even the "others" can solve the riddle of the self. To the most elementary question—is he intelligent? is he good? is he brave?—no answer is forthcoming. Caught between the desire to reveal himself and the fear of being penetrated by another conscience, Stendhal can only complicate the illusive quest of the self. And the mask he learns to wear in order to camouflage his intimate being does not, of course, help him unveil himself in his own eyes.

The yearning for lucidity and self-knowledge does indeed

coincide with the need to dissemble. The intruding glance is wished for and feared at the same time. Hence the importance of disguises and the fictional joys of the incognito. "I would wear a mask with pleasure, I would change name with delight" (*Souvenirs d'Egotisme*, 1415). In the curious text entitled *"Privilèges du 10 avril 1840,"* he imagines that some superior decree endows him specifically with the ability to become *another*: "Twenty times a year, the grantee will be able to change himself into the being he wants. . . ." The basic urge behind the dream of metamorphosis is to remain impenetrable. Such fantasies of masquerades are obviously related to the fiction-making impulse. They also cast light on the theme of a privileged *locus* where personal freedom could prosper, hidden and unmolested.

The temptation to dissemble and disguise, to hide what counts most, is an early trait of Henri Beyle. It is, from the outset, bound up with the act of writing. He admonishes his sister: "Say nothing of all that to anyone [. . .]. Do give up the bad habit of reading to anyone the letters I write to you"—"Above all do not show this letter to anyone. . . ." To invoke youth's natural embarrassment, or *pudeur*, in the face of elders is not enough in this case. What is involved is a deliberate stance. In another letter to Pauline, à propos "fools"—that is à propos the "others"—he advises: ". . . let's prevent them from glossing our behavior by hiding our actions" (*Corr.*, I, 8, 19, 69). In fact, the letters to Pauline turn out, in large part, to be a didactic exercise, a correspondence course on the art of secretiveness. But to hide what? Henri Beyle would answer—and Stendhal the writer was to turn this into a major theme: the "superiority" of sensitive souls who are always hated by the common herd called society. "You must hide your superiority, and enjoy yourself alone, in your room, reading a book that entertains you" (*Corr.*, II, 240). The dissembling intentionality could not be more explicitly linked to the notion of solitude and withdrawal. "One must become a hypocrite," he advises, long before conceiving of the figure of Julien Sorel.

Yet this "superiority" which asks to be hidden cannot be equated with banal arrogance: lies and silence are to protect a sensibility that, far from strength, is experienced by Stendhal as supreme vulnerability. "In all my life, I never talked of that which mattered to me; the least objection would have hurt me to the quick" (*Vie de Henry Brulard*, 165). In depth, it is the idea (or ideal) of happiness that wants to be concealed. Is that not literally the Duchess's advice to Mosca when she becomes aware that the Prince is intensely angered by the "sight" of happiness? "We must keep our love a secret . . ." (*Il faut cacher nos amours* . . . [II, 140]). These subterfuges of Beyliste lifes-manship are revealing of the bond between fervor, deception, and disguised freedom. "Is not lying the only recourse of slaves?" (*Vie de Henry Brulard*, 135.)

Concealment of "happiness," but also happiness of con-cealment. "What is the use of going so far afield to seek hap-piness; it is right under my eyes" (II, 176). Fabrice's sense of discovery, during his secret stay in abbé Blanès' tower, is re-vealing in a number of ways: the tower foreshadows the prison; the joys of a panoramic view suggest a possible mas-tery over his past and his self; the satisfactions of the overview are inseparable from the comfort of invisibility. Fabrice has indeed found a "convenient place to see without being seen" (II, 174).[9] Still this is not enough; between the imaginary gen-darmes and himself he places an improvised screen: ". . . a tattered scrap of old linen which he nailed against the window and in which he made two holes for his eyes" (II, 176). It is hard to attribute such voyeuristic camouflage to practical cau-tion. Stendhal makes a point of invoking the irrationality of *l'âme italienne*. What is involved is a fundamental retractility. For Stendhal, as for his heroes, lucidity is conceivable only from within a shelter. Hence the recurrent image of the hid-den seer: Armance "hidden in the attic of the castle, behind a blind" can observe all the details of Octave's departure (I, 125); the ladies of Königsberg, in *Le Rose et le Vert*, watch the movements of the *messieurs* in the street by means of special mirrors affixed to their windows, while they themselves remain invisible, protected by "blinding metallic sheets" (II, 1074-1075).

Ideal joy, to be sure, is attained only when the seeing eye is seen. But such yearned-for enchantment is not devoid of deep apprehension. The emergence of another's glance is tolerable only from within a protective enclosure.[10] Prison ultimately provides a revelation—including that of love. In the meantime, the fleeting lyric moment requires the protection of the night. Julien discovers the delights of "vague and sweet reverie" during the evening hours in the gardens of Vergy (I, 279). Lucien Leuwen responds to the harmony of *soirées enchanteresses* in the woods. Fabrice sheds tears of happiness, "protected by deep night and vast silence" (II, 166). Gilbert Durand has related these nocturnal delights, part of a larger motif of claustrophilia, to Armida's enchanted gardens.[11] The comparison with Tasso is not arbitrary. *La Gerusalemme liberata* is mentioned in the opening pages of *La Chartreuse*. As for the dream of invisibility and of magic metamorphoses, it would seem grafted on another Renaissance reference, Ariosto's *Orlando furioso*: "I often think of Angelica's ring; it would give me supreme pleasure to change into a tall, blond German, and thus to walk in Paris" (*Souvenirs d'Egotisme*, 1416).

This desire to disappear and to seek refuge in another body is intimately associated, as the "Privilèges du 10 avril 1840" indicate, with the keenness of the glance. Once again a magic ring confers special powers. "When the grantee carries on him or on his finger, for two minutes, a ring he will have held for a moment in his mouth, he will become invulnerable." Such invulnerability can be achieved also through insertion into an alien body-fortress. "Twenty times a year the grantee will be able to change into the being he wants. . . ." Better still: ". . . four times a year and for an unlimited period each time, the grantee will be able to occupy two bodies at once." The wish for invisibility is bound up with the wish for perspicacity. The *privilégié* is most sharp-sighted when he is not exposed to another's seeing eye. Invulnerable, he will ten times per year enjoy "an eagle's eyesight." He will be "lynx-eyed." Article 21 is more precise still: "A hundred times a year, he will be able to see what any person he wishes is doing. . . ." With one significant reservation: ". . . with total exception of the woman he loves most." In the last analysis, any extreme form of happiness in Stendhal calls for obscurity and silence.

Walls, masks, impersonations, function not merely as protective screens; they insure existential freedom. Enclosure and constraint serve the sense of becoming and of discovery. An accepted necessity allows the cultivation of that form of spontaneity Stendhal calls *l'imprévu*. Such a devious quest of the authentic self evidently involves the dialectics of role-playing and spontaneity (the *rôle* and the *naturel*). At the outset of his first night with Mme de Rênal, Julien reverts, we are told, to his "natural role." The oxymoron stresses the fundamental compatibility of the two apparently irreconcilable terms. Play acting, on first thought, appears as the contrary of naturalness. This in itself points to an important ambiguity of Julien's character: the more he allows himself to be inspired by *le rôle de Tartufe*, the more clearly this indicates that he is not naturally a hypocrite. Yet a role can become a second nature. By wearing a mask, by merely trying it out, one risks seeing it adhere to one's face. Hence the Stendhalian fear of the definitive role. Mosca, about to surrender to jealousy, recognizes the danger: ". . . once I have spoken the fatal word *jealousy*, my role is marked out forever" (ii, 155). Dialectically, however, *rôle* and *naturel* are interlocked in Stendhal. To play at being is a way of seeking or inventing one's self.

The frequent surprises experienced by Stendhal's protagonists—surprises stemming from their own actions and reactions—are proof that they are not inhibited by a fixed image of the self. Fabrice's astonishment upon arriving in jail is typical: "Could I be one of these men of valor of whom antiquity has given some examples to the world? Am I a hero without suspecting it?" Thirty-five years earlier, Stendhal jotted down in a notebook entitled "Pensées de Paris" a remark that suggests how dear this thought was to him: ". . . the true hero performs his beautiful deed without suspecting that it is beautiful."[12] The opposite of a role? Yet only a temporarily assumed role holds out the promise of a similar revelation.

Every actor knows it: freedom of movement comes when the part is well learned. Stendhal is keenly sensitive to the interrelations between a fixed scenario and the joys of improvisation. He himself never spun his fictions more freely than on a pre-established canvas. His characters, too, affirm their freedom to the extent that they accept the rules of a game. Mosca's charm and efficiency on that stage called the court of Parma have much to do with his not being duped by his own part. Inversely the court (". . . where he played such a beautiful role" [II, 119]) is theatrical—in other words a *game*—only for those who, like Mosca, remain generously available for what truly matters. Carried by the game, they can also dominate it. Surely it is not by chance that the Duchess's favorite pastime is *commedia dell'arte*, where the set outline of a plot allows for improvisation. Comedy within comedy: ". . . I have played a part on stage for one hour, and for five hours in the princess' room" (II, 429). Another passage, rich with theatrical vocabulary, explicitly stresses the alliance between role-playing and spontaneity. Having "staged" (*mis en scène*) and masterfully played in the *Audience de Congé* (Chapter 14), the Duchess withdraws from action to consider what idea she ought to form about "the scene that has just taken place." Stendhal adds (we know already that her conduct is unpredictable even to herself): "She had acted at random, for her own immediate pleasure . . ." (II, 256).

To freedom through constraint corresponds protection through silence. The author's devious intrusions, the dissemblings of his irony, are part of a general rhetoric of obliquity which shields the lyricism embodied by his heroes. "Fabrice had an Italian heart; I crave the reader's pardon for him . . ." (II, 166). This typically Stendhalian strategy finds its echo and commentary in his autobiographic writings, which constantly refer to the poetry of the unsaid or the unsayable. "I have never been able to speak of that which I adored; such a discourse would have seemed to me a blasphemy" (*Henry Brulard*, 151). Hence the frequent conditional sentences in his novels, these hypothetical structures that allow for the treating of a fictional situation as though it were real, and to create ironically a fiction on fiction. Hence also the dream of a meta-language, of a special private code, to say that which cannot be said: ". . . I would like to be able to write in a sacred language." This wish expressed in *Promenades dans Rome* is significantly placed after the still more revealing wish to be understood only by "persons born for music" (i, 72).

Does this refusal-wish account for Stendhal's stylistic casualness, his apparent *disinvoltura*? The fear of verbal "blasphemy" is no doubt a form of withdrawal, modesty in the sense of the French word *pudeur*. The word does indeed come up in relation to his own sensibility and to his own writings: ". . . *mes compositions m'ont toujours inspiré la même pudeur que mes amours*" (*Henry Brulard*, 151, 97). Such a rift between the sign and the referent does not, however, in Stendhal's case imply the priority of the spoken or the written word. "The subject outdoes the saying," he observes on a number of occasions, appropriating some lines attributed to François I:

> *Qui te pourra louer qu'en se taisant?*
> *Car la parole est réprimée,*
> *Quand le sujet surmonte le disant.*

What Stendhal sings is his nostalgia for silence. "With those I loved too much, mute." The shadings of regret and self-reproach suggested by this cryptic notation are a negligible price to pay for a certain type of happiness. Stendhal not only values silence; he considers it the irreplaceable sign of bliss. His ideal salon is the one where he would not have to play the role of wit, where he could listen and even forget his own presence. Behind the apparent bluntness of a letter to his friend de Mareste, one perceives deep-lying satisfactions he associates with having neither to shine nor even to talk: "*Le soir, société très gaie, très musiquante, très foutante, où je suis admis volontiers et sans avoir besoin de parler et de briller.*" Writing

Vie de Henry Brulard, he stumbles on this lovely formula: "I willingly lapse into the silence of *happiness*" (*le silence du bonheur* [248]). Passion and speech are, as it were, incompatible. Already in 1804, twenty years before writing his first novel, he remarks in *Filosofia Nova* (II, 123): ". . . the more passionate one becomes, the more speech fails one."

A sacred language. . . . It would seem that it is through fictions of prisons that the dream of silence and special mediation was to be fulfilled. In all his constructs, Stendhal surrenders to the taste for messages by special intercession: secret graphs, codes, special meanings conveyed by opera recitatives, indirect signals. Not to speak clearly can be a deliberate strategy. Thus Duchess Sanseverina makes use of a particularly ambiguous fable by La Fontaine to communicate her meanings to the Prince. But such indirections cannot be viewed as mere tactical devices, nor even as part of a larger "elliptical" mode.[13] They most often serve what is most precious in Stendhal's fictional world: intimacy at a distance. The prisoner's cell, locus of inaccessible love, is also the symbolic place where secret messages and long-range mediation achieve this exquisite and ideal intimacy.

It is the writing process itself which, in the last analysis, is situated by Stendhal in an ideally confined space. "What a lovely place, the Grande Chartreuse, to write a tragedy!" (*Journal*, 534.) An almost dreamlike sequence, in one of his earliest texts, adumbrates the images of the *"prison aérienne."* The young Henri Beyle imagines a "delicious valley" rich in "contours"; each of the contours in this emblematic topography represents a given passion. This valley, enclosing all times and all countries, is perfectly horizontal. But here is the exception. At the center of the valley (the Farnese Fortress will also stand at the center of a vast plain), there is the region of artists and philosophers: "They live in an immense tower construction situated exactly at the center of the valley." The recognizable motif of elevated enclosure does not, however, constitute the sole interest of this early text (1804). According to Stendhalian logic, these superior inhabitants of the tower are endowed with *perfect vision* as well as *invisibility*. *"Leur vue est infiniment pénétrante . . ."*—*". . . rien n'arrête leurs regards . . ."*—*"Leur vue est parfaite."* But also: *"Cette tour est invisible à tous les yeux autres que ceux des savants et des philosophes."*[14]

The most significant thematic structures of Stendhal's mature work affirm themselves in this juvenile vision. Not only is freedom conceived in ascensional and separatist terms (the different artists climb to "varying heights"); but the most fundamental freedom is clearly associated with the act of writing. And this act belongs properly to the privileged world of claustration. Thirty years later, not so very long before writing *La Chartreuse*, Stendhal jots down the following observations concerning the "animal named writer"—observations that might well serve as epigraph, or conclusion: "Have you ever seen, benevolent reader, a silkworm that has eaten its fill of mulberry leaves? The simile is undignified, but it is so apt. This ugly animal no longer wants to eat. It needs to climb and weave its silken prison."[15]

‖ 6 ‖

Victor Hugo:
The Spaceless Prison

Where would thought lead if not to jail?
—William Shakespeare

THE NEW VOICE

"On voit le soleil!" (One sees the sun!) This cry of the Condemned Man in Hugo's *Le Dernier Jour d'un Condamné* is
quoted from memory by Dostoevsky in the letter he writes
his brother on December 22, 1849, a few hours after the
macabre scenario of his sham execution. Imperial grace came
at the last moment: the death sentence was commuted to hard
labor. But the resuscitated man was never again the same.

The French quotation in the letter to Michael refers to the
short chapter XXIX of *Le Dernier Jour d'un Condamné*. The
literary reference was part of a private language: Dostoevsky's brother was indeed later to translate Hugo's novel. And
chapter XXIX is central to the novel, as well as dramatically
relevant to Dostoevsky's situation. The nameless protagonist,
obsessed by the image of his head which the guillotine will
transform into an object, desperately invokes his grace, even
at the cost of life imprisonment. Dostoevsky had perceived
the importance of the sun in this fiction about incarceration
("I love the sun," whose "warm" and "gay" rays trace luminous figures symbolizing life and freedom—III, 659-660);[1]
and he had himself experienced the temporal anguish of a
deadline inflicted with precision. Hugo's title, echoed by the
capitalized indication *Quatre Heures*, at the end of the text,
proposes suspense in the face of an ineluctable immediate future. This slow-motion death—"this six week agony and
day-long death rattle" (III, 700)—was to be relived by Dosto-

evsky in *The Brothers Karamazov*, where he evokes the condemned man, unable until the last moment to believe that he will die, reassured because two streets still separate him from the scaffold. Such a *repetition* in the double register of lived experience and the act of writing testifies, through a symbiotic exchange, to the existential density of Hugo's fiction.

It is likely, moreover, that the Bicêtre prison of *Le Dernier Jour d'un Condamné*, as much as personal memories of forced labor in Siberia, colored *The House of the Dead*. Turgenev felt that Dostoevsky, in the episode of the prisoners' bath, had attained Dantesque grandeur. But is not the immediate model once again Hugo's fiction? The riveting of the convicts' iron collars and the departure of the chain gang in chapter XIII (Hugo had documented himself *in situ*, but had also just read the *Mémoires* of Vidocq) are translated into a tableau of a grimacing humanity set in hell. It is presented as a visual experience (the Condemned Man is spectator before becoming himself a spectacle): livid faces of prisoners behind their bars; burning eyes, convulsive movements; clenched fists raised in a gesture of defiance. And it is an experience in sounds: the rattling of the chains, the curses and the strident laughter, the cacophony of voices. The demon-convict remains a thematic feature in the work of Hugo: the convict's laughter, "echo of the demon's laughter," continues to be heard some thirty years later, in the pages of *Les Misérables*. When the chain gang, the infamous *cadène*, is glimpsed through the innocent eyes of Cosette, this hallucinatory vision points back to the inferno of the earlier novel. Hugo is quite explicit: "Dante would have believed he saw the seven circles of hell in motion" (XI, 651).

Two literary traditions converge in *Le Dernier Jour d'un Condamné*: the Last Judgment, or *Dies irae*, looming over the Western tradition; the more specifically romantic motif of solitary confinement, symbol of a hellish enclosure in the self. His sentence read, the Condemned Man goes into a state of stupor (*ivre et stupéfait*); he feels that a "revolution" has taken place inside him. He has discovered his incurable otherness:

". . . now I clearly perceived something like a fence between the world and me" (III, 661). This new man deciphers his destiny on the four walls of his cell.

Hugo's short novel set a trend; it precedes the texts of Stendhal, Dostoevsky, Andreyev, Sartre, Camus, Malraux, in which the prisoner, in a *cachot* deprived of Pascalian vision, undergoes an apprenticeship in the absurd. To be sure, Hugo draws on well-known images and *topoi*: oozing walls, tempting windows, glimpsed or yearned-for sky, a benignly smiling jailer, dreams of escape, poignant graffiti, the sight of birds associated with the voice of a young girl, typical prison sounds (grating of bolts and locks, jarring of iron staircases), the chaplain's visit, the attachment of the prisoner to his cell (*"Je l'aimais, mon cachot"*—III, 68). And it is true that Vigny, in *Cinq-Mars*, had already evoked the "strange revolution" (*étrange révolution*) undergone by the prisoner confronting death. But the experience evoked by Vigny remains abstract: it is a meditation on eternity in the tradition of Pascal's *cachot*.

The experience suggested in *Le Dernier Jour d'un Condamné* is of a visceral nature: imprisonment and confrontation with death are proposed in the register of fear and frailty. The Condemned Man is simply not a "hero." The dialogued preface, *"Une Comédie à propos d'une tragédie,"* rightly stresses this aspect: ". . . what a horrible idea to develop, to probe, to analyze, without sparing us a single one, all the physical torments, all the moral tortures, that must be experienced by a man condemned to death, on the day of his execution!" The Condemned Man himself jots down the symptoms of his animal-like terror: headaches, excessive perspiration, cold, shivers, burning eyes, elbow pain, convulsive shudders—symptoms whose cause will also be the cure in "two hours and forty five minutes"! (III, 700.) For fear functions in a temporal perspective; it makes the present exclusive and intolerable.

Here lies the originality of the novel: Hugo confines his protagonist to a present that separates him from his past and denies him his future. Jean Massin speaks of the tyranny of the present indicative, of the cruel presence of an "ironic future."[3] The imagination of the Condemned Man is in fact forced to play on a negative future, a future radically deprived of a consoling dimension. "I think [. . .] that I will no longer think tonight" (iii, 685). Fictional technique and temporal perspective are closely wedded: the "diary" rhythm prefigures Sartre's *La Nausée* ("They have just brought me food . . . I have tried to eat . . ."—"A man has just come in . . . " —iii, 694). Hugo also seems to strive toward what will be known as the interior monologue. The solipsistic use of the first person singular, much like the enclosure within the present indicative, confines the character in rhetorical and metaphoric terms. Hugo seems aware of the temporal and subjective challenge: the intellectual "autopsy" is referred to as a detailed, technical record of the intellect's ultimate motions (*procès verbal de la pensée agonisante*—iii, 664). Once again we encounter Dostoevsky. Some five decades later, in the introduction to his tale *Krotkaia* (1876), discussing the relationship between reality and the fantastic, he imagines a hypothetical and invisible stenographer, and gives as his model Hugo's "masterpiece" *La Dernier Jour d'un Condamné*.

Dostoevsky rightly stressed the oneiric precision of Hugo's text. If *Le Dernier Jour d'un Condamné* is a novel of ideas, nothing could be further removed from a rational demonstration. The death penalty, as well as images of crime and punishment, are a lifelong obsession with Hugo. Beyond the ideological rejection of the guillotine (even where later he was to justify the Revolution), beyond the early personal encounter with the scaffold, the rigors of the "law" are in his mind obscurely associated with an underlying family drama.[4] And many years later, in 1862, he claimed still to hear the "frightening cry" of a woman being branded—a spectacle he witnessed in 1818 or 1819, and which allegedly determined his vocation to "fight for ever against the evil actions of the law."[5] This vocation is confirmed by the 1832 preface, which suggests that the novel, written under the influence of Beccaria, should be read as a denunciation of capital punishment.

But this preface, published three years after the novel, and linked to the fiction-pamphlet *Claude Gueux*, unduly stresses the propagandistic nature of the text. Capital punishment is a live topic at the time.[6] Vigny, in *Cinq-Mars*, had protested against judicial murder. Hugo, in his preface, calls for a complete reworking of the penal code; he raises the question of the scaffold in revolutionary times: the specter of the political guillotine announces the haunted imagery of much later historical works, as well as the central themes of *Quatrevingt-Treize*. In a striking passage where the substantive *misérables* appears, he even sketches out the criminal career of Jean Valjean. All this, however, has little to do with the text of the novel itself. The inspiration of *Le Dernier Jour d'un Condamné* is hallucinatory rather than polemical. The prison, a monstrous presence (*espèce d'être horrible*), imposes itself as structure and as metaphor. This personification of the edifice leads to visionary contamination between the walls, the body, and the mind:

> . . . it is prison incarnate, it is Bicêtre made flesh. All is prison around me; I find prison in all its forms, in a human form as well as in the form of bolts or iron bars. The wall is a prison of stone; this door is a prison of wood; these turnkeys are prisons of flesh and bone. Prison is a horrible creature, complete, indivisible, half edifice, half human being" (III, 680).

Incarceration here suggests specular polyvalence. If *Le Dernier Jour d'un Condamné* is indeed a novel of ideas, it is as a game of *reflection*, a drama of intelligence casting the image of its own thought back to itself. One of the officials finds the prisoner "rather pensive." He has good cause, as we have seen ("I think . . . that I will no longer think tonight"). Is not this novel the account of a mind's self-observation as it watches itself move toward death, "thought by thought" (*pensée à pensée*—III, 700)? *Pensée* and *idée* are among the most frequently recurring substantives, as well as the personifying pronouns that refer to them. The opening signals are telling.

The first chapter, barely forty lines long, repeats the word *idée* three times, and the word *pensée* four times—not to mention the infinitive *penser*. To which must be added at least six pronouns referring to that "infernal thought" capable of jealousy, of assuming all sorts of personified forms, of making heard its tyrannical voice, of adhering to the walls of the cell.

Hugo was moving towards a drama of "ideas." In the notes and fragments collected under the title of *Feuilles paginées*, which belong mostly to the feverishly active year 1827, a figural correspondence is worked out between the images of the skull, the wall, the scaffold, and the intellect. "Each paving stone of the place de Grève [the place of public executions] is perhaps a naked skull"—a sentence that is echoed almost exactly in chapter XLIV of the novel. And just after the image of the *coupe-tête*, which unavoidably summons the specter of the guillotine, this elliptic jotting: *"C'est le pugilat de deux idées."* These fragments are bound up with another terse remark obviously related to the novel: "They say I exaggerated the guillotine."[7]

The rift between the thinking head and the head-as-object cannot be reduced to black humor. The fixation is only logical: what is at stake is precisely the head. Repeated puns stress this fixation. On the day of the execution, the "merchants of human blood" renting seats with head-splitting calls *"criaient à tue-tête"* (III, 709). The victim recalls how once, crossing the place de Grève, he turned his head so as not to see the guillotine. Soon it will be different: *"Je ne détournerai pas la tête"* (III, 692). When he sees the crowd waiting for his own execution, and hears them scream *"Chapeaux bas"* (Hats down), he remarks to the priest: *"Eux les chapeaux, moi la tête"* (III, 709). Slang also provides ironic images of disjunction. Hugo displays a range of convict *argot*, largely gleaned in Vidocq's *Mémoires*: the protagonist learns that the head is called the *Sorbonne* (when it meditates) and *la tronche* (when the executioner cuts it—III, 663). The cleavage between the head as object and subject is thus translated into metaphor by what Hugo con-

siders the supremely metaphoric language of misery: the
verbe-forçat. The language of the law further reifies the "thinking head" (the *"tête qui pense"*) by throwing it into what is
called the "balance of justice" (iii, 664). The public prosecutor
asks specifically for the *head*.

The head fixation focuses on a more basic split: the *separation* from the trunk. The Condemned Man imagines the
priest's remaining with him until "the head is here and the
body there" (iii, 694). He puzzles over which part the ghost
will choose: "Is the specter head or trunk?" (iii, 702.) He sees
himself as "something" foul (*immonde*): a head on the one
side, a trunk on the other (iii, 690). A double principle gov-
erns this body-object obsession: the head as an internal and an
external reality; the glance of the subject and the glance of the
other. At the beginning, in the episode of the chain gang, the
victim is still the observed observer; as the text progresses, he
increasingly views himself as the seen but unseeing object.
Hence the insistence on his execution as spectacle. The words
"spectacle" and "spectator" recur with frequency, invariably
to suggest a morbid fascination ("avid" curiosity, "avid and
cruel spectators"). The crowd, also viewed in terms of *heads*
("sea of heads," "mob of heads")—a horrible and hateful
mob pushing for a good view of the gruesome solemnity—
becomes the symbol of the *other* who rejects him within himself (iii, 707-711, 706).

Locked up in his own being, the prisoner experiences what
Baudelaire, in a different context, was to call "man's fearful
marriage to himself." The novel opens with the observation
that he must henceforth live alone with his "thought" (*"j'ha-
bite avec cette pensée, toujours seul avec elle . . ."*). The obsession
with the head thus assumes from the outset the value of a
tête-à-tête: an intimate confrontation that confuses object and
subject. Explicit mentions of a face-to-face in the cell stress
the motif of the split personality. He finds himself *"face à face"*
with his condemnation, *"seul à seul"* with an idea; holding his
"heavy head" in his two hands, he withdraws into his own
"self." Courage itself is defined through the acceptance of

a tête-à-tête with the fixed idea: "Well then! Let's be coura-
geous with death, let's grip this horrible idea with our two
hands, and let's stare into its face" (III, 701).

This confrontation operates in fact as a major metaphorical
inversion. For it is not so much prison that imposes itself as
the locus of a fixation; that fixation truly "possesses" and im-
prisons him. It is external reality that here assumes a figural
value. The opening signals of the text once again give precious hints. Chapter I begins and ends with the identical verb-
less exclamation ("Condemned to death!"), thus locking the
chapter on itself, and prefiguring the locked-in structure of a
novel whose very title begins with the terminal adjective
"last" (*dernier*). The beginning of the opening paragraphs
("Now" and "Before") establishes more than a contrast between life outside and inside of jail: it signals an initiation to a
new sense of time. "Each minute had its own idea": the notion of mental mobility is further stressed by the words "fantasies," "arabesques," "embroider," "unfold" (*dérouler*). But
that was *before*. *Now* temporal dynamics have been arrested.
"Now I am a captive." From the outset, the text, through a
shift in temporal perspective, internalizes the enclosure. The
third paragraph provides the pivot. The prison image is
turned upside down: ". . . my mind is imprisoned in an idea."
From that point on, the development follows its own logic:
the prison-thought is inscribed on the walls of the real prison
("*cette fatale pensée écrite dans l'horrible réalité qui m'entoure*").
This in turn establishes a correspondence between interiority
and exteriority; it links the notion of writing to the metaphor
of the wall.

The essence of metaphor is in the reversibility. The obsession of imprisonment becomes the prison of obsession. But
this is not a one-way operation. The correlative thought-
edifice is a recurrent feature in Hugo. In *Notre-Dame de Paris*:
". . . *tout édifice est une pensée*." Inversely, Frollo states: ". . . I
carry the dungeon within me."[8] The reference to the great
bell of Notre-Dame, the *bourdon*, suggests that Hugo's mind
was already elaborating basic images of the historical novel.

The intertextual bond between the two works is in fact deeper still, as hinted by the analogy of the two cavities, tower and skull, in chapter XXXVI of *Le Dernier Jour d'un Condamné*. "There is something like the sound of bells that shakes the cavities of my brain. . . ." As for the "almost co-substantial" coupling of a human being (Quasimodo) and an edifice (the cathedral), it is the obverse of the personification of the prison-edifice (*"espèce d'être horrible"*—III, 680).

Conversely, the incarcerated brain becomes a prison. Hugo plays on the container image. The brain pulsates against the walls of the skull (*"les parois du crâne"*—III, 699). The figure is a familiar one in Hugo's work. In *Les Misérables* we shall again find these inner partitions of the prison-brain, the *"cloisons de notre cerveau."* This metaphorical network relates to the notion of poetic vision. The image of the skull, the *cerveau muré*, must be read against that other image of the captive brain, somber restricted area where "doubt" weaves and suspends its spider-like web on the ceiling of its dungeon.[9] Doubt, but also visionary transcendence. There is more than plot to explain why, in *Quatrevingt-Treize*, that other Condemned Man, the dreamer-soldier Gauvain, experiences his intensest vision beneath the double vault of a real as well as figural dungeon: the *voûte visionnaire* of his brain confirms the convertibility of the metaphor.[10]

A nightmare, according to Bachelard, is a dungeon.[11] The Condemned Man's cell is also the locus of a specific anguish: the walls on which his destiny is written, walls literally "covered with writing" (graffiti, bizarre drawings, fragments of thoughts left behind by former prisoners) and which assume the function of a "strange book," keep alive a more fundamental question about the production of the text itself. To write or not to write? At this level, the novel obliquely deals with the writer's vocation. Chapter VI assumes a special status: it focuses sharply on the confrontation with the idée fixe (*seul à seul avec une idée*), but also raises in explicit terms the problem of *writing*. "Since I have the means to write, why wouldn't I? But to write what?" Prison punishment and poetic vocation are thus bound up; yet a gap is made manifest between saying and doing.

The opening signals once again have proleptic value. The "before" at the beginning of the second paragraph evokes the portrait of a man who, even though he is not called a poet, possesses a poetic nature. His youthful mind is described as "full of fantasies." He speaks, much as an artist might, of his gifts. "There was a permanent feast in my imagination." From the "stuff" (*étoffe*) of life, he elaborates "endless arabesques": he weaves and textures. But this former self is now dead; the man supremely endowed for the joys of sensibility and creation has vanished. All that remains are vestigial clues. Unlike Claude Gueux, who does not even know how to read, the Condemned Man had a study (a "cabinet") into which he retreated to work and converse with friends (III, 702). He is a man of culture; he knows Latin. And his first contact with capital punishment is literary: he remembers "having read in some book" that all men are condemned to death (III, 662). But these vestigial memories are also the signs of a cultural malaise, and more precisely of the malaise of culture itself. The Condemned Man is scoffingly addressed as "marquis" by the sardonic convict who inflicts on him his slangy eloquence and brutal laughter. Faced with this verbal realism, symptom of the realities of misery and of crime, the protagonist experiences his refined education as guilt, while suffering from an "honest" man's revulsion for the outlaw: "I recoiled with horror" (III, 688). Significantly, he is afraid of physical force. ("Had I refused, he would have struck me with his heavy fists"—III, 690).

The discovery of legal and social alienation is indeed coupled with the intuition of a more fundamental estrangement. The rift within the self is the reflection of a painful awareness: the presence of the "other," embodied not by abstract judges, but by the hostile crowd, the *horrible peuple*—laughing and screaming—in whose presence cultural refinement is not even worth a sneer. Hence a fascination akin to hatred that fuses into a single otherness the convict as well as the spectators of the execution. The "others," with their "atrocious snickering" and their fingers pointed at him, are like demons about to assault his cell (III, 673-674). The crowd waits for him with a furious joy. Hence also the prevailing notion of the spectacle and the aggressive glance. The presence of "avid and cruel spectators" moreover stresses a particular form of guilt. The collective glance takes on its full intensity during the nightmare that peoples his cell with figures carrying their head in their left arm. They shake their fists at him. Only one figure does not accuse him: the parricide (III, 669). The affective network parricide-eye-guilt, central in Hugo's work, spreads beyond the confines of this novel.

But what the novel does suggest within its own confines is that the poetic spirit, *plein de fantaisies*, dies, or is denied, only to allow for the emergence of a new consciousness. To write is henceforth conceived as a tragic activity: one writes on the wall, with one's own blood. The Condemned Man thinks of his daughter who might read him: ". . . she must know . . . why the name I leave her is covered with blood" (III, 706). The old man is dead: the reborn consciousness knows that its place is with the victims, amidst the captives of this world. It knows that a "significant affinity"—as Albert Béguin put it—binds the destiny of the poet to that of the prisoner.[12] Ever since "Le Poète dans les Révolutions," Hugo did not tire proclaiming this affinity.

> La prison est son sanctuaire,
> Et l'échafaud est son trépied.

Le Dernier Jour d'un Condamné marks, however, a turning point. Theme and private phantasms have come to merge.

Dostoevsky too, in his moving letter to his brother, records the death of the esthete. The "head" that has lived for art has been brutally severed. (The image of decapitation, since Dostoevsky had been threatened with the firing squad, is clearly another allusion to Hugo's novel.) Nonetheless he declares, a few paragraphs later, that life without the possibility of writing would be intolerable. And here is the point:

writing will never again be the same activity. The new man becomes another: *a man* among men. Hugo liked to sum up his life with the terse formula: *"solitaire, solidaire."*[13] This lapidary statement supports Georges Poulet's contention that no writer has lived out more intensely the "solitude of the self" and the "solitude of the world"; and yet the one exists only to the extent that it is fused with the other. "There is no real otherness because there is no real personality."[14] And indeed, the Condemned Man remains nameless; his own daughter, who does not recognize him, calls him "Monsieur" (III, 704). Is this not because, at the heart of this novel, Hugo has situated the problem of the writer who strips himself of his own physiognomy, so as to find a voice which will never again be quite the same?

TO ESCAPE IS TO BE SAVED

This depersonalized, though by no means anonymous, voice henceforth speaks for the world. A rhetoric of space characterizes Hugo's image of the poet: conversations with the ocean, boundless visions, the seer's attraction to immense perspectives that guide him toward the unexplored center of an enigma. The prison seems forgotten. The cell appears incompatible with this glance toward the unknown.

Hugo likes to pose as nature's privileged interlocutor; he sees himself as the bard of freedom and movement. Whether he flees the city, stares at windswept clouds, interrogates the tumultuous surface of the sea, freedom and space are linked in a rather conventional manner. Mountains symbolize proud independence. Flight toward the upper regions repeatedly tempts his imagination. Hence the frequent image of the open or half-open window, and the many dreams of levitation. All is in motion; all in fact *is* movement. Everywhere Hugo senses the sexual urge (the *rut*) of infinity. He associates poetic genius with the lack of all restraints. Constriction of any sort is for him a symptom of decadence. What he exalts above all is the potential of man, a potential defined in "anti-prison"

terms. "*Le monstre a le carcan, l'homme a la liberté,*" proclaims
the oracular voice of the "Bouche d'ombre." God *wants* freedom, explains the Angel of Rationalism in the philosophical
poem *Dieu*. This statement, less simplistic than appears at
first, casts light on Bishop Myriel's decision, early in *Les Misérables*, to have all locks removed. His house, before he
moved into it, was armed with bolts and locks "like a prison
door" (xi, 69).

The prison image, even when projected in such preteri-
tional terms, thus remains a permanent feature in Hugo's
work. Some of the oppressive visions of incarceration and
degradation can be traced to early encounters with brutality:
human limbs hanging from trees along an Italian road, scaffolds and bodies glimpsed by the young boy during his early
travels in Spain. A case could also be made for strictly literary
influences. The setting and the props of some of his works
seem to be borrowed from Gothic fiction: rattling chains, spiral staircases, threatening fortresses. Keys, corridors, traps,
are constantly mentioned. Frollo, who communicates secretly
from cloister to church, seems to come straight out of a novel
by Lewis or Ann Radcliffe. Even more suggestive of this
Gothic influence are the haunted houses, the living structures
(Notre-Dame sets itself in motion, its heavy columns become
gruesome legs), the edifices that bury and are in turn buried
alive.

Yet, for Hugo, this is not a passing fashion. His fascination
for macabre scenes and for detailed accounts of tortures (red-
hot pincers, molten lead, wheels and racks, ships and shred-
ding flesh) is part of a larger vision. *Les Voix intérieures*, which
offer the bucolic notes of "A Virgile," also impose the convulsive images of "A Albert Dürer": forests of monstrous
trees, with twisted branches, knotted underbrush, contorted
vegetation—threatening excrescences that seize and crush.
The whirlpool, the vortex, the abyss are even more fundamental obsessions. "*Gouffre amer*" is not merely a cliché, con-
veniently rhyming with *mer*; it is a key formula. Text after
text alludes to the love-fear of the vertiginous fall, of the trap,
of the gaping void. This terror of the fall, in *Dieu*, is qualified

as the *"formidable amour de l'abîme."* Hugo's Satan is a prisoner of infinity.

In his arsenal of terror, Hugo treasures of course more precise images of constriction and incarceration: oneiric ceilings (the *plafond effrayant*) in *"A Celle qui est voilée"* (IX, 339); endless varieties of webs and spiders; chains of all sizes (the "titanic" chain hanging from the axle tree near the Thénardier inn is a chain "worthy of a convict-Goliath"); caves and caverns; visions of granitic, geometric, immobilizing shapes, such as the heavy stone fortresses in *Les Burgraves* and *La Légende des siècles*.

Certain stone nightmares bring to mind Piranesi, whose name comes up in various contexts. In *Les Orientales*, Hugo had already projected a somber tower of Babel, a formidable "pile of towers" (III, 133). One of the settings of *Marie Tudor* is a room with stairs leading one does not know where. The immense edifice in "La Pente de la rêverie," a prefiguration of the metaphysical wall of *La Légende des siècles*, is an avatar of the Biblical tower. Babel is indeed a recurrent motif; it rhymes with Abel. In fact, Cain is never far off—and Cain is for Hugo the embodiment of crime and of bad conscience.[15]

The poem in which the Piranesian perspective is explicitly brought to bear on the Babel image is "Puits de l'Inde! . . ." in *Les Rayons et les Ombres* (*"Effrayantes Babels que rêvait Piranèse!"*)—a crucial poem which juxtaposes dizzying stairs and ramps, chaotic pilings-up of walls and landings, dark and damp cells, spiders in crypts, oozing partitions, threatening structures that seem to come to life. Dripping and trickling (the *suintement* of the "cold drop" is elsewhere compared to a tear of infinity—IX, 315) suggest the action of time: a drop can *in time* hollow out an immense well. In one of the early episodes of *Dieu*, a drop of water scoops out gigantic holes, builds vast pediments, titanic portals, huge temple-like structures. Wherever these Piranesian effects appear—apocalyptic visions, intermingling images of scaffolds, archaeological rubble and massive prisons haunted by Michelangelesque silhouettes—the result is a figure of incarceration.[16]

To this must be added a wide range of subterranean images

(the underground hole, the labyrinth, forms and beings buried alive) suggestive of entrapment in hell. Even in the luminous *Orientales*, the repeated epigraphs drawn from Dante reveal darker preoccupations. Every reader of Hugo's poetry—even the early one—is familiar with the broadening spirals that lead towards underworld Last Judgment scenes. The repeated image of the labyrinth is equally striking: the Paris sewer system in *Les Misérables*, this gut of the modern Babylon, is filled with ducts, caeca, blind alleys, crypts, ancient cells. The Roman sewer in *Les Châtiments* is another hideous intestine whose fetid, suppurating quality suggests contamination and moral pathology. *"Je suis le regardeur formidable du puits,"* Hugo writes in *Dieu* (*O.H.*, p. 22). He likes to define himself as the one who looks searchingly into the pit. Subterranean horror fascinates him, as does the theme of the *inferi*: not only because he cannot tolerate the idea of eternal punishment, but because he is haunted by the notion of death-in-life. Hence repeated scenes involving people buried alive: feeble voices of half-buried soldiers after the battle of Waterloo; Jean Valjean accepting the stratagem of being buried; the condemned man in *Torquemada* forced to descend step by step into the hole that is to be walled up.

Hugo's vocabulary betrays this central obsession: the words *carcan*, *écrou*, *fer*, *cachot*, *geôle*, *trappe*, *oubliette*, *barreaux*, *grilles*, *soupirail*, *cage* (of iron, bronze or stone), *cellule*, *bagne*, *verrou*, *captif*, *boulet*, the verbs *garotter* and *murer* appear with striking frequency. The prison image serves as metaphor for a wide range of ideas: the restrictive rules of neo-classical tragedy (negative value), Eschylean fate (positive value), insomnia, states of alienation. As soon as monastic rules or values are brought up, the prison image almost automatically appears. In *Les Misérables*, the correlation is thematized: the convent of the Petit-Picpus, a blissful refuge for Cosette and Jean Valjean, is for the latter a lugubrious reminder of the penitentiary. Throughout his work, Hugo mobilizes images of incarceration, as well as of tortures, physical degradation, and jail-rot. The digression on slang in *Les Misérables* becomes a pretext for evoking the underground jail, the hell-like sepulcher below the Châtelet. Elsewhere, he conjures up hallucinatory figures from myth, from literature, or from historical legends, such as Dante's Ugolino (whom hunger in jail drove to feed on his children) or the Man with the Iron Mask, whom he planned to make the hero of his drama *Les Jumeaux.* [17]

Many texts of Hugo in fact take place in prison, or turn around the theme of imprisonment: *Le Dernier Jour d'un Condamné, Claude Gueux, Marie Tudor, Les Burgraves, Les Misérables, La Fin de Satan* (an important section of which is entitled "La Prison"), *L'Homme qui rit* with its penal cave and ritual of torture—not to mention diverse poems on Napoleon as the great captive. *Notre-Dame de Paris*, Hugo's first elaborate fiction, can be read as systematic variations on the theme of claustration. Frollo is walled in by his books (solipsism of the intellect), just as Quasimodo is walled in by his deafness and his misshapen body. Spiritual deformity is in turn converted into metaphors of incarceration: Quasimodo's soul is a chained psyche, in a dark cavern filled with blind alleys. Even sexual repression and sadistic urges are translated into prison images. Frollo's lust convulsively lifts the "chain of vows"; he yearns to copulate with his victim in her sordid cell, while proclaiming (motif of moral deformity): "I carry the cell within me." Conversely, the cell-like room of the archdeacon, as well as the cathedral itself, are viewed as spaces of confinement. As for the numerous literal chains and literal jails in the novel, they seem to correspond to the private obsession which his wife Adèle, without suspecting the full meaning of the image, projects in *Victor Hugo raconté par un témoin de sa vie* (IV, 1192): the poet, about to begin *Notre-Dame de Paris*, bought himself ink, a heavy woollen sweater, locked up all his clothes so as not to be tempted to go out, and "entered into his novel as into a prison." [18]

A poetry of escape is elaborated through the metaphor of enclosure. Melodramatic flights take on moral and metaphysical meanings. In the cloistered night of *Dieu*, one hears the "fleeing" of the winds (*évasion des vents*—O.H., p. 27). Accounts of prisoners' escapes are proposed as exploits of the highest order: Jean Valjean's repeated achievement against all odds, that of thirty prisoners in *Les Misérables* who manage to vanish through the canal of the latrines, the mysterious disappearance of Claquesous, the suspenseful escape of Thénardier. Such exploits are considered with something akin to awe. Hugo marvels at these "bold inventions of the penitentiary." The link between artistic genius and the prisoners' escape feat is made explicit: *il y a des Benvenuto Cellini au bagne* (xi, 587). These dynamics of escape ultimately transform even the most sordid escapee into an inspired individual. "The effort toward liberation is no less surprising than the wing beat toward the sublime" (xi, 691). For Hugo, every escape is an allegory of the creative act. Poets, he explains in *William Shakespeare*, have revelatory "*échappées*" which allow them to pierce the clouds. (The substantive *échappée* means not only breakaway, but glimpse, and even vision.) "An escape is a cure" (*Une évasion, c'est une guérison*), he writes in *Les Misérables* (xi, 412). What is involved is the liberation of the soul, the freeing of the spirit. The "fearful thirst for freedom" sanctifies man, metamorphosing stupidity into instinct, instinct into intelligence, intelligence into genius (xi, 691). All nature strives towards liberty. It is the itinerary of spiritual progress and universal redemption. The comet flying through space appears to Hugo as a sinister world cast loose in search of absolute purity:

> *Est-ce qu'on ne voit pas que c'est une échappée?*
> *Peut-être est-ce un enfer dans le ciel envolé.*
>
> (xv, 753)

PRISON AS INCUBATION

This dream of metaphysical freedom and of total redemption carries us to the heart of Hugo's visionary world. Originally, however, the prison obsession operates at the socio-political level. The dream is at first limited to the destruction of all physical jails.

> *Saint-Lazare—il faudra broyer cette bâtisse!*
> *Il n'en restera pas pierre sur pierre un jour!*
>   (VIII, 708)

This demolition-wish in *Les Châtiments* reflects a rebellion against all abuse of power. Prison, in this context, is both symbol and symptom of social injustice. Hugo turns vehement when speaking on behalf of the victims and the disinherited. Christ, Socrates, Jean Huss appear to him as archetypal figures of glorious outcasts. He prides himself on being the champion of a "damned" humanity, on being one of the first "socialists" (IX, 255; XII, 274). His hatred of the jailor is equalled only by his hatred of the hangman. The horror-fascination for the scaffold that allowed him to imagine the anguish of the Condemned Man still animates, many years later, the noble figure of Saint François de Paule in *Torquemada*. It could be said of Hugo what he himself said of Bishop Myriel in *Les Misérables*: "To have seen the guillotine was for him a shock. . . . The scaffold is a vision."[19]

There is ample evidence that Hugo documented himself in some detail on prison conditions: the convict scenes in *Le Dernier Jour d'un Condamné*, the workshop in *Claude Gueux*, the Force prison "punishment chamber" in *Les Misérables*.[20] An abandoned fragment of the latter novel is entirely given over to prison mores. Prison slang fascinates him.[21] When he was elevated to the dignity of Pair de France, he made use of his new prerogatives to visit the jail of the Conciergerie. In *Choses vues*, he describes this inspection: the feeling of darkness and oppression, an odor *sui generis*, the death-cell, the torture chamber. The visit stimulates his imagination. In 1847, he is at it again, visiting a death row. In 1855, he asks the Provost of Guernesey for permission to visit the island's prison. "L'Echafaud" of *La Légende des siècles* draws on this new inspection. Not only the décor (the thickness of the walls, the quality of light and air) holds his interest, but the psychology and behavior of the prisoners.

Society is severely indicted. For it is society that breeds crime. The father stealing bread for his child, the child forced to work under inhuman conditions, already live in a prison-hell. In *Les Châtiments*, Hugo evokes the horrible cave-dwellings of Lille, where a sordid sub-proletariat dies a daily death. The real prison, where these victims of the social order unavoidably end up, accelerates the process of degradation. Prison soils and distorts. It is ironic and revealing that Inspector Javert, the inverted image of the redeemed criminal Valjean whom he pursues, was born in prison.[22] A chapter of *Les Misérables* is entitled "Embryonic formation of crime in the prison incubation" (*Formation embryonnaire des crimes dans l'incubation des prisons*). Injustice produces and justifies hatred. What does one hear in the penitentiary? "An immense curse, gnashing of teeth, hatred, desperate malice, an enraged cry against the human association, a sarcastic outburst against heaven" (xi, 426).

This curse, seeming to rise out of one of Dante's *bolge*, must be met with immense love and pity. Higher even than the demands of justice, such love and pity are the supreme glory of the visionary poet—the *mage*. In the famous poem "Les Mages," in *Les Contemplations*, Rousseau, Voltaire, and Beccaria meet in the same stanza to wrestle with hatred. And later, in *William Shakespeare*, when Hugo examines the function of the modern poet, it is to proclaim once again that the *mage* of the 19th century, a child of the Revolution, must first of all be a brother to all the oppressed, the outcast, the damned (xii, 309).

The political significance of the prison image is a permanent feature of Hugo's writing. For him also the Bastille is the chief symbol of the Ancien Régime. But, like Michelet, he is aware that the Revolution has not put an end to the Bastille. The political symbolism logically becomes more pronounced as he moves away from his early conservative position. By the time he writes the vituperative *Les Châtiments*, after Louis Bonaparte's coup d'état, all of France appears to him as a huge iron cage. And beyond the metaphor, he glimpses the suffering of the political victims: in French Guinea, in Blidah, in airless African penitentiaries. From his own exile, he predicts that the inflammatory torches of rebellion will soon fill Paris with awe and hope, that the hour of retribution is near. *"Brisez vos fers, forcez vos geôles,"* is his impassioned call to civil mutiny (VIII, 684, 696, 716). The "sacred right" of Revolution haunts Hugo more than ever, after his conversion to Republican ideals. His last novel, *Quatrevingt-Treize* (1874), echoes his fear of popular violence expressed in the 1832 preface to *Le Dernier Jour d'un Condamné* (IV, 484): "In times of revolution, watch out for the first head that falls. It makes the people thirsty for blood" (*Elle met le peuple en appétit*). Yet—at the surface at least—Hugo seems to have appeased his doubts (but how is one to reconcile hatred of violence and belief in history's justice?) by absolving Revolutionary excesses as a necessary remedy, by pitting the transitory against the eternal order.

> *Les révolutions, qui viennent tout venger,*
> *Font un bien éternel dans leur mal passager.*
> (IX, 254)

It is because France towers as the "mother of revolutions" that its political enslavement by Napoleon-the-Little appears to him as a particularly hideous crime.

THE DARK CAPTIVE

The myth-making process is more fundamental, however, than historical considerations. Even in the most political lines of *Les Châtiments*, where Hugo's indignation enjoys free rein, it is the image of the glorious Convict (the *forçat*) that prevails. This image of the demonic convict, merging with that of the social and political victim, ultimately assumes metaphysical significance. For Hugo, as for Dostoevsky, the penitentiary is

the house of the dead, the locus of the *Dies irae*, of a living
hell-death (an *affreuse mort vivante*—xi, 206), but also of a possible redemption.

The penitential symbol of rebellion and damnation is first a
symbol of the status of man. "Mankind is in jail" (*Le genre
humain est au cachot*), cries out Gwynplaine in *L'Homme qui rit*
(xiv, 350). Echoes of Dante blend with echoes of Pascal. It is
in the philosophical poems of *Les Contemplations* that this
image of the *cachot* is most insistent. In the mournful poems
"Pauca Meae," man is shown as a convict weighted down by
a heavy chain. In "Pleurs dans la nuit," he is the somber prisoner (*reclus ténébreux*) behind iron bolts and inflexible doors.
In "Ce que dit la bouche d'ombre," he is the regal captive, the
majestic convict, sobbing in his oppressive cell. The motif in
fact becomes redundant. In *Dieu* (*O.H.*, p. 128), man
glimpses the world through a hole in the prison wall; his one
dream is to escape. Yet escape poses a serious problem. For
man *is* prison; the fallen spirit has been transfixed into matter.
Hugo's vision implies metempsychosis and a hierarchy of
spirits, beings, and things. The oracular voice from the dark,
the *bouche d'ombre* explains: "*L'ange devient l'esprit, et l'esprit
devient l'Homme.*" The fallen spirit, transfixed into matter, becomes the jail. The lapsed soul has been transmuted into
man-prison, animal-prison, tree-prison, stone-prison. But
this degradation also means nostalgia for what was lost.
Hugo's Lucifer cries out his hope for an upward movement:
"*Laissez-moi remonter, gouffres!*" Hence the title promising redemption: *La Fin de Satan*. The end will be the beginning: the
law of Hugo's world is a return up to daylight.[23]

Hugo's originality, with regard to political and theological
thinking, is to situate incarceration within man, to make of
man's own guilt his jailor. What is the "hidden cave" in *Les
Burgraves* if not the metaphor of remorse, the private enclosure where the memory of crime continues to ooze? The
spider is caught in its own web. Once again the "voice of
darkness" is oracular, as it states the nature of this self-
incarceration: "*Toute faute qu'on fait est un cachot qu'on s'ouvre.*"

This formula casts light on the figure of Cain which haunts the poet's imagination. Psychoanalytic criticism tends to interpret this figure as the expression of Hugo's guilt toward his rival-brother who died insane. And surely the figure of Cain has intimate meaning. But does it relate only to the brother? Is Cain not the archetype of all of nature's perverters, the "ancestor of the dark creatures," as the poet puts it in *La Fin de Satan*? The nail, the stick, and the stone that served for fratricide have become War, Gallows, and Prison. Above all, Cain is the eternal prisoner of his immured conscience. For crime is the true dungeon: Cain cannot flee from the eye of God (x, 441-442).

The paradox is flagrant: on the one hand, there is the horror of crime and punishment; on the other, prison becomes a holy place. Prison horror leads to nightmarish realism. The typical prisoner is described in his agitated immobility, permanently re-awakening to his desperate condition.

> *Le captif, va, vient, tremble: il fait de vagues pas,*
> *Sent à son pied sa chaîne et s'arrête farouche,*
> *Boit à sa cruche, mord à son pain noir, se couche,*
> *Se lève, se rendort, tressaille, et, réveillé,*
> *Dit: Où suis-je? qui suis-je? et tâte un mur mouillé.*
> (La Fin de Satan, x, 1780)

Yet in the earliest *Odes* (i, 811) prison is already called a sanctuary. The paradox is of a metaphysical nature: the convict is compared to the devil, and the devil in turn presented as a convict; inversely, the convict appears as a Promethean visionary, as hero and angel ("infamous angel" to be sure, and "hideous hero") and ultimately, in the final pages of *Les Misérables*, as a radiant, deified figure. Jean Valjean, in the apotheosis of his death, becomes Christ-like.

The pivot of the paradox is the theme of redemption. Here Hugo's ambiguities toward solitude become most revealing. He condemns solitude without reservations. It is a curse. "All of hell is in this word: solitude," he writes in *La Fin de Satan*. Solitude dehumanizes; it is a form of castration. The world, in

the eyes of Hugo, is a "totality where no one is alone" (*Dieu*,
O.H., 133). To cut oneself off from others is suicide. It is also
a moral desertion. Woe to him who abandons his brothers!

> *Malheur à qui dit à ses frères*
> *Je retourne dans le désert.*
>   (VI, 27)

What is at stake is more fundamental than a moral precept.
Hugo thinks of isolation with what amounts to sacred horror.
His love of children, his need to surround himself with
human presences (his exile was complete with wife, family,
and mistress!) reflect this fear of "detachment." His poetry
thematizes and symbolizes this rejection of solitude. The
Comet, in *La Légende des Siècles*, emerges from its hideous isolation to prevent the "fearful celibacy of the void" (*l'effrayant
célibat de l'abîme*—XIV, 934). And the Human Spirit, at the
outset of *Dieu* (*S.G.*, 27) asseverates that it is horrible to be
alone.

Aloneness is however the apanage of genius. Imagination
functions at that price. That no doubt is why Hugo insists on
the dangers of reverie, which he associates with solitude. He
warns a fellow writer suffering from depressions: "Solitude
brings sadness; reverie has a disturbing effect" (*Choses vues*).
The important poem "La Pente de la rêverie" opens with the
warning not to "dig" beneath the surface of reality, not to
penetrate into the uncanny dream world. The slope and the
spiral lead to madness (IV, 426). Ultimately, the dreaming
mind becomes another jail. How indeed is one to extricate
oneself from the dreaming self? "What a Gordian knot is our
reverie!" Hugo exclaims in *William Shakespeare* (XII, 246).
"Inner servitude, there is true slavery!"

The topos of the skull-as-prison is thus clearly bound up
with the notion of infinity compressed inside the mind of the
poet.[24] In almost Baudelairian lines, Hugo describes this
skull-dungeon, this *caveau muré* complete with symbolic
spider (doubt) and spider's web (paralysis of the will):

L'homme, esprit captif, les écoute,
Pendant qu'en son cerveau le doute,
Bête aveugle aux lueurs d'en haut,
Pour y prendre l'âme indignée
Suspend sa toile d'araignée
Au crâne, plafond du cachot.
(IX, 358)

But the ambiguity remains: solitude means Moses on the "mountain" as well as Satan in the "abyss."

Toute solitude est un gouffre,
Toute solitude est un mont.
(IX, 203)

This ambiguity is didactically illustrated in the long digression on convents in *Les Misérables*. The monastic life, with its mortification of the flesh, is a wasting away, a form of emasculation, a parasitic teeming hostile to progress, a basic dehumanization. Yet in those same pages on the Petit-Picpus convent, monastic virtues are extolled: the practice of equality and fraternity, the venerability of voluntary exile and renunciation, prayer as an opening unto the unknown. Behind it all, a personal note: the image of the convent is associated with the figures of the mother and the fiancée. Some of Hugo's intimate childhood impressions go back to the Parisian house and garden situated on the ground of the former Feuillantines convent.

Anchoritic and cenobitic aspirations compete with each other throughout his work. In his earliest poems, the "isolated cell," as well as the hermit's "desert," appear to him as privileged settings for the visionary poet. As an epigraph to his 25th Ode, he quotes Calderon's lines in praise of the *amena soledad* (III, 463). Long before his own self-imposed exile, he described himself, in a sumptuous line, as "the banished, proud and solitary king" (*le roi banni, superbe et solitaire"*—II, 500). Solitude is the apanage of the strong. When Hugo qualifies himself as *l'homme des solitudes* (the plural gives it a special dimension), he raises himself to the level of the free and mighty figures of his poems: the Cid who claims to be his own cage and his own key; Masferrer, a lonely "eagle" inebriated with space; Welf, fierce and free in his tower. It is a tragic, but also a creative solitude. Divine inspiration is to be found far from the crowd:

> *Dieu t'attend dans les solitudes;*
> *Dieu n'est pas dans les multitudes.*
>
> (VI, 26)

And so is love. Hugo's dream world favors the happy enclosure, the privileged garden: memories, no doubt, of the conventual childhood garden "closed in by high walls," of the "solitary garden," evoked by the Condemned Man, which later appears again as Cosette's and Marius' love paradise in *Les Misérables*.

As for visionary solitude, it is often conceived in terms of altitude or flight into space (IV, 388). The poem "Magnitudo parvi" (IX, 204) tells of vatic solitude that leads to the impenetrable realm of *le démesuré*—a favorite notion of Hugo, meaning the creatively excessive, the immoderate, the boundless. Solitude, in this prophetic perspective, implies an expansion toward infinity. These fervent stanzas do indicate that, despite his horror-fascination, Hugo also conceives of a happy prison. If indeed enclosure is a refuge (Esmeralda in the Rat's Hole of the Recluse, Valjean in the confined space of the Petit-Picpus), it also functions as the locus of inner freedom. The four walls of the cell serve the reverie of superior souls. Indeed Hugo reinforces the image by reversing the terms of the metaphor: intellectual concentration becomes the equivalent of prison walls (". . . *ces absorptions profondes . . . qui emprisonnent même le regard et qui équivalent à quatre murs*"—XI, 649).

Visionary occultation is the obverse of spiritual flight. In either case, the prison symbol serves the dream of freedom. Salvation through prison is the exemplary itinerary of Jean

Valjean. The Petit-Picpus convent—a prison shelter for the escapee—is a necessary stage, just as the escape through the sewer system implies an ascent through the fall. Valjean sees the light in the darkest hour. In *Choses vues*, Hugo explains: "When one is imprisoned one finds light in the darkest cave." Not everyone of course is up to such trials. Hence the ambiguous status of solitude. "Solitude disturbs those it does not illumine" (vii, 966). But, on the other hand: "In profound souls isolation develops a particular wisdom that goes beyond man" (xv, 557).

That goes beyond man—such potential for grandeur and illumination justifies the conception of the mythic convict, of the Promethean *forçat*. The titan-slaves of *La Légende des siècles* are his brothers. The prodigious satyr who, before the assembled gods, sings a paean to Man, reflects in his eyes the stolen fire. Prometheus, for Hugo, is "vanquished righteousness" (xii, 247). He is the chained liberator, admirable in the bitter enjoyment of his own tragedy.

A psycho-historical transfer brings myth to bear on autobiography. Hugo reads Napoleon as a modern Prometheus. On the rock of Saint-Helena, he is the "captive giant" hallowed by misfortune. Several poems ("Deux Iles," "Lui") reveal him in a tragic pose. The most striking image appears in the famous "L'Expiation," where he is shown nailed to the hideous rock, with a vulture eating away at his heart. The "Homeric spectacle" of this chained Titan is again evoked in "Le Retour de l'Empereur."

The autobiographical elaboration is obvious. Hugo himself had a vocation for exile. In his juvenile *Odes* he already assumed an exile's pose. As for the real period of exile, after Louis Napoleon's coup d'état in 1851—a self-exile he voluntarily prolonged—it only strengthened his vocation. Grandiloquent lines in *Les Châtiments* express his pride:

> *Je t'aime, exil! douleur, je t'aime!*
> *Tristesse, sois mon diadème.*
> (viii, 616)

This stance of tragic joy is of course bound to the conviction that all great poets have been exiled, that exile of some sort is a requisite for greatness. In 1824 (Hugo is barely 22 years old), he observes: "Dante was banned before he became a poet" (ii, 473).

Such glorification of exile is hardly distinguishable from glorification of imprisonment. In Hugo's terms, the shadow of the prison bars casts a light comparable to a saint's nimbus or glory.

> *J'admire, ô vérité, plus que toute auréole,*
> *Plus que le nimbe ardent des saints en oraison,*
> *Plus que les trônes d'or devant qui tout s'efface,*
> *L'ombre que font sur ta face*
> *Les barreaux d'une prison.*
>
> (viii, 274)

Even these lines have an autobiographic ring; they were addressed to his sons who, as editors of *L'Evénement*, had been jailed. Hugo later generalized, ironically: "Where would thought lead if not to prison?" (xii, 158.) After all, Voltaire's career began in the Bastille! But there is also the almost religious conviction that the prisoner, much like the pauper, is venerable. In a discarded fragment of *Les Misérables*, Hugo recalls that Tertullian named prisoners and slaves the "preferred ones," the *praelati*.[25] To suffer is to deserve. In "Dolor" (*Les Contemplations*), suffering is blessed for providing a key to heaven: *"Les souffrances sont des faveurs."* In the poem "Liberté" (*La Légende des siècles*) this spiritualization of the prisoner is more explicit still. "Wherever a prisoner cries and screams, God is witness" (*"Partout où pleure et crie un captif, Dieu regarde"*). The prisoner-martyr becomes a mediator between the human and the divine.

THE ABOLISHED PRISON

The mediating witness is of course the poet as defined in "Les Mages." Hugo proclaims the vatic mission of the visionary artist. Dark witnesses of space (*noirs témoins de l'espace*): the spatializing of the search for the ideal is a common topos. What characterizes Hugo is that elevation appears as flight; the movement towards light first implies a cage and the ability to make one's way through bars.

> *Ils sont le vrai, le saint, le juste,*
> *Apparaissant à nos barreaux.*
> *Nous sentons, dans la nuit mortelle,*
> *La cage en même temps que l'aile.*
> (ix, 360-361)

The effort to attain is bound to the discovery of a breach. The political context—in *Les Châtiments*, Hugo sees art as a chain-breaking activity (viii, 599)—banalizes the prison metaphor. Its full force is achieved as soon as it is transposed to a metaphysical context. In *Dieu* (*S.G.*, 78) Hugo asserts that the thinker, navigator-explorer of the infinite, always dreaming of a beyond, sets out to *climb space*, or better still to force his way into a beyond through an act of transcendental burglary. The word "effraction" is here converted into a redemptive signal. The *in* comes to signify *out*.

This double action of flight and breakthrough, linked in either case to the theme of imprisonment, symbolizes the visionary enterprise of the "Mages" determined to find the cleft in the wall. The wall, as a poetic figure, looms in fact everywhere in the work of Hugo. Walls, barriers, ceilings represent the fascination of the unseen. The black curtain of "La Vision de Dante" and the wall of violence in *Dieu* imply partitions that conceal the mystery of things. They suggest the immured unknown. At the beginning of *Notre-Dame de Paris*, Hugo writes that there is something utterly intriguing about a "wall behind which something goes on." The idea of a wall that prevents and promises a revelation, the "incurable desire" to peer over it, are to be found throughout Hugo's work. The high walls of the Feuillantines garden—the garden of his childhood and of first love—surely contributed to the sense of mystery and impenetrability.

In a broader perspective, the wall signifies spiritual blindness. In the 13th *Ode* ("L'Antéchrist"), the poet has Satan erect a "funereal wall" between man and heaven. But the image also functions as the symbol of the hidden God, the *Deus absconditus*, who sets man "on the black side of the dark barrier" (IX, 330). In any case, the wall implies a larger space; it indicates that the world is not confined. "To disappear is to reveal oneself" was the original title of the poem "Suprématie" in *La Légende des siècles*. In *Dieu*, a sinister lock, a heavenly latch, an immense bolt protect divine mystery. As for man, in solitary confinement, imprisoned like a fly "beating against dim windowpanes," he seeks an opening (*O.H.*, 25). For he will never be content to remain on this side of the wall. The sequestered soul will search for a way out. Flashes of light open up hallucinating vistas. Now and then the obstacle becomes almost transparent; no longer a wall, nor even a fog-bank: a web. How is one to prevent the prisoner's yearning for escape; how quell man's desire to crash into the infinite? Who can say, asks Hugo, "you will go no further"? Thus the "Mages" assail the unknown:

> [*Ils*] *parlent à ce mystère,*
> *Ils interrogent l'éternel,*
> *Ils appellent le solitaire,*
> *Ils montent, ils frappent au ciel.*

> (*They speak to this mystery,*
> *They question the eternal,*
> *They summon the recluse,*
> *They ascend, they beat at heaven's gate.*)

The image of the breach extends and elevates the cell imagery. Certain key verbs (to open, pierce, bore, slit, gape, crack) correspond to the desire to cross over and reach an invisible goal. Everywhere perspectives are glimpsed through narrow openings; mists or veils part, affording limitless views. Booz, in his dream, sees the gate of heaven "ajar." "La Pente de la rêverie" begins in front of a window, symbol of a thousand perspectives that each gust of wind reveals to the poet's glance. In "Magnitudo parvi," the eye pierces through the mirror. Everywhere there is the search for openings, for "fatal chinks" (*brèches fatales*).

Imagination is the great diver sounding the deep. *"Mes yeux plongeaient plus loin que le monde réel"* (My eyes plunged farther than the real world). The verbs "to sound" and "to dive" are also privileged terms. *"J'ai plongé dans le gouffre et l'ai trouvé profond."* In "La Vision de Dante," there are two gates: one opens onto ethereal space, the other is the mouth of the nether regions. This passage to the *inferi* is a recurrent feature: the ever-broadening spiral in "La Pente de la rêverie," the enormous spiral in "Après une lecture de Dante," the descent towards the invisible in the Parisian sewers, the Titan's escape through the well he digs (*La Légende des siècles*). But this descent is an ascension. "Whether one moves up or down, one only goes towards God," says the slave-architect in "Le Travail des captifs." By virtue of digging, one rediscovers light. Thus in *Dieu* Hugo speaks of the "supreme ascension of the fall." Death itself, at the end of the poem, is described in terms of a breakthrough.

The prison imagery thus encompasses the entire range of man's spiritual adventure. "Earthly claustration is an escape to heaven," Hugo writes in a notebook of 1860.[26] The remark casts light on a series of recurring images: the prophet who sees the world open up through a crack; the gaze of the solitary dreamer whose vision extends beyond the stars; vast panoramas glimpsed from cells; narrow enclosures with "the sky for a ceiling." In *Dieu* (*O.H.*, 110), paradise is descried through dungeon slits.

This rip caused by the "wind of infinity" (*Dieu*, *O.H.*, 24), this partition that intensifies the hunger for the absolute, imply the desire to navigate on the twin seas of time and space. Yet there is terror in this desire. The will to fathom the unfathomable is arrogant and perilous. The vatic dreamer becomes a "prowler along heaven's barrier," about to commit a crime—the crime of Icarus or of Nemrod, who, in his flying cage, takes off to conquer space and is then punished by God (*La Fin de Satan*). The terrifying ether should discourage even

the hardiest. "Plein ciel," a poem of utopian aeronautics, describes this spatial terror:

> *Pas si loin! pas si haut! redescendons. Restons*
> *L'homme, restons Adam . . .*

Dieu begins with the advice to remain within the limits of
mankind, locked within the human circle. The Sibyl in *La Fin
de Satan* also counsels sedentary prudence. God wants to be
contemplated, not looked at.

This terror in the face of the infinite explains the mortal pal-
lor and dreadful cry of the poet at the end of "La Pente de la
rêverie." One runs the risk of madness when confronting
limitless space. There is nothing to hold on to. Infinity itself
becomes a prison. One feels, as one of the voices in *Dieu* explains, thrown "into space, yet into jail." *Inferi* proposes the
image of an unwalled prison of the impalpable, a prison-space
where nothing arrests the upward drift. These spaceless con-
finements are named *lazarets de l'infini*. Beyond the uncanny
prison-globes and planet-jails stretches out an eternity that
tolerates no intrusion.

Yet Hugo sings of the "wild will" (*folle volonté*) to fathom
the unfathomable. Whatever the danger or impossibility of
the venture, man wants to affirm himself in space; he aspires
to read "the infinite work and the eternal poem." What
counts is the joy of liberation. For if Hugo's God remains
hidden, he nonetheless wants man's emancipation from the
shadows; he wants for man a freedom that delivers him from
eternal hell. A double liberation: as humanity moves towards
light, it also moves towards forgiveness.

Redemption, in Hugo's terms, could in fact be called *prison
abolished*. "*L'univers Châtiment monte à l'univers joie*" (*Dieu*,
O.H., 140). Such indeed is the meaning of Saint François de
Paule's words in *Torquemada*: "Never a chain, never a cell."
The notion of progress has been transposed to the metaphysical realm. Just as social progress will abolish life imprisonment and capital punishment, so an immense pardon will re-
integrate Judas amidst the elect. "Pardon is greater than Cain"

(*Dieu*, *O.H.*, 91). In the name of the victims, Hugo invokes pity for the jailor as well as for the hangman (ix, 313).

Joy in redemption, yes. But first comes the experience of confinement. Numerous passages describe universal pardon through the image of the abolished jail. "No eternal hell" (*Pas d'enfer éternel*) says the *bouche d'ombre*, the voice from the dark: a good enough reason for rejecting, or rather for transcending the penal notions of Christianity.[27] "No eternal hell," repeats the Angel in *Dieu*. For it is inconceivable that God punishes eternally and that paradise is a balcony overlooking the gallows. "No prison is eternal"—was already man's dream in the poem "Océan" (*La Légende des siècles*). And in the last lines of *La Fin de Satan*, at the instant of great pardon, God explains: "prison once destroyed abolishes Gehenna" (*la prison détruite abolit la géhenne*). Joy in redemption; nothing could be clearer. But for liberation to acquire its full beauty and meaning, it was first necessary, as in the case of Jean Valjean in *Les Misérables*, to know imprisonment and darkness; it was necessary to go through the evil narrows (*rétrécissement vicieux*) of the sewer. There, however, the light and the exit were to be found. For no one knows better than the prisoner the longing for a lost paradise.

Nerval's Privileged Enclosures

FACETIOUS PRISONS?

"Politique (1831)," originally entitled "Cour de prison," is one of the most graceful poems of *Petits Châteaux de Bohème*. Its wistful sadness and flexible workmanship bring to mind Verlaine.

> *Dans Sainte-Pélagie,*
> *Sous ce règne élargie,*
> *Où, rêveur et pensif,*
>   *Je vis captif,*
>
> *Pas une herbe ne pousse*
> *Et pas un brin de mousse*
> *Le long des murs grillés*
>   *Et frais taillés!*
>
> *Oiseau qui fends l'espace . . .*
> *Et toi, brise, qui passe*
> *Sur l'étroit horizon*
>   *De la prison,*
>
> *Dans votre vol superbe,*
> *Apportez-moi quelque herbe,*
> *Quelque gramen, mouvant*
>   *Sa tête au vent!*
>
> *Qu'à mes pieds tourbillonne*
> *Une feuille d'automne*
> *Peinte de cent couleurs*
>   *Comme les fleurs!*
> . . . .

The combination of a masculine rhyme and a four-syllable verse at the end of each stanza conveys the impression of broken movement, of interrupted flight. The meter serves irony.

The six-syllable lines lead to the claudication of the briefer verse. We are far indeed from André Chenier's famous *Iambes* which also describe a prison experience, but in the register of indignation.

> *Le messager de mort, noir recruteur des ombres,*
> *Escorté d'infâmes soldats*
> *Ebranlant de [son] nom ces longs corridors sombres*

To be sure, Nerval's poem draws on stereotypes of prison poetry: the wall, the bird, the wind, the glimpsed or remembered space. Yet in spite of the imagery and the literal meaning, the rhythmic pattern maintains an atmosphere of ease.[1]

The motif of the facetious prison, blending parody and melancholy, recurs in Nerval's work. "Sainte-Pélagie en 1832," first published in 1841 in *L'Artiste*, is a humorous text. The narrator, arrested for disturbing the peace, explains that he will never be a Silvio Pellico, but that he has known a real cell and seen the pale light of dawn filtered through barred windows. Waiting for daybreak and food, he and his dissolute companions evoke legendary prisoners who overcame their suffering by growing a flower or taming a spider. Then, feeling the pangs of appetite, they remember the tortures of Dante's Ugolino. But all ends well: they dine together gaily. Prison has in fact become so pleasant that the narrator requests to remain until the next day. The request is, however, not granted: he is set free, and not even allowed to finish his meal. Nerval concludes playfully: "I was about to give the spectacle of a prisoner forcefully thrown out of his jail."[2] This text, ironizing on a literary tradition, develops in its own self-conscious way the theme of the happy prison.

A similarly humorous imprisonment is described in the last three chapters of *Les Nuits d'Octobre*, where the travelling narrator, in search of *realism*, finds himself arrested and jailed in Crespy-en-Valois for having forgotten his passport in Meaux. The dream he has in his cell is filled with images explicitly attributed to Poe, Dickens, and Ainsworth. Masters of that "realism" he ironically wishes to emulate, they are all creators of scenes of incarceration. Once again, de-mystifying parody seems to take over. The narrator claims to be disappointed because the vault, which goes back to the time of the Crusades, has been patched up with concrete. "I was offended by this luxury; I would have liked to raise rats and to tame spiders." And there are other disappointments: the vault is not oozing humidity, the feather bed is equipped with a comfortable quilt.

But the reader must beware. An unspoken anguish underlies these apparently smiling pages. The irrational arrest corresponds to a no less irrational sense of guilt. *Vagabondage, essayisme, réalisme, troubadourisme exagéré*—these are snatches of sentences formulated in the indictment. In his dream, the narrator appears in court, facing a tribunal cut out against a background of "deep shadows." It is a literary guilt, perhaps a more secret guilt also, barely hinted at. The adventurous excursion ends in good fun, to the accompaniment of the gendarme's surly but fundamentally good-natured voice.

Nerval's smile often resembles a grimace of anguish. Ever since his earliest writings, dark humor presides over images of captivity. In *La Main enchantée* (1832), Eustache Bouteroue, locked up in a cell of the Châtelet for having slapped a judge, exercises his wit by metaphorizing the jail into a *vêtement de roc*. Here too, significantly, the narration turns around an absurd guilt, or rather an undemonstrable innocence. When the protagonist loudly proclaims that he is innocent, the jailor gently but firmly replies, in a tone calculated to calm down excitable inmates: "By golly . . . where do you think you are? We have only that kind here."[3] The answer is doubly ironic: it pretends to agree with the prisoner, while affirming ambiguously the essential innocence of any man in jail.

The prison motif haunts Nerval. Historic jails seem to charm him as they did other romantic lovers of local color and picturesque effects. He too was a reader of Latude and Casanova. The 12th letter of *Angélique* evokes, in tourist manner, Abélard's tower, as well as the underground cells and the prison where Louis the Debonnair was held captive by his children. The end of the chapter mentions the purchase of a book about the abbé de Bucquoy, with its title facing an engraving of the Bastille, the inscription "The Hell of the Living" (*L'Enfer des vivants*), and a quotation from the *Aeneid*: *Facilis descensus Averni* (sic). In a later addition to this passage, Nerval quotes André Chénier's famous lines on the hell of the Bastille and "holy liberty."

The book is in fact already mentioned at the beginning of *Angélique*, and for a good reason: the story of the abbé comte de Bucquoy had been fully developed in the text of the *Faux Saulniers* (1850), of which *Angélique* was an integral part before being detached and made into a separate story of *Les Filles du Feu*. This *Histoire de l'Abbé de Bucquoy* is almost entirely set in prison (at the For l'Evêque, in Soissons, in the Bastille) and shows that Nerval had been a most attentive reader of various so-called documentary texts on state prisons published during the Revolutionary years, in particular *La Bastille dévoilée* (1789) and probably also the *Mémoires Historiques et Authentiques sur la Bastille*. All the commonplaces of this kind of literature reappear: the eight towers of the Bastille, the oubliettes, the cruelty of the jailors (a governor's nephew tries to rape one of the prisoners and drives her to suicide), the ingenious efforts to make contact with the other captives or with the outside world (letter codes by means of knocks, pens and ink fabricated with pigeon bones and diluted soot)— nothing is left out, not even the macabre descriptions of the putrid corpse reminiscent of Pétrus Borel's collection of horrors in *Madame Putiphar*. As for the planned, aborted, and successful escapes (complete with ropes made from bed sheets and chair wicker, filed bars, drilled walls, crossings of moats filled with water and mud), they are no doubt inspired, as were so many adventures of this kind in 19th-century literature, by the famous exploits told in Latude's *Mémoires*. Romantic literature plays endless variations on this escape heroism.

THE "FANTASTIQUE SÉRIEUX"

Much of this might appear as a peculiarity of literary history, were it not for the tight link existing, throughout Nerval's work, between the motifs of enclosure, escape, and freedom. Personal experiences more significant than being arrested for disturbing the peace left their scar. The fear of madness and of commitment are echoed in his work: Hakem's stay in the Moristan insane asylum, Raoul Spifame's imprisonment in Bicêtre, the narrator's descent into the private hell of *Aurélia*, which proposes to describe a sickness that occurred entirely in the "mysteries of [his] mind." Nerval's taste for travel and aimless wandering is the psychological obverse of his claustrophobia. Enclosure and vagrancy remain simultaneous temptations.

Variants of close confinement constitute metaphoric avatars of the prison theme. Grim prisons, joyful prisons: Nerval's privileged fortresses suggest either an impossible search for a lost reality, or a dream-promise of the superior bliss of freedom. The *chateau périssable* of projected ideals or of past innocence remains, however, fundamentally disquieting. Seen from a distance, Beit-Eddin, the ancient residence of emirs in *Druses et Maronites*, resembles a fairy-tale castle. From close up, the only inhabited part of the ruins turns out to be a jail (II, 473-474).[4] Terrifying castles and dungeons— the indispensable features of the *fantastique sérieux* he discusses in his essay on Cazotte—continue to tempt him.

Labyrinths, corridors, the network of narrow city streets —places of quest and perdition—exercise an even stronger attraction. A revealing transfer of images occurs early in *Les Nuits d'Octobre*, in the chapter entitled "Capharnaum":

> Corridors—endless corridors! Stairs—stairs one climbs up and down, and up again, whose lower part always dips into a black water perturbed by wheels, under huge arches of a bridge . . . through inextricable constructs! To climb up, down, or to wander through the corridors—and this during several eternities—could this

be the punishment to which I am condemned for my faults? (Chapter xvii.)

This passage, whose key terms (corridors, stairs, climbing up and down, tangled constructs, eternity, condemnation, mysterious guilt) suggest a Piranesi-like incarceration, follows hard on the evocation of an urban landscape of which the *arches de pont* are a logical dream extension. The city-labyrinth and the city-hell are obsessive images in Nerval. Through contamination and analogy, they confer on apparently trivial episodes a thematic and structural weight that a first reading does not always reveal. The exploratory drive (*fureur d'investigation*) that propels the narrator through the streets of Vienna at the beginning of *Voyage en Orient* should not be attributed to frivolous tourism. The compulsive roaming is directly related to the obscure joy of being led to the "most tangled part of the city," to the need to lose himself in the private myth of a maze (ii, 131). Yet this sense of loss is in itself illusory, theatrical. Parisian hell in *Les Nuits d'Octobre* (Chapter x) proposes Dantesque visions of La Pia and Francesca. But the secret of Paris, as Nerval confides in one of his notebooks, is that captivity itself is an appearance, that the prison-city provides numerous openings for escape (i, 863).

Nerval's work refers to many enclosures that are not walled up, to prisons that are not truly locked. The pyramids, with their low vaultings and mysterious galleries, appear to him as the ideal setting for an initiatory performance of *The Magic Flute*. The underground palace Soliman built in the Kaf mountain, so that after death he would escape the laws of decomposition, remains accessible to the humble mite. The microscopic arachnid undermines the pillar of the throne, making it collapse and thereby liberating the humiliated spirits (ii, 674–676). The subterranean world in the *Nuits de Ramazan* is both a figuration of hell and a privileged place for the fiercely independent sect of Adoniram. In this inner topography, volcanoes and grottoes are places of both terror and hospitality. Princess Setalmulc, sister of Caliph Hakem, sits in her labyrinthine dwelling, in the remotest corner of a room whose wrought ceiling imitates a stalactite grotto (II, 414). Nature and artifice end up by resembling each other; they blend in an atmosphere of a Thousand and One Nights. A disquieting correspondence is established between dissimilar places. The convent whose walls lock up the inaccessible woman in *Sylvie*; Madame Carlès' "pension," a place shut off on all sides from "external nature" (*Druses et Maronites*, II, 381); the seraglio, in *Nuits de Ramazan*, the setting for a dangerous escape adventure—all these enclosures allow for a characteristic blending of a sense of mystery, the joy of discovery, the dream of a secret loophole. Walls, as well as thresholds, veils, and barriers, are essential to Nerval's mental landscape.[5]

It is, however, the theater that provides the most suggestive recurrent image, linking together notions of encincture and flight, barriers and openings, pleasure and anxiety, veils and rendings of delicately woven textures. In *Sylvie*, the theater is indeed the point of departure of reverie and unrest. The prefatory dedication of *Les Filles du Feu* evokes the actor Brisacier, who wound up identifying with the roles he played. A letter to Alexandre Dumas shows us Nerval at Baden Baden, imagining that he is on a make-believe opera stage, looking at the set and the props (28 August 1838). Theater metaphors pervade landscape descriptions. In *Voyage en Orient*, Lausanne offers an "opera perspective"; the Munich square resembles those "unlikely sets" (*décors impossibles*) that theaters sometimes venture; Syra displays to the traveller-spectator a décor that is equally "impossible"; the row of houses along the river Nile looks like a *décoration de théâtre*; Constantinople, another *décoration de théâtre*, should be admired without visiting the wings (II, 16, 27, 93, 279, 694). The theater represents for Nerval a temporal and spatial experience embracing, within the same privileged locus, a diversity of moments within a singular duration. The narrator, in *Sylvie*, sits in the stage boxes of the same theater "every night." At regular hours he participates in a repeated ritual. The same moments are played over, immobilized in the ceremonial of art. The actress, true "apparition," is compared to the "Heures divines" standing out against the background of the Herculaneum frescoes (I, 589-590). On the one hand, the theater creates the illusion of distance, making the close-by seem unrealizable; on the other, the theatrical experience is the threshold to the unreal, nourishing dreams, conflating illusion and reality, suggesting an eventual *passage*. In these rites, distance is transformed into immediacy. In *Les Femmes du Caire*, Nerval observes that the theater is unique in providing the illusion of possessing the feminine unknown: "... *il vous donne l'illusion de connaître parfaitement une inconnue*" (II, 210). The true exit of the enclosed theatrical space opens unto the ideal.

THE ESCAPE WITHIN

These metaphors are interesting not because they betray fixations but because they are marshalled thematically. Proust saw Nerval's work as a model of sickly obsessiveness (*hantise maladive*).[6] But the model is of course a structured *literary* mediation of haunting private motifs. Enclosures and walled-in landscapes function at a number of levels. They suggest latent apprehension, anxiety in the face of the so-called "real" world. Imagination, symbolically captive in a miserable dwelling, knocks against the windows of its hovel "like an imprisoned insect" (II, 151). There is anxiety in the face of the to-be-discovered secret. The city again functions symbolically, revealing gradually its hidden districts to the visitor, in particular the unknown Oriental city, with its walled streets and veiled women. But it is the theater, with its curtain and illusionist sets, that provides Nerval with the metaphors most suggestive of the exhilaration and ache of an illusive presence. The restless teasing of the riddle is in fact the sign of a more radical interrogation of identities. Caliph Hakem, in the Moristan prison asylum, wondering whether he is God or simply caliph, has great difficulty assembling the "scattered fragments" of his thoughts (II, 424). In *Aurélia*, this fragmentation, symptom of a long illness affecting the recesses of the mind, logically calls for images of subterraneous corridors. These obsessional motifs confirm the link between theatrical and claustral images.

The condemnation to a sense of perpetual wandering in dark, indeterminate, Daedalian spaces reflects Nerval's anguished fascination as he confronts his madness—an anguish and a fascination intensified by mirror effects that compel him to *see himself* in the act of wandering. Nerval indulges in his alienation: the image of the mental labyrinth becomes the privileged figuration of his private hell. In *Aurélia*, he compares the entrance of the underground realm of Fire to the veins and vessels "that meander in the lobes of the brain" (I, 765). The metaphor, by inversion, reconverts the image into a clinical reality. As for the notion of hell, it is explicitly stated. In the preface to *Les Filles du Feu*, dedicated to Alexandre Dumas, the substance of *Aurélia* is unmistakably announced: "Some day I shall write the story of this 'descent to hell' " (I, 502).

Yet the fantasy world of Nerval, so hemmed in and oppressive, also appears reassuring. Enclosure is protective. Weakness calls for a refuge, just as alienation seems to seek an asylum. Georges Poulet defines Nerval's nostalgia for the singular, yet repeated moment: "He sees himself surrounded by himself. His past dances the round about him."[7] The fact is that Nerval wishes to step within the circle; he yearns to penetrate into the enclosed space—prison, asylum, or underground labyrinth—to find a shelter or stronghold that might restitute his lost vigor. He dreams of a breakthrough, of an escape *within*. At the very outset of *Aurélia* he speaks indeed of "breaking through" (*percer*) the gates of ivory and of horn which separate him from the invisible world. But the early signal of a transcendental flight is quickly followed, in the same paragraph, by the image of a shady underground world (*souterrain vague*—I, 753).

Nerval's labyrinths are not necessarily malefic.[8] Places of confinement and of secrecy, they also protect against the erosive workings of time. Behind the yellow façade of the uncle's house in *Sylvie*, behind the closed green shutters and the locked door, the ancient furniture is perfectly "preserved." The old prints, the antiquated engravings, the stuffed dog— all the objects in this scene suggest a comforting fixity (I, 612). In *Aurélia*, there is talk of very old necromancer-kings whom powerful cabbalists "locked up" in "well kept" sepulchers to preserve them from the ravages of death, while the treasures that were to protect them against the anger of the gods were buried in *vastes souterrains* (I, 777-778). Similarly, Tubal-Kaïn explains to Adoniram that he had long galleries dug to serve as "retreats" for his tribe, that the stones of the protective pyramid were cemented with "impenetrable" bitumen, and that he personally "sealed" the little door of the narrow passageway which was its only opening. According to Nervalian logic, the image of these underground dwellings, where water itself is "imprisoned," corresponds to the supreme instinct of preservation that impels Tubal-Kaïn to seek reentrance into the pyramid (II, 629-630).

These places of conservation also confer strength and freedom. Against the granitic fortresses and inaccessible caverns of Kaïn's descendants, even Adonaï's tyrannical might remains inoperative. The immunity is of a spiritual nature. The fear of death, made manifest through dreams of regenerative survival and magic confinement, implies the release of the soul. The inaccessible palace within the Kaf mountain is destined to protect Soliman against decomposition. It is also to rejuvenate his exiled spirit. If Soliman does not succeed in his quest for immortality, this has to do with the limitations of his character. Tubal-Kaïn, however, succeeds. And this success, in the context of his inner, subterranean world, means that his "soul [is] freed" (II, 630). The parallel between the survival of Tubal-Kaïn and the rebirth of the necromancer-kings in their well-guarded sepulchers is obvious. The underlying unity of Nerval's work is indeed unmistakable if one grants the relation between an image such as the stuffed dog in the uncle's house (*Sylvie*, Chapter IX) and the buried talismans in the underground passages in *Aurélia*. Magic hollows and secret chambers correspond to the same temporal anguish and the same dream of an escape through closure.

This notion of a salvational confinement, of a metaphoric prison escape, casts light on Nerval's symbolic descent to the nether regions. His *descentes aux enfers* are quests aimed at transmuting disaster into victory. Hence his taste for stories of incarceration and feats of escape (the abbé de Bucquoy, Raoul Spifame), as well as his fascination for accounts of inner liberations. The powers of the imagination seem multiplied in any state of detention and oppression. Real imprisonment, just as confinement within one's own madness, brings about a *multiplication* of the personality. The Nervalian "double" manifests itself by preference in a circumscribed and restricted intimacy. The paradox of a spiritual freedom attained within prison walls is confirmed by a teasing observation jotted down in a text entitled "Sur un Carnet": "The jailor is another kind of captive.—Is the jailor jealous of his prisoner's dreams?" (I, 866.)

Nerval's mental itinerary, though it implies a negation of what is not at the center, quickly becomes centrifugal. The imaginary monk's cell opens onto space; it is the threshold to transcendence. Francesco and Lucrèce, in *Le Songe de Polyphile*, escape from their convent and monastery to meet in a mythological otherworldliness: ". . . in their double dream, they crossed the immensity of space and time" (II, 79). Yousouf, in *Histoire du Calife Hakem*, similarly experiences temporal and spatial release: ". . . the spirit, delivered from the body, its weighty jailor, escapes like a prisoner whose keeper falls asleep, leaving the key in the cell's door." Hakem's *double* describes the joys of a flight, in a state of spiritual inebriation, through "atmospheres of unutterable bliss" (II, 404). The image—an old one—is that of the soul freed of its worldly frame.

Man's mortal condition thus assumes for Nerval the form of a captivity that must de denied. Spiritual correspondences, allowing glimpses of the mystery of things, derive from the awareness of limits. "Presently a captive on this earth, I converse with the choir of stars participating in my joys and sorrows!" This sentence in *Aurélia* (I, 810) sums up a cosmic dialogue entirely founded on the double notion of bounds and liberation. Madness itself is projected through the dual image of the cell and of its negation. A "strip-tease" of insanity illustrates this escape through the hell of consciousness-turned-jailor: the narrator, while walking and singing, takes off his "terrestrial clothes," waits for the soul to leave the body, and has a vision of the "unveiling" of the sky (I, 760-761). Madness, the cause of a literal and metaphoric seclusion, remains throughout Nerval's work the symbol of a liberating immurement. Raoul Spifame, within the triple walls of Bicêtre, is convinced that his dreams are his life, and that his prison is but a dream (I, 85-86).

This text, ironically entitled *Le Roi de Bicêtre*, is of central importance. Raoul Spifame, "a suzerain without seigniory," bears an uncanny resemblance to his king Henri II. He commits such weird acts that his family decides to have him committed. The one who takes himself for the king is locked up in a madhouse, locked up with a fanatic who takes himself for the king of poets. Nerval's authorship of this text has been questioned. Yet the themes are so unmistakably his own that any doubt seems unwarranted. Spifame's jail is a reality from which he escapes, not by loosening the bars (though a brief episode does exploit this romantic cliché), but through the illusion of happiness which metamorphoses his prison into a palace, his rags into brilliant finery, his miserable meals into opulent feasts. The end of the story is not only ironic, but logical and deeply meaningful. Spifame has been caught again after a successful escape. The king, however, touched by the gentle madness of this unhappy nobleman, refuses to have him sent back to the madhouse. He gives orders instead that Spifame be "kept" in one of his "pleasure castles." The place of internment and the place of contentment ultimately become indistinguishable.

The ironic treatment of the prison theme leads us back to

texts such as "Sainte-Pélagie en 1832" and the Crespy-en-Valois episode in *Les Nuits d'Octobre*. Only in the major texts, the irony cannot be read as a frivolous literary exercise or as facile parody. The recurrent prison metaphors, combining self-punishment and self-justification, linking the search for a secret to the anxiety of dreams and to the fear of insanity, suggest an ambivalent state of captivity. Escape itself is fraught with insecurity. Nerval thus assumes a special status in the literary tradition of escapism. His prisons are essentially happy prisons. But, unlike Stendhal, in whose work the notion of freedom is elaborated within the four walls of a cell, where love and the inner life are discovered inside the symbolic Farnese Tower, Nerval grants himself only intuitions of freedom and velleities of escape. It is a freedom that cannot be attained, an ineffective freedom, always to be questioned. Nerval's prisons themselves are in the last analysis unstable, and their images interchangeable. That is surely why Nerval's jailor is not jealous of his prisoner, but of his propensity to dream.

‖ 8 ‖

Baudelaire:
Confinement and Infinity

In truth the prison, unto which we doom
Ourselves, no prison is . . . —Wordsworth

. . . élire domicile dans le nombre . . . —Baudelaire

CENTRALIZATION, EVAPORATION

"Have you noticed," Baudelaire inquires in one of his letters,
"that a stretch of sky, glimpsed through a basement window,
or between two chimneys, two rocks, or through an archway
(. . .) gives a deeper sense of infinity than a vast panorama
seen from a mountaintop?[1] This notion of the amplifying
power of constricting forms is dear to Baudelaire. He expresses it more tersely in the *Salon de 1859*, about a painting in
which two chunks of rock frame an expanse of sky and sea:
". . . infinity seems deeper when it is constricted" (. . . *l'infini
paraît plus profond quand il est plus resserré*—1070).[2] The remark
applies to the painter's perspective, but also points to basic aspects of Baudelaire's art and personality.

Baudelaire is no doubt the poet of escape, dreaming of a
departure for the unknown, contemplating in his imagination
the ideal ship setting sail for exotic regions. "Our soul is a
three-master in search of its Icaria," he writes in "Le Voyage." To travel beyond known realms, to reach the unknown—that is his poetic project, especially if this voyage, as
in the case of "La Vie antérieure" or "La Chevelure," is to be
accomplished through the ecstasies (*transports*) of the senses.
The artful, languorous delights of synesthesia correspond to a
tireless quest for the inaccessible which, in his terms, defines
the greatness of Romanticism.

Yet this same poet of escapism and expansion is also the

poet of intimacy and circumscription, longing to be protected, coddled, girt in. His verse and his prose evoke the
mundus muliebris, the intensely feminine ambiance of the alcove; they reveal him as a refined interior decorator, fond of
antiques, of elegant ceilings, of heavy curtains that shut out
the world. Sedentary like those cats whose mysterious presence fascinated him, Baudelaire sings of privileged moments
whose memory remains a private affair, or can be communicated only in a whisper. Much like Samuel Cramer, the caricature of the artist-hero in *La Fanfarlo*, he longs for narrow
spaces (*espaces très étroits*).

This apparently incompatible mixture of escape dreams and
of a walled-in intimacy is characteristic of Baudelaire. His
work is colored by the fear of evaporation (a devilish subver-
sion of human will), as well as by the project to bring into a
balanced juxtaposition the passive delights of ecstasy and the
prerogatives of self-control. The paradox informs some of his
richer poems—such as "La Chevelure," in which the dialectics of passivity and desideration operate throughout[3]—and is
explicitly summed up in a prose poem "Les Projets": "Why
force my body to change places since my soul travels so
freely?" (266.) For projects, as Baudelaire understands them,
remain intentions whose realization would be distressing in
the extreme. Such an interiorization of spatial desire of course
increases its intensity. Hence the central image of the port,
ideal locus of controlled dreams and of a dandyish equilibrium between movement and immobility.

"Evaporation and centralization of the *self*. All is there,"
Baudelaire asserts, at the beginning of his diary *Mon Coeur mis
à nu*, as though to provide himself with a key to his own character. The two poles of Baudelairian anguish could not be better defined. "Centralization" and "evaporation," as well as
their synonyms, are recurrent terms in his vocabulary. Centralization is also condensation and concentration. Baudelaire
translates admiringly Emerson's statement about the hero's
self-possession: "*Le héros est celui-là qui est immuablement con-
centré*" (1126). As for evaporation or vaporization, their

synonyms are even more numerous: *expansion, volatilisation, déperdition, dissipation.* Gaston Bachelard was struck by the frequency, in Baudelaire's writings, of the adjective *vaste* and the prefix *ex*.[4] Spatial amplification does indeed correspond to his notion of the privileged moment. In *Fusées*: "There are moments in one's existence when time and space are deeper, when the feeling of existence is immeasurably increased" (1256).

Expansion is deemed desirable, concentration necessary. Yet Baudelaire feels he cannot attain the one, and is not capable of the other. He fences himself in to dream, and dissipates himself in concentration. Much like the victims of hashish, in *Les Paradis artificiels* (365), whose eyes stare in the direction of infinity and who experience the weird sensation of slowly disintegrating while *being smoked*, he does all he can to compress and repossess himself, but in vain: he only disperses himself while remaining his own prisoner.

Other antinomies confirm this passive quest for the infinite. In "Chacun sa chimère," Baudelaire diagnoses the "indomitable need to wander" (*invincible besoin de marcher*—236). Elsewhere he refers to the hatred of one's dwelling, to the "*grande maladie de l'horreur du domicile*," in terms reminiscent of Pascal (243, 1284). Yet this dreamer who sings of the passion for travel, this invalid who desires to change beds, is essentially a poet of immobility. Like the philosophical owls in his poem "Les Hiboux," meditating without making a move, he fears tumult and motion.

> Leur attitude au sage enseigne
> Qu'il faut en ce monde qu'il craigne
> Le tumulte et le mouvement.

Just like the statue of the sphinx in "La Beauté," he hates "*le mouvement qui déplace les lignes*" (20). *Homo duplex* no less than the fictional Samuel Cramer, he indulges in excessive "habits of seclusion and dissipation," while remaining faithful to purely mental orgies. This duplicity is brought out sharply in his review of Charles Asselineau's *La Double vie*, where the

expression *homo duplex* refers precisely to such a double
intentionality—dream and reality—which induces those who
are temperamentally made for family life to long for distant
travels, and induces men of action to dream of a sedentary
life, "locked up within a few square feet" (658). The two
tendencies inform the same consciousness, endowing it with a
chronic frustration.

Solipsism has its dialectics. Baudelaire flaunts the aristo-
cratic pride of solitary pleasures. "Dandyism," as he understands it in *Le Peintre de la vie moderne*, is in large part cult of
the self (1178). But he has to admit that such a cult is not a
simple matter of choice, that it is a true vocation of self-
inflicted and self-observed suffering. The dandy is condemned to live, even sleep, in front of a mirror (1273). His is a
reflected existence; no escape is possible, not even a respite. If
drugs and intoxication interest Baudelaire so much, it is because they illustrate a servitude that blurs and blends subject
and object: the "frightful marriage of man with himself"
(*l'épouvantable mariage de l'homme avec lui-même*—372). Images
of a lucid and impotent confrontation with the self intensify
the irony of some of his finest poems, such as "L'Héautontimorouménos" and "L'Irrémédiable." The "luminous
abyss" (*gouffre lumineux*) in which the dandy-prisoner-of-self
admires his Narcissus-like face corresponds, on the
metaphoric level, to images of falling and sinking.

If therefore Baudelaire evokes the addict's illusion of divin-
ity, if he denounces the alluring fetters of drugs, it is because
he is only too aware of the dangers of spiritual onanism trans-
forming the self into the center of the universe. While he saw
the highest aim in being a "great man" and even a saint *"for
oneself"* (1286, 1289), and felt that genius meant irreducible
otherness (*L'homme de génie veut être* un, *donc solitaire*—1294),
he also asserted that true poets have the ability to *"sortir
d'eux-mêmes,"* to forget themselves and merge with the
"other."[5]

> *Et je me couche, fier d'avoir vécu et souffert dans d'autres que
> moi-même.*
>
>   (Les Fenêtres, 288)

This basic contradiction, which parallels the antithesis of centralization and evaporation, is summed up in a pithy formula of *Le Peintre de la vie moderne* dealing with the artist-dandy who "espouses" the crowd: *"C'est un 'moi' insatiable du 'non-moi'* . . ." (1161). The formula casts light on Baudelaire's taste for anonymous immersion in the flow of city streets, the *bain de multitude*. The praise of Constantin Guys' "Parisian" art is genuine, but is also a pretext for a more important thematic development. To be an observer-prince in the heart of the capital signifies "settling in the number"; it originates in the nostalgia for the fugitive "other," the *non-moi*. And beyond that fluctuating and unstable other-than-myself, there is the yearning for the infinite.

Baudelaire's city themes cannot be reduced to a passion for local color or to the jarring seductions of Baron Haussmann's urban renewal. The "perfect stroller" (*parfait flâneur*) discovers the supernatural, stumbles on poetic invention. Such epiphanies come about through the conjunction of encincture and perspective, isolation and communion. Commenting on Charles Méryon's etchings—the subject once again is Paris—Baudelaire speaks of openwork allowing for dramatic "depths of perspectives" (1083). In *Fusées*, he refers to a religious communion with the self through collective inebriation: *"Ivresse religieuse des grandes villes.—Panthéisme. Moi, c'est tous; tous, c'est moi"* (1248).

The anonymity of the crowd and the privacy of the room are complementary attractions of this city poetry. The image of the capital, filled with the disquieting tumult of "human liberty," implies binary structures: immensity and seclusion, individuality and incognito, solitude and multitude. Yet these are false oppositions. The terms themselves turn out to be convertible. *"Multitude, solitude: termes égaux et convertibles pour le poète actif et fécond"* (243). The room becomes an asylum, an insular or monastic refuge in the metaphoric city-ocean (*noir océan de l'immonde cité*) where church steeples are the masts, and the soul is in constant danger of shipwreck. The opposites of contact and claustration, opening and enclosure, remain in permanent semantic tension. Baudelaire stresses the horror of aloneness, while extolling its virtues.

His is, however, not a banal conflict between the social and the creative self. From childhood on—that is the way he chooses to see himself retrospectively—he feels a vocation of a *destinée éternellement solitaire* (1275). This fated solitude is enhanced by compensatory images of glory and purity. "There is nothing I like better than to be alone," he proudly writes to his mother.[6] In an important article on Théophile Gautier, he glorifies the aristocrats of solitude (678-679). His imagination endowed pariahs with a special beauty. As for the spiritual value of solitude, Baudelaire was convinced that it not only gave access to *"vast contemplations"* (953), but had a regenerative and redemptive value. In a curious passage of one of the prose poems, Baudelaire attributes Robinson Crusoe's salvation to solitude: ". . . *elle le rendit religieux, brave, industrieux; elle le purifia . . .*" (1608).

Baudelaire, like his contemporary Flaubert, is haunted by images of monks and monasteries, drawn to the paintings of Zurbaran and the "monastic caricatures" of Goya (1018). He too views as the artist's ideal the ascetic conquest of solitude. But are conquest and victory possible for him? Is his claustrophilia not largely due to passivity and abdication of will power? The refuge-chamber serves to exclude and protect. It is a correlative of the fear of degradation, of the shame that comes with failure. "I shall lock myself up hermetically," he announces in a letter to his mother.[7] To work, that is the implication. But mostly to surrender to voluptuous daydreams that require no effort, to indulge in what he himself, in "La Chambre double," calls a "bath of laziness" (*bain de paresse*) and to surrender to "hothouse sensations." Time itself vanishes in this "atmosphere of stagnation" (233-234). The place of concentration becomes the place of dissipation.

THE PARTITION. THE FESTIVITY WITHIN

The cellular space, no less than the tropical island and the port, becomes one of the *luoghi ameni* of this special world. In "Les Sept vieillards" claustration relates to terror in the face of the absurd:

> *Je rentrai, je fermai ma porte, épouvanté,*
> *Malade et morfondu, l'esprit fiévreux et trouble,*
> *Blessé par le mystère et par l'absurdité!*

In "L'Examen de minuit," the persona of the poem seeks to hide in the darkness of his room. The key terms in the prose poem *"A une heure du matin"* (immersion in darkness, double lock, barricade, separate) all hint at the soteriological merit of the four walls. The poet wishes explicitly to "redeem" himself in the silence and solitude of the night (240-241). Even the big city, though external to the protective garret or hovel, is metamorphosed into a partitioned space: *"La nuit s'épaississait ainsi qu'une cloison"* (35). This famous line in "Le Balcon" evokes the Paris of the twilight hour, the dubious and bizarre moment "when the sky's curtains close" (1162). Lovely passages describe the tender, imprecise colors of dusk, the charm of nightfalls, *"voilés de vapeurs roses."* "Crépuscule du soir," a text Baudelaire considered particularly "Parisian," introduces him into the heart of the night—the accomplice of the criminal and of the sinner—by means of a specific image of enclosure: ". . . the sky / Closes slowly like a vast alcove. . . ." It is significant, moreover, that the images of the hospital and of the bordello—other places of solitude and confinement—should be an integral part of this vision of Parisian hell. The parallel is not fortuitous. Suffering and vice, death and eros, constitute inescapable couples. The escape wish grows only the more pressing. The inner jail ultimately vivifies imagination and vision. In "Paysage," the poet proposes to close all shutters and all doors in order to build for himself, in the heart of darkness, palaces lit up by unreal suns. But this highly private festivity, this nocturnal *fête intérieure*, which is to deliver him from anguish, in fact only supplies the fireworks of illusory freedom.

Baudelaire recognizes the danger. Hence the *horreur du domicile*: he knows that the four walls of his room cuddle him, only to let him fall in his own esteem—hence also a basic distrust of the much-praised solitude. Like many children, he experienced an acute sense of isolation in school; he later re-

called school tyranny with bitterness, comparing the dormi-
tory to a jail. His childhood letters published in recent years
suggest, however, no tragic pose at that time. On the other
hand, the subsequent remarriage of his mother, providing
him with a Hamlet complex, seems to have been cultivated
by him as a traumatic affair: he felt both powerless and
excluded. Significantly, it is to his mother that he complained
most bitterly of his "awful loneliness." "I am alone," he
writes to her in a moving letter dated May 6, 1861, "without
friends, without a mistress, without a dog and without a cat
[. . .]. I have only the portrait of my father, which remains
mute."[8] The paternal silence is like a reproach inscribed on
the wall.

Thematically, this terror of solitude is linked to Satanism
and guilt, to the very notion of evil. "After debauchery, one
always feels more alone, more abandoned," he jots down on a
loose sheet devoted to his moral hygiene (1265). The prose
poem "La Solitude" casts an even grimmer light on this
solitude-in-sin. "I know that the Demon is fond of haunting
arid places and that the spirit of murder and lewdness is powerfully inflamed in solitude" (264). The desert landscape associated with Saint Antony's temptations is the central setting
for the lesbian *"femmes damnées,"* sinning "seekers of infinity"
(chercheuses d'infini—107-108). The sedentary refuge of his
room becomes a symbol of paralyzing ennui, of temporal oppression, of the implacable tyranny of all deadlines. Charles
Mauron suggests that Baudelaire's claustrophobia comes with
the shame of not facing up to his inner freedom.[9] It is without
a doubt in this context of a humiliating and oppressive claustration that Baudelaire felt the keenest affinities with Edgar
Allan Poe for whom, he thought, all of America was a "vast
prison."[10]

THE SEALED HORIZON

Baudelaire indeed views Poe's moral and psychological suffocation as an anachronistic and therefore timeless replica of his

own condition. The poet-pariah is in metaphorical captivity. Poe's favorite imagery—heavy doors, somber walls, low and oppressive clouds, victims buried alive, hidden and anguishing secrets—found a brotherly echo in his own imagination. In the *Salon de 1859*, he describes all true artists as "locked-in spirits" (*âmes enfermées*—1097). The poem "Sur Le Tasse en prison" presents the soul of poetry as being crushed by the four walls of "Reality." The engraving by Goya that perhaps most obsessed him depicts a victim trying desperately to emerge from his tomb, while evil spirits—demons and gnomes—push down with all their might on the stone he will never be able to lift (1019). This horror-image of the unmovable lid, the *couvercle*, is a basic motif in Baudelaire's work. It must be read side by side with all the other visions of crushing architectures. It is not merely the taste for the macabre trappings of the Gothic novel that draws him to Pétrus Borel's descriptions of "dungeon horrors and tortures" (725). He himself imagined colossal ruins, gigantic bridges, "Nineveh-like constructions inhabited by vertigo" (1084). His notes contain a curious project, probably for a poem, all filled with galleries, stairs, caeca, labyrinths, masses of oozing and cleft rocks about to tumble down and crush human brains. He sees himself trapped: "I cannot find the exit" (317). The titles of certain projected works are equally revealing: "Death Penalty," "The Trap," "The Stairs," "Prisoner in a Lighthouse" (312-314). Elsewhere we read of "death penalty for a forgotten crime," of anguish and guilt in "unknown apartments" (316). The prison image—the poet uses the striking expression "*l'ennui de nos prisons*" (124)—becomes the metaphor of the guilt and grief of living. The "chambers of eternal mourning" in the poem "Obsession" suggest a symbolic inner confinement that transforms every escape wish into conscious illusion.

A negative claustration. "Spleen LXXVI" sums up this spiritual sickness through funereal images of drawers, pyramids, burial vaults, paupers' graves—images of contain-

ers imprisoning defunct objects and suggesting the death of
the soul:

> *Je suis un cimetière abhorré de la lune,*
> *Où comme des remords se traînent de longs vers*
> *Qui s'acharnent toujours sur mes morts les plus chers,*
> *Je suis un vieux boudoir plein de roses fanées . . .*

As for "Spleen lxxviii," an allegory—in the sense Baudelaire
gives this word—of the human condition, its texture and
structure fully exploit variations of the jail motif: low, heavy
clouds; oppressive lids (*couvercles*); dark and damp cells; rotting ceilings and walls; falling rain imitating prison bars; spiders weaving their web in the recesses of the mind's secret
dungeon:

> *Quand la terre est changée en un cachot humide,*
> *Où l'Espérance, comme une chauve-souris,*
> *S'en va battant les murs de son aile timide*
> *Et se cognant la tête à des plafonds pourris . . .*

Clusters of related images in other poems contribute to the
same metaphoric network: images of entrapment in "L'Irrémédiable," of suffocation in "La Destruction," of crushing
weight in "Le Guignon" and in the prose poem "Enivrez-
vous." The numerous echoes and correspondences between
the private notes and the published poems stress insistently
the notion of a temporal burden which Baudelaire himself
glosses in a commentary under the heading *Hygiène*: "At
every moment we are crushed by the idea and the sensation of
time" (1266).

The sickness of will power diagnosed in the prefatory
poem "Au lecteur," the paralyzing duplicity described in
"L'Héautontimorouménos," are the psychological corollaries
of these metaphors of infernal oppression. The "sealed horizon" (*horizon plombé*) and the "frozen sun" (*soleil de glace*) in
the grim sonnet "De Profundis clamavi" leave no doubt as to
the association of ideas and images. The burial vaults of "unfathomable sadness" in "Les Ténèbres" provide an even

clearer illustration of the sense of condemnation. In *Métamorphoses et Symboles de la libido*, Jung quotes a text by Nietzsche in which the prisoner, immured in himself, lifeless and literally petrified, is compared to a corpse crushed by innumerable weights: the figure is that of the self-absorbed psyche dreaming to be buried alive.[11] Jung's commentary might well have taken as its point of departure Baudelaire's "La Cloche fêlée," in which the poet's soul is seen as "agonizing" in futile efforts, crushed under a heap of corpses.

This claustration within the self is confirmed by countless tropes that—much like the imagery of the "Spleen" poems—assimilate the brain to a macabre container, an infernal locus, or more precisely still, to a prison cell: the brain wrapped in a shroud in "Brumes et pluies"; the setting for a mental Walpurgis Night, an orgy of demons in "Au lecteur"; a mental retreat (*thébaïde*) in the *Salon de 1859*. . . . The spider, the prisoner's traditional companion, silently spinning its web in the brain-jail, is of course also a symbol that psychoanalysis identifies.[12]

THE HAPPY CAGE

Baudelaire's motifs of confinement seem to function within the larger theme of self-destruction. Yet the obsession with confinement also relates to the yearning for infinity. The idea proposed in the *Salon de 1859* (". . . infinity seems deeper when it is constricted . . ."—1070) is poetically echoed in a number of texts. The narrower and the darker the alcove, the easier the evocation of distant continents. It is in the most compressed setting that the reverie of an elsewhere is the most intense. It is there also that one can surrender to such reverie with the greatest impunity, without the risk of having to translate desire into action. Drawers, chests, caskets, wardrobes, perfume bottles are the repositories of hidden essences and secrets; their locked-up treasures provide access to infinity and immortality. In his very Proustian poem "Le Flacon," Baudelaire revealingly evokes Lazarus in the act of tearing his shroud.

Perhaps the most rewarding text concerning the ambiguities of Baudelairian nostalgia is *Le Poème du Haschish*,
whose opening section is entitled *Le Goût de l'infini*. A fictional victim of the drug describes her vision: she sees herself
first in a very small and very narrow boudoir, then in an indeterminate locale surrounded by prison bars, yet opening on all
sides onto space (368). On the one hand, there is the clear notion of claustration; on the other, a real sense of spatial
ecstasy. The cage becomes a "beautiful" cage, a "sumptuous"
cage, the ideal setting for a fairy-tale deliverance (Sleeping
Beauty is indeed evoked); and the prison, in which strange
birds imagined by the lady-dreamer celebrate her liberating
captivity, becomes a *prison magnifique*.

But why is the cage presented simultaneously as happy and
malefic? Does Baudelaire merely wish to suggest the ecstasies
of opium while denouncing its obvious dangers? The implications are clearly more far-reaching. The theme of escape,
specifically toward the infinite, is at the heart of Baudelaire's
work. "I am never well anywhere, yet I always believe that I
would be better off elsewhere . . ." (283). This statement in
the prose-poem "Les Vocations" might serve as epigraph.
The "elsewhere" remains throughout a transcendental reality.
Baudelaire's mind's eye aims at the unseeable. The *goût de
l'infini* manifests itself in his critical texts as well. For
Baudelaire's notion of infinity involves not merely the dream
of flight and elevation toward the "limpid spaces" (10); it corresponds to the marvelous and deeply disturbing poetic fac-
ulty. Still in the *Salon de 1859*: "The imagination is the queen
of truth, and the *possible* is one of the provinces of truth. It is
positively related to infinity" (1038). And in his article on
Théodore de Banville, he defines the lyric sensibility as a dila-
tion, as a soaring toward a "higher region" (736). But far
from providing reassurance as to the spirituality of artistic
fervor, the analogy remains disquieting. Man's vices, according to Baudelaire, also point to the *goût de l'infini* (348).
The seductive and threatening figure of beauty fails to answer the question as to its divine or infernal origin (*Viens-tu du
ciel profond ou sors-tu de l'abîme?*). The nostalgia for worlds

beyond is not without peril. Still in *Le Poème du Haschish*, Baudelaire identifies the *dépravation du sens de l'infini* (349)—a depravation that precedes and goes beyond the experience of opium. And the happy, sumptuous cage becomes the scene of inauthenticity, the scene of false departures and illusions of flight.

THE PORT; FALSE FREEDOM

The dreamed-of means of escape, in many other texts, point to the same principle of intoxication: the intoxication of wine granting access to "artificial paradise"; the intoxication of crowds and of large cities; the intoxication of the senses opening onto an illusive infinity. Illusive, because the dream of take-off implies abdication and immobility. Sleep, "the adventurous voyage of every night" (354), may well be the most adequate symbol of this false movement. What Baudelaire seeks is not transcendence, but mediation and intercession. His exercises in synesthesia allow for such escapism by proxy. Music has this function. The metaphors are telling: music makes one "set sail" (65), sweeps one away as do the waves of the sea, explores altitude (*creuse le ciel*), "gives the sense of space" (1296). Wagner's compositions are like *enlèvement*;[13] they lift into the air, provide the illusion of being freed from the laws of gravity. The listener to music circulates in the upper regions (1213-1214). The link with drug addiction is made explicit. In his essay on *Tannhaüser*, Baudelaire compares the beatitude provided by music with the "dizzying conceptions" of opium.

This sense of infinity has little in common with a mystic's experience or with the bold visionary thrusts of a poet such as Hugo. Baudelaire confines himself to equivalents and substitutes. Total experience, or just plain experience, frightens him. He is haunted by infinity because it terrifies him. In "Le Gouffre," which begins with an evocation of Pascal, there is talk of "the awesome and captivating space" (the latter adjective here assumes a quite literal meaning): the poet is as though paralyzed in front of the immense void. "All I see is infinity through all the windows," he sighs. "Les plaintes d'un Icare" recall the tragic end of the one who wished to embrace space. "Le Couvercle" suggests the terror inflicted by the mystery of a hostile sky.

> *Partout l'homme subit la terreur du mystère,*
> *Et ne regarde en haut qu'avec un œil tremblant.*

Similar images of fright are related to the "sting" of infinitude in "Le *Confiteor* de l'artiste" and the "inaccessible azur" in the sonnet "L'Aube spirituelle."

The incommensurable remains appalling. But it is the imagined boundlessness of the self that truly dismays him. The *femmes damnées* are condemned to flee the bottomless abyss of their desire:

> *Faites votre destin, âmes désordonnées,*
> *Et fuyez l'infini que vous portez en vous!*

Yet flight is unthinkable. "Yesterday, tomorrow, always, shows us our image" (126). The only possible escape-voyage is death. Baudelaire seeks—so he states in "Obsession"— stark emptiness and darkness: ". . . *le vide, et le noir, et le nu!*" And this because the inner limitlessness, the inner "infinity" he carries in him and wants to flee in vain, is his freedom. It is this freedom which, in the last analysis, terrifies him—hence the symbolic appeal of the prison house of illusions, the lavish mental cage where, by means of the subterfuges of fancied release, he can remain immured while relishing the spectacle of actions he will never perform.

Sartre's indictment of Baudelaire is focused on the bad faith of the eternal adolescent who does not want to do, but to *be*—who chooses to see himself as already posthumous, as an inert freedom.[14] There is no doubt that Baudelaire dreads above all to extricate himself from what he likes to consider his unavoidable destiny. Denying all true motion, he ultimately conceives as the only voyage possible the one that implies the immobility of death:

> *O Mort, vieux capitaine, il est temps! levons l'ancre!*
> *Ce pays nous ennuie, ô Mort! Appareillons!*

Travel images in his work are consistently linked with passivity and indolence. Spatial desire is transmuted into premature satiety. The travel project leads to non-departure and non-realization: ". . . what is the use of executing projects. . . ?" (266.) The famous poem "L'Invitation au voyage" is in fact an invitation to settle in a supremely ordered world of quiet, rest and inactivity:

> *Là, tout n'est qu'ordre et beauté,*
> *Luxe, calme et volupté.*

The dream is that of a cozy interior. The *humeur vagabonde* characterizes the ships coming from afar, not the protagonists of the poem.

The pattern is: non-voyage and a false departure. Baudelaire is fully aware of his duplicity, as he admires the authentic traveller: "*les vrais voyageurs sont ceux-là qui partent / Pour partir*" (122). For the poet there is at best the image of departures: ships setting sail, or waiting in a port to set sail. Even the image of the port, as Baudelaire develops it in a number of texts, confirms the non-occurrence of the voyage. The port for him is a place of reverie and security, or, more precisely, the setting for a safe reverie about departure. Ideal Baudelairian locus of controlled dreams, of a dandyish equilibrium between motion and stability, the haven ("*séjour charmant*," as he puts it in the well-known prose poem on the tired soul—292-293) opens up, yet locks in. The word *séjour* (stay, sojourn, abode, resort) clearly signifies a sedentary existence. It stresses the elegant, even haughty, pleasure of the disenchanted protagonist who, in a reclining position, contemplates without any ambition or even curiosity the movements of "those who leave," of those who have the will to leave: the *others*.

THE RECESS. THE CITY

Infinity through constriction: we have come full circle. Baudelaire's taste for enlarged perspective is complemented by the need to protect himself against this enlargement of vision. The contradiciton rehearses the Romantic dream of escape into the prison of dream. The safety of the port, the safety of jail and of poetic intoxication, are paralleled by the figural safety of the urban cell, the private nook, from within which the cityscape is glimpsed. The landscape of stone stands as though in defiance of the "natural" landscape. The city—this "dream of stone" caressed by the mist—offers him, especially when viewed through a protective window, the reassurance of lapidary stasis, as well as the *spectacle* of mobility and freedom. Paris has a hold on him. Though he pretends to envy Flaubert, leading a provincial existence near his mother in Croisset, he does not join his own in Honfleur. The poetry of the capital takes on a central importance in his work. The modern metropolis, with its fugacious crowds, its hidden quarters, its horrors and its hell, becomes the symbol of a metaphysical paradox: freedom and necessity coexist. It is the place of shame and of revelation, the place—as Baudelaire puts it in *Le Peintre de la vie moderne*—of an "astonishing harmony" as well as of the "tumult of human freedom" (1161). The scenery of stone and mist is also the background against which the drama of *evaporation* and *concentration* is played out.

Baudelaire's work thus casts light on the status of any megalopolis in the modern imagination. An outgrowth of the industrial revolution, responsible in physical and economic terms for a collective enclosure, the great urban center—wasteland or penitentiary, place of proliferation and of anguish—is perceived as the point of intersection between the unique destiny and the anonymous, the multiple, the infinite. Baudelaire speaks lyrically of the crossing (*croisement*) of innumerable relations in large cities. But he also speaks of the protective barricades of his private cell. It is not a coincidence if his tragic figures of exile—Andromache, the thirsty swan, the tubercular Negress—are first of all seen as captives of the inhuman city, whose infinite sadness and longing for infinity are projected against the immense wall of the Parisian fog.

|| 9 ||

Huysmans:
The Prison House
of Decadence

J.-K. Huysmans, poet of cozy interiors, in also a city poet. Like Baudelaire, whose strident modernity he imitates, he enjoys merging with the crowds. He too seeks out abandoned districts, and relishes the spectacle of industrial ugliness. Certain cityscapes are favored: labyrinthine old streets, leprous walls covered with excrescences, polluted waters, underground passages.[1]

This urban scene is sordid but emblematic. The following is Huysmans' description of the rue de la Santé, a "prison lane" where he likes to dream and meditate:

> He knew this street from way back; he often went there for melancholy walks, drawn to it by its homey provincial poignancy. For it lent itself to reveries, as the walls of the Santé prison and of the Sainte-Anne insane asylum were to the right and convents to the left. Air and daylight penetrated into the street; but behind, all seemed to become dark. It was, so to speak, a prison lane, bordered by cells where some were forced to undergo temporary punishment, while others willfully suffered eternal retribution.[2]

Reverie is here directly bound to confining walls. The description proposes a double image of incarceration: the involuntary confinement of prison and insane asylum is set against the implicit freedom of conventual life. "Temporary" sentences confront "eternal" justice. Spiritual salvation is implied in the notion of voluntary suffering. The darkness of the confined spaces seems to open onto an atemporal order. The antithetical parallelism is developed in the lines that follow. Huysmans imagines a Flemish primitive painting depicting, on the one side, prison cells filled with thieves (the archaic word *larrons* points back to the crucifixion scene); and, on the other, conventual cells where the image of the crucifix is specifically in evidence. On both sides of the street one finds the same stone jugs. The repetition of this pictorial detail signals a false antithesis. The thieves and the crucifix belong to the same symbolic context.

Cloister and prison tend to merge in the work of Huysmans. In *La Cathédrale*, the protagonist's strolls through Chartres always lead back to the city jail and other oppressive buildings. He views all places of detention as "springboards for old dreams." And these dreams, "old" because deep-rooted and archetypal, seem to require architectures that combine rigidity with suggestions of spiritual flight. The *forme haute et rigide* of prison walls conjures up conventual images (*le mur de clôture élevé par un Carmel*—I, 276). Conversely, the words that recur most frequently to describe the monastic ambiance are terms of imprisonment: *écrouer*, *incarcérer*, *geôle* (II, 107-110).

La Cathédrale glosses the symbolic value of the cellular regime. The Middle Ages are for Huysmans the high point of civilization because that period knew how to *surround* man, how to encircle or invest him, not for the sake of oppression but for edification. Walls place the confined individual in "direct relation with heaven." The cloister cleanses the soul (Huysmans puns: "*émonde les âmes*") of worldly concerns (II, 281-282). *L'Oblat* evokes bygone times of religious fervor when the "contemplative life" was typically locked up behind severe walls and sealed doors, when the expiating impulse led the "*ermites volontaires de la nuit*" to bury themselves alive (I, 165-174, 180). Textual reminiscences are numerous: the Trou au rat and the Sachette episodes in *Notre-Dame de Paris* are specifically mentioned. Huysmans had indeed been struck by the theme of reclusion in the work of Hugo. Folantin, the unheroic hero of *A Vau-l'Eau*, carefully re-reads "the mysterious and penetrating chapter on the Petit-Picpus convent, in *Les Misérables*."

City strolls, preferably along narrow streets, correspond to figurative deambulations: the metaphor is internalized. Referring to his sick soul forced to stay "indoors," Huysmans elaborates images of the "internal castle" (*château interne*), circumscribed spiritual abodes, shrunken spaces, doors that will not open (*La Cathédrale*, 1, 54). Durtal's internal walks (*promenades en lui-même*) suggest a quest-like wandering and a sense of foreboding. Other bookish memories come to the surface: ". . . facing these chambers of the soul, dim with mist, he imagined a strange association of the Revelations of Saint Theresa and a tale by Edgar Poe." Such a duality is confirmed by the notion of a privileged prison within the prison of solipsism, which for the time being, however, remains inaccessible to himself: ". . . the rooms surrounding the central cell, the one reserved for the Master, were bolted and fastened with rivets that could not be unscrewed, and triple bars— inaccessible." The quest, it would seem, is from the outset doomed to the outer rooms of this inner castle, confined to the limbo of the "vestibule."

The "castles of the soul," inhabited by boredom and mourning, cannot be dissociated from the symbolism of Parisian promenades. The image of the wall looms like a dark mirror. The cityscape has a specialized function in the work of Huysmans. He loathes the modernized Paris of Baron Haussmann, the large boulevards and wide perspectives brought about by the Second Empire's urban renewal. His favorite quarters allow for the reverie of enclosure. *La Bièvre*, which extols the pleasures of leisurely strolls in search of an almost disappeared river, plays complicated variations on the image of incarceration. Pretending to deplore the evils of industrialization, Huysmans weaves a densely metaphoric text: the river Bièvre is "locked in," "garrisoned" (*casernée*), "committed to jail" (*écrouée* in endless *geôles*), asphyxiating in long "tunnels." Everywhere there are walls, vaults, under-

ground passageways, labyrinths. If a door opens, it is to allow
a glimpse of a "prison corridor" (11, 12, 21-22). In *Le Quartier
Saint-Séverin*, walls are even more massive and oppressive.
The ancient streets are a network of dark trenches (*lacis de
tranchées noires*), galleries contain grim air-holes (*soupiraux*),
porches and doorways are strengthened by iron bars. At cur-
few time, the inhabitants of this gloomy district barricade
themselves behind thick walls whose stones seem to shed
black tears (*larmes d'encre*). The streets that attract him are like
compressed communication trenches (*boyaux comprimés*): the
rue du Chat-qui-Pêche resembling a fissure (*simple fente*) between two walls; the rue de la Huchette with its sooty walls
and latticed houses—a street all blackened like a coal-box
(*charbonnière*—30-31, 39, 54-55).

The obsession with walls generates figurative developments. Cyprien, the hero of *En Ménage*, sees everywhere
a "wall of misfortune" (*mur de débine*). Conversely, the
metaphor tends towards concretization. The esthete-
protagonist of *A Rebours* decides to "bind his walls like
books" (24): the image links the psychic need to the physical
presence of the text. Huysmans stresses the virtues of ugly
weather; he enjoys describing the "delicate lashes of a driving
rain" (*A Vau-l'Eau*, 8), in order to draw the reader's glance
into the cozy *inside*. The endless squalls of a Chartres winter
lend a protective beauty to the priest's apartment, even
though it smells of stagnant water and of provincial stuffiness.
Similarly, the "solemn darkness" and cellar odors of the large
nave enfold the drenched *promeneur* in *La Cathédrale* (I, 9-11,
71, 94).

Despite ambulatory dispositions, all of Huysmans' writings disclose a terror of space. He loves his book-lined study:
between him and the hostile *outside* there is the window,
closed yet transparent, which grants the comfort of a protected reverie. The mere thought of a move, or only of a trip,
fills him with anguish. The memory of travel produces dizziness (*vertige*). He relives the fright he experienced as the train
crossed a suspended bridge, the awesome sensation that all

was swallowed by "immensity" (*La Cathédrale*, I, 16-19). But spectacular landscapes are hardly needed to provoke panic. The sky in *En Rade*—the title refers to the need for protection and immobility—gives the protagonist a sense of vertigo: *"le vertige des yeux perdus dans l'espace."* Jacques Marles, overcome by the "sensation of the unknown," is specifically unsettled by cloudless August days; he suffers, in Mallarmean fashion, from the "nudity," the "cruel blue," and "ferocious" openness of midsummer days when nothing obstructs the horizon (*En Rade*, 96, 147, 170). What unsettles him most, in the dilapidated castle where he sought refuge, is the impossibility of locking oneself in. He inspects the place with alarm, searching for "solid closures." It is hopeless: ". . . there was no wall, no hedgerow; everybody could come in" (73-74).

Huysmans' dyspeptic heroes, lounging in overheated rooms or idly dreaming in sinecure government offices, cultivate the delights of claustration. An ecstatic expression comes over Monsieur Folantin's face as he thinks of his apartment. Amusingly, his colleague interprets the expression as an anticipation of sexual pleasures. In fact, Folantin is a confirmed misogynist. Yet the interpretation is not far off the mark. The anticipation of pleasure might easily be viewed as a nostalgia for the womb, a memory-yearning for the maternal refuge. The text invites such a reading, in particular references to his mother "locked up from morning till night, in a glass cage" and to his cousin enclosed in a provincial convent (*A Vau-l'Eau*, 68, 13-14).

Huysmans repeatedly places childhood under the sign of monastic withdrawal. The preface of *A Rebours* invokes an "ancestry of beguine convents and cloisters" (*ascendances de béguinages et de cloîtres*). The importance of *interiors* is made explicit in his earliest texts. The notion of marriage or concubinage, in *Les Soeurs Vatard*, is but a nostalgia for shelter: ". . . he dreamt of a well-closed room." Or again: "He desired, at any cost, to find a deliverance, a haven where he could run aground . . ." (281-282). Enclosure assumes a multiplicity of values: the joys of inertia, the appeal of asceticism, the seduction of a sordid setting. The steam-filled atmosphere and the pungent smells in *Les Soeurs Vatard* are described with obvious relish. Huysmans insists on the "putrid emanations," on the harsh stench (*puanteur rude*) of latrines (14). In *Marthe* the house is called a slum, a hovel, an *affreux terrier*, whose walls "piss yellow droplets" (29). Yet enclosure is also associated, from the very start, with esthetic experiences. Huysmans explains his taste for Dutch paintings: ". . . they satisfied my needs for both *reality* and *intimacy*. . . ."[3]

These esthetics of intimacy can be traced to a quasi-morbid attachment to the four walls of his room. *Sac au dos*, one of Huysmans' earliest texts, provides a striking illustration. The narrating soldier, fresh from the Franco-Prussian war, still suffering from the promiscuity of barracks, cattle cars, and army hospitals, is jubilant as he returns to the hothouse atmosphere of his room, to the soft welcome of his old armchair and bed. The narrator imagines a silent mass celebrated in this intimacy. The following passage might well have disturbed Zola and his other "naturalist" friends: it foreshadows Huysmans' decadent writings and the ambiguities of his religious imagery:

> I rediscover my dwelling as I left it; my trinkets and my books seem to bid me welcome. I light all the candles so as to see them better. It's a *Te Deum* of colors, a hosanna of flames! (191-192.)

The room remains the privileged locus of padded existence. Huysmans' imagination furnishes these ideal spaces with wing-chairs and with the discreet presence of a devoted housekeeper patterned on the stereotyped *servante de curé*.[4] The ecclesiastic note is not fortuitous; the sybaritic ascete has metaphysical aspirations. Allusions to Pascal are deliberate. Discussing Verlaine's *Poésies religieuses*: "It is striking how few, especially among the artists, can remain alone with themselves in a room."[5] And in a letter to Zola: "At bottom, Pascal was right: we must remain in our room."[6] Hence the importance of doors—when they fail to lock, other ways must be found. Jacques Marles, feeling unprotected in the overly accessible castle, wedges a chair against the entrance door to give himself at least the illusion that it cannot be opened from the outside (*En Rade*, 28).

Key words (haven, shelter, refuge, asylum) straddle the physical and metaphysical registers. Various tropes encourage this ambivalence. Describing physical well-being in a heated room, Huysmans speaks of keeping one's "soul" all nice and warm (*chaud à l'âme* comes closer to a pun); inversely, the heat emanating from the stove is associated with the sound of prayers filtering through the cloister bars.[7] Symptomatic phobias inform the dream of cuddling in a hothouse cloister: fear of the obscene "health" of the outside world; congenital aversion to the "vile crowds"; queasiness produced by any form of promiscuity, especially involving body functions: "I am at home, in my own toilet! And I say to myself that one must have experienced the promiscuity of hospitals and camps to appreciate the value of the washbasin, to savour the solitude of those places where one can in comfort drop one's trousers."[8]

This self-relish suggests a refusal of freedom, the fear of spending oneself. Huysmans' characters wish to "close the cage" from within; they seek a guarantee against disintegration. Huysmans contrives the word *s'évaguer*, punning on the resemblance with *s'évader* (to escape), but playing on the etymon *vague* (errant, ill-defined, imprecise). For him release means loss of substance. The sexual connotation becomes obvious. The fear of spending himself is closely bound up with mysogynic motifs. The numerous observations on besotted husbands, all entangled in women's skirts, cannot be read merely as traditional jokes. Too many passages express the terror of the feminine body. When confronted with marriage, Folantin withdraws horrified at the thought of "suffering a woman's touch in every season, of having to satisfy her. . . ." It is revealing that this physical aversion is traced back to "woman's original flaw" (*tare originelle de la femme*). The solution is to indulge occasionally with professionals in a repul-

sive hygienic exercise. The "stable of the senses" is opened
from time to time. It is to be led to the slaughterhouse-
brothel, where the *bouchères d'amour* operate with deadly efficiency. As for the contempt for feminine forms which
Huysmans attributes to the monstrous Gilles de Rais (a 15th-
century nobleman who tortured and killed children), it is not
enough to invoke sadism and sodomy. It is the *odor di femmina*
that is abhorrent: ". . . this smell of woman which all sodo-
mites abhor."[9] No wonder that this abhorrence is, at a more
prosaic level, linked with the fear (and memory) of venereal
disease! Folantin still smarts at the thought of having to walk
in pain to his office.[10] Even dyspepsia, as well as other digestive troubles affecting Huysmans' character, must be read as a
characteristic lack of appetite, a secretly wished-for atony.

The allurements of impotence account for strategies of
withdrawal. The theme of *absence* manifests itself at various
levels. Huysmans shuns the light; he dreams of a sunless existence. Certain letters to Zola, whose *Germinal* he read as a
"lamento of Darkness," make this very clear: ". . . I do not
like the sun which awakens my neuralgia; or rather I might
like it in the manner of Rembrandt, that is glimpsed through a
basement window. . . ."[11] Night remains the sought-for ambiance. Des Esseintes' mother, tired genetrix of a tired race,
cannot tolerate daylight (or any light, for that matter) without
suffering from nervous disorders. With her son, this allergy is
translated into esthetic value. The hero of *A Rebours* chooses
his furniture and fabrics to suit artificial light (*lumières factices*);
he prefers to be up at night and sleep during the day; his mind
seems to function "in contact with darkness" (20). His passion for interior decorating involves the artifices of the night.
He "composes" his boudoir: surrounded by mirrors, this specialist of shifting tones arranges his lighting so as to transform
the color of human flesh into a painter's carnation. Night itself becomes factitious. And while human nakedness, in this
opulent bordello atmosphere, is transmuted into color and
form, objects are personalized into assuming an erotic charge.
Des Esseintes conceives of pieces of furniture mimetic of

feminine orgasm, "imitating the contractions of [woman's] pleasures, the twisting of her spasms, through the undulations and wrigglings of wood and brass . . ." (99). For piquancy's sake, he introduces into this setting a large white bed whose "artificial candor" he relishes almost more than the rest.

Such "spaces" of artifice where erotic desire fulfills and exhausts itself through a system of transfers are essentially oneiric. Des Esseintes' house in Fontenay is uncannily silent. The two old servants communicate with no one, and are required by their master to wear at all times heavy felt slippers. Doors are well-oiled; the floors are padded with thick rugs. As for the study, it is protected by the upholstered walls of a corridor, and "hermetically closed" (28-29). Such a dream locus only stimulates erotic fantasies of impotence.

For there can be little doubt that the fascination with sexual inadequacy determines a number of metaphoric constructs. Sexual expenditure is always associated with a crushing sense of fatigue. The bachelor's lot appears as eminently desirable. *En Ménage*, one of the early novels, deplores the "misery of a shared bed (. . .), the fatiguing bore of required caresses . . ." (10). Faced with the amorous performance, Huysmans' heroes are convinced that they are not up to the task, that they are "sad paladins." Thrusts of the libido are defined in terms that hardly disguise latent impotence. A late and false summer in a pre-winter setting: ". . . *cette canicule exaspérée flambant tout à coup, dans un novembre de corps, dans une Toussaint d'âme.*" The text usually becomes more explicit: "Worn out, exhausted, lacking true desire, calm, sheltered from crises, almost impotent. . . ."[12] The convulsions of the flesh, especially the routine activity of "conjugal sweat" (*sueurs conjugales*),[13] produce nothing but disgust. Yet erotic imaginings are only whipped up by the refusal of a regular sexual commerce. Huysmans' characters dream of sophisticated, backbreaking caresses inflicted on them. They are haunted by images of emasculating professionals who confirm them in their passivity and fear of being drained. The skilled hetaera appears in these fantasies as a voluptuous torturer who leaves the victim undone.[14]

The fascination with the bitch (*pouffiasse*) is part of a voyeuristic complex.[15] Huysmans' imaginary erotic scenes imply non-participation. The description of a woman admiring a powerful cuirassier suggests the relief of not being himself put to the test. Envy of the strong male is transmuted into esthetic appreciation. "With one glance, she seems to assess the strength of his shoulders, the power of his legs and of his back, his promising animal looks. . . ."[16] Prurience is heightened by such strategies of esthetic withdrawal. The same *Croquis parisiens* indulge in olfactory suggestions of feminine intimacy (evocations of arm-pit odors in "Le Gousset") coupled with visual pleasures typical of a spectator's desire: "Women are never more desirable than when their close-fitting Oxford cloth dresses, sticking to their bodies like wet shirts that emprison them, outline every shape from top to toe" (135). Elsewhere, it is by proxy, through the obsessed, semi-legendary figure of the murderous sex-maniac Gilles de Rais (a contemporary of Joan of Arc!), that Huysmans indulges in his phantasms: the trees, with their branches, their holes, their orifices, appear to him transfixed in an "immobile fornication."[17] His taste for excess tolerates in fact no compromise between abstinence and debauchery. To his friend Landry he writes: ". . . I believe it easier not to go to bed with a woman than not to indulge in filthy practices with her. I am an old lecher [*un vieux cochon*] of your type. . . ."[18] But whether the point of view is that of the decadent esthete as in *Croquis parisiens*, of the amateur of fashion appreciative of close-fitting dresses, or of the mediating legendary figure, the perspective and criteria are always those of artifice. Revealingly, it is in a discussion of the painter Félicien Rops that Huysmans declares the causal link between continence-in-solitude and orgiastic fantasies (*délire orgiaque*): ". . . the truly obscene are the chaste."[19]

Statements such as these cast light on the tight bond between images of enclosure and reveries of impotence and

eroticism. Huysmans mentions the revolt of the senses in
cloisters, the saints' tortures of the flesh in their desert, precisely after having stressed, à propos Félicien Rops, the libertine workings of the mind in any state of confinement and solitude. The dialectical relation between continence and licen-
tiousness must, however, not be attributed simply to a taste
for the forbidden. Huysmans links this taste for depravation
to a deeper sense of profanation, to unhealthy religious reveries, to a disturbing flirtation with the Church. "Ever since I
moved close to the Church, my belief in filth [*persuasions d'or-
dures*] has become more frequent and more persistent." This
morbid perception is at the heart of Huysmans' metaphor of
enclosure. Confinement turns out to be libidinous, especially
in its religious connotations: ". . . all mystical reveries end up
in filth [*cochonnerie*]."[20] One is reminded of Flaubert's *La Tentation de Saint Antoine*—one of Huysmans' favorite texts—in
which the diabolical Hilarion denounces the saint's ascetic
withdrawal from the world as a supreme refinement in corruption. "You hypocrite, who wallow in your solitude the
better to surrender to the debauchery of your desires!" Images
of self-enclosure arise almost automatically whenever Huysmans conjures up orgies of the imagination. About the sala-
cious daydreams in *En Route*: "they always acted out, behind
the lowered curtain of his eyelids, fairy plays whose acts
hardly ever varied" (37). Or better still: ". . . she undresses
behind the lowered curtain of my eyelids; at the thought of it,
I am overcome with abject weakness" (*affreuse lâcheté*—131).

But if the subtle corruption of reclusion reanimates an inhibited libido, the metaphor of claustration is not limited to
that register: it exorcises, transmutes, brings about sublima-
tion. The imagery of enclosure succeeds in inverting what is
assumed to be the usual relation between psychological motivation and the act of writing. That act becomes determining.
Thematic variations on containers (bottles, boxes, drawers,
wardrobes, the *gousset*), as repositories of a secret, suggest the
topos of a revelatory essence. *En Rade* provides a typical illustration in the form of a musty old room: "This smell almost

moved him, for it brought up coddling visions of a wan past; it was like the last exhalation of forgotten scents . . ." (69). In a sentence Baudelaire might have written, Huysmans evokes the *âme des flacons*, the soul of those bottles opened long ago which lingers on in these dead chambers. The soteriological theme is clear (salvation through survival, victory over time): the container is here the figure of extra-temporality.

Proust, who was an attentive reader of Huysmans, also comes to mind. Not only is the cloister image frequently associated with childhood memories, but the description of the monastic *locus amoenus* (*En Route*, 34-35) elaborates a specific symbolism of the receptacle. Folantin experiences the surprises of involuntary memory: an operatic aria brings to life the image of his grandmother; for a moment, he has in his mouth the taste of the biscuits she used to give him when he was a child. This experience in synesthesia is logically connected to the image of the precious receptacle: ". . . during the third act, Folantin no longer thought of his grandmother, but his nose was suddenly filled with the smell of an old box he had at home . . ." (53-54).

For both Huysmans and Proust, the notion of salvation proves inseparable from claustrophilia. At the center of Proust's novel there is the intimacy of the room from which young Marcel enjoys the season's "total spectacle"; or, better still, the key image of Noah's ark from the heart of which, in a darkened world, the locked-in consciousness glimpses the invisible.[21] With Huysmans, the early yearning for the enclosed space, for the *bienheureuse rade*, also leads to the image of the "padded ark" (*arche capitonnée*).[22] The logic of such associations brings out the basic importance of the "refined reclusion" (*thébaïde raffinée*) which is the subject of *A Rebours*, and is revealingly qualified as a "warm, immobile arch" (10).

The cell remains Huysmans' *chambre spirituelle*. His craving for cloisters, his nostalgia for abbey inns, his notion of monastic delights, are proclaimed in dithyrambic passages that sing of cellular joys. Between the material inventory of the tiny, white-washed rooms of La Salette monastery, and the sensation experienced by the hero Durtal, there is the gap of a mystery. Is his, however, a genuine religious experience? "Durtal remained there, with his elbow on the table, and an infinite sweetness filled him; it felt like the blossoming out of a soul that slowly rediscovered itself."[23] To be sure, Huysmans suggests that there is no solution of continuity between the physical joys of curling up and the conception of a spiritual refuge in a religious context. The phenomenon of the soul's "expanding in the company of Christ" he attributes to the constraining virtues of the cloister. But is such a *mystique expérimentale* to be equated with the esthete's ecstasies, or with the secret pleasures of the solitary dreamer who indulges in his own personality at the very moment he pretends to forget himself?

This peculiar notion of salvation involves the writer's vocation as well as the conditions of writing. The two are moreover closely wedded within the context of "modernity"—a word and a concept dear to Huysmans. In *L'Oblat*, Durtal, who calls himself a "drug-addict of the Divine office" (*morphinomane de l'office*), continues to evoke the expiatory solitude of hermits; but, in reality, he views claustration primarily as a prolonged withdrawal to an ideal study, confined by walls of books. The setting of his "monastic" existence leaves little doubt as to the telescoping of images. "He lived in his large study with its book-clad walls." Father Gévresin having willed him his private library, even the bedroom walls are now covered from floor to ceiling with books!

The redundant wall imagery, associated with the bequest of an ecclesiastical library, is part of a system of transfers that tends to confuse religious and esthetic images. Even the window, which separates the outside from the inside by means of a confined glance, is a pretext for a system of exchange. Durtal sets up his desk near the window: ". . . he daydreamed, prayed, meditated, took notes."[25] Prayer and meditation do point to religious activities—though the latter leaves room for ambiguity; but the two verbs that frame the sentence obviously relate to the occupations of scholar and poet: daydreaming (*rêvasser*) and the taking of notes. Even more telling is the avowed intention of using piety as a cover for the pursuit of esthetic values. In the following passage, all hinges on a metalepsis: the *"bibelots pieux"* (pious trinkets):

> At bottom, what he needed was to obtain from the abbot in whose cloister he would confine himself the permission to bring his books with him, to keep at least some pious trinkets in his cell. Yes,—but how was he to explain that secular texts are necessary in a monastery, that from the point of view of art it was indispensable to immerse oneself in the prose of Hugo, of Baudelaire, of Flaubert. . . ?[26]

The "point of view of art": the passage is explicit. The meaning pivots around the adjective "pious." Even the word "trinket" (*bibelot*) ironizes the metaphor. For the subject is indeed religion—but the religion of art, the cult of The Book. Huysmans is of course not the only high priest of this cellular cult. Mallarmé's themes of closed shutters, of thick curtains, of pieces of furniture heavy with locked-up secrets, of rooms containing time, are all placed in the service of The Book.

If Huysmans rightly considered *A Rebours* as his central work, this is hardly for the simple biographical reasons given in the preface he wrote twenty years after the novel, when he viewed it as the early sign (*amorce*) of his eventual religious conversion. Huysmans must have read his own text as a linguistic and cultural system of transfers and exchange. Much has been made of the so-called "phases" of his literary career: naturalism, decadentism, spirituality. Such neat separations allow the biographer to tell a story of linear progress toward faith. But the richness of texture of *A Rebours* depends, on the contrary, on the synchronism of categories, on the simultaneous co-existence of jarring elements. To be sure, the novel is a breviary of decadentism. Des Esseintes suffers from neurosis. Delighting in "deliquescence," ensconced in his hothouse atmosphere, this sickly sybarite succeeds in undermining his own perversions of asceticism. The ultimate de-

scendant of an exhausted stock, warped product of consan-
guineous and even incestuous relations, Des Esseintes suffers
all manners of ills: anemia, eye trouble (he cannot bear the
daylight), neuralgias, lack of appetite, digestive disturbances.
His sexual needs belong in the annals of psychopathology:
complicated preparations, acrobatic caresses, refinements in
the art of inversion. His exaggerated estheticism leads him to
prefer literary works, such as Petronius' *Satyricon*, depicting
"the vices of a decrepit civilization," or paintings suggestive
of lewdness and perversity. Gustave Moreau's *Salomé*, stressing the lascivious dance, affects his nervous system through
"scholarly hysteria" (48, 83-84). As for his own "decadent"
exploits, they are well known: the live turtle shell inlaid with
precious stones; the "mouth organ" filled with various al-
coholic distillations by means of which he plays mute sym-
phonies on his palate; imaginary voyages; cultivation of
"syphilitic" flowers; crime conceived as one of the fine arts.
The unnatural is more than an addiction; it is a philosophy:
". . . artificiality appeared to Des Esseintes as the distinctive
sign of man" (35).

But if the novel is outwardly "decadent," its deeper intentionality is metaphysical. Pessimism itself is in the service of a
quest. The theme of *ennui* inherited from scorners of "reality"
such as Baudelaire corresponds to a nostalgia for the absolute.
This may well be the symbolic meaning of claustration in *A
Rebours*. In his *thébaïde raffinée*, Des Esseintes locks himself up
with his books and becomes intoxicated with solitude. Yet
the artificiality of his existence, away from what in almost religious terms he calls the *pénitentier de son siècle* (the prison
house of life), forces him into direct confrontation with the
absolute of nothingness. The negative religious temptation
becomes particularly strong in Chapter VII:

> His propensity for artifice, his need for eccentricities,
> weren't they the consequence of specious studies, of
> extra-mundane refinements, of quasi-theological specu-
> lation? They were, in fact, raptures, thrusts toward an

ideal, toward an unknown world, toward a distant
beatitude desirable like those promised us in Holy Scrip-
tures (120).

The bond between artifice and spirituality is confirmed in an
admiring reference to Flaubert. Huysmans quotes the Chimera's declaration in *La Tentation de Saint Antoine* ("I seek
new perfumes, larger flowers, untried pleasures"),[27] which
leads him to elaborate on the fever of the unknown, the un-
fulfilled ideal, the dream of transcendence through the *au-delà
de l'art* (163). The horror fascination with nature, which is the
chief symptom of Bovarysme (Emma indeed laments over
the "inadequacy of life"), and also leads Des Esseintes to the
"certainty that no new happiness was possible" (275), can be
interpreted only as an inverted idealism that sees in artifice a
principle of revolt.

Des Esseintes' quip is well known: "*La nature a fait son
temps*" (Nature has had its day). The remark, tersely summing up the decadentist program, takes on full significance
when read into the mainstream of anti-naturalist thought.
Here too Baudelaire's aphoristic voice can be heard: "Nature
teaches nothing"—"All that which is beautiful and noble is
the result of reason and reckoning"—"Good is always the
product of artistry." The young artist in Baudelaire's short
novel *La Fanfarlo* would gladly "repaint" all the trees, the entire landscape.[28] Des Esseintes expresses a similar fondness
for "made-up" nature (the landscape's *maquillage*); he imagines a plain covered with a fine powder, smeared over with
white cold cream, and trees coated with chalk (38). The time
has come, he feels, to replace nature with artificial creation.
This rebellious impulse, which betrays a deeper need for
transcendence, finds its coarsest but also most symbolic expression in the final episode of the nutritious enema. Des Esseintes interprets this inverted manner of feeding as the
crowning achievement of his life. Physical deviation implies
in this context a real sense of liberation. The rectal feeding is
like a declaration of independence. "It would be delicious, he

said to himself, if one could continue this mode of nutrition even in good health. . . . What a telling insult in the face of old Nature whose uniform demands would once and for all be smothered!" (318.)

This hostility to nature helps explain the strongly ambivalent attitudes towards modern science. For it is the same Huysmans, indignant about the vulgarian *moeurs américaines* and horrified by the "lonely suppository" called the Eiffel Tower, who has Des Esseintes proclaim his admiration for the locomotive as the perfect example of an "animated and factitious creature" (36). Machines and steel constructions are, in fact, given a special status in *L'Art moderne*. According to Huysmans, the architects and engineers of the Gare du Nord have created an outstanding piece of "contemporary art." What is involved is a taste largely determined by negative factors. "Modernity" functions in relation to the "terrible life" of great cities; it is defined by the awareness of pervasive ugliness. In his contradictory reaction to science viewed as a creative disfiguration of the natural world, Huysmans recapitulates the inner contradictions so typical of the Romantic imagination. The steam engine fills him with a characteristic mixture of "admiration and fear."[29] There can be no doubt that the prestige of the machine is always associated in his mind with a rebellion against nature. Thus the "horrible magnificence" of engines is evoked in almost therapeutic fashion when the insipid landscape creates in him a sense of nausea. "How petty this landscape seems in comparison with a factory scene, or the hull of a ship lit up by the flames of the furnace!" Huysmans even turns ecstatic, conceiving the sex act of industry as the trope of a purely artificial creativity, singing of ironworks copulations, of steel embryos born of the furnaces' matrix (*matrice des fours*).[30]

The centrality of *A Rebours* is, however, not due entirely to the synchronism of the themes. More fundamental still is the pervasive prison image. The joint is a specific notion of modernity implying both a mystique and a withdrawal. Gustave Moreau appears, in *L'Art moderne*, as the embodiment of this seeming contradiction of modernity and spiritual escapism: "He is a mystic locked up, in the heart of Paris, in a cell impenetrable to the noise of daily life which angrily beats at the doors of the cloister" (152). The prison-monastery symbol conveys, throughout Huysmans' work, the concept of "modernistic" escapism. Certain rhetorical figures—for instance *après-midi internés* in *La Cathédrale* (I, 290)—look ahead to the thematic metaphors of Gaston Bachelard. One even finds the Bachelardian notion of *eaux immobiles*: "It is a contemplative body of water [*eau contemplative*] in perfect harmony with the self-communing life of cloisters."[31]

Huysmans' writing provides an inventory of prison themes. *Prison-torment*: the endless grief (*inépuisable navrement*) of being alone in a room, yet the glorification of meaningful suffering. His sympathy for Villon, detained in the deepest dungeon, has to be read in this dark light. Conversely, the refusal of mirth underlies his aversion to Saint Francis, whom he associates with insolent health and the Italian sun.[32] *Prison freedom*: worldly concerns (*siècle*) are the true penitentiary and Paris is the true world of forced labor (*le bagne*). *Prison spirituality*: this is the logical consequence of a thematic inversion. Hence the symbolic importance of the mad sinner Gilles de Rais, who, in jail, suddenly "reversed his soul."[33] The mystic artist, Huysmans declares in his preface to Rémy de Gourmont's *Latin mystique*, works in a cell. *Prison of art*: the esthetic perspective is never absent. The confrontation with nothingness is essentially the poet's business. The finite allows of the quest for the infinite; it will always be the artist's task to illustrate this confrontation with nothingness as a privilege. *Prison of decadence*: the very notion of inversion translated into a system corresponds to the "decadent" ideal. Huysmans does not merely turn upside down the customary notions of freedom and constriction; in his prison house of artifice he continues to juggle with factitiousness. Des Esseintes aims at nothing short of "*reversing* theatrical optics." His perversity thus transcends the contriving of a false monastic cell; it involves the inverting of the inversion. He seeks to create "a sad thing with joyful objects," to place elegance in the service of fake poverty. This double inversion is best summed up in the description of the complicated floral arrangements: "After the artificial flowers aping real flowers, he desired natural flowers that would imitate false ones."[34]

Metaphoric prowess does not exorcise Huysmans' essential duplicity with regard to the monastic ideal. On the one hand, there is the fear of the real monastery, withdrawal in the face of the "austere ugliness" of all places of penitence and of prayer.[35] A letter to Leclaire is explicit: "Cloisters are beautiful in dreams, but awful in reality. Surely salvation is more unlikely there than out in the world."[36] But even the "monastic" dream is less that of an ascetic existence than of an artistic community, or of a propitious setting for the solitary artist. In either case, the claustral concept has an esthetic value. Ambivalence, however, prevails even in this esthetic context. The cloister is "useful for the preparation of a work"; but will he be able, behind such thick walls, to "fabricate" his books? Durtal finally hits on a compromise: the life of an oblate, associated with a religious community but not bound by vows. Unquestionably a practical solution: ". . . the oblate's existence is beneficial above all to artists; it provides them with monastic grace. . . ."[37] But the solution also implies the dream of an association for the cult of art—a substitute religion. In *La Cathédrale*, he invokes the "chimera of an abbey, more literary, more artistic"; he surrenders to vague fantasies, seeing himself as a "monk in a debonair convent ministered to by a lenient religious order in love with liturgy and art" (I, 305, 298).

In *L'Oblat*, this yearning leads specifically to the image of an artists' colony. There is, however, a new reversal: it is no longer the artist who needs "monastic grace," but the church that needs art. Father Felletin could not be more explicit: ". . . we need scholars, well-read people, artists . . ." (II, 19). There can be no doubt that, in the face of recent political developments—a law of 1901, hostile to religion, almost led to the dispersion of all religious orders—Huysmans was play-

ing on the word *congrégation*. Yet the attempt to save religious
congregations under guise of communities of scholars and artists cannot be reduced to a strategy of camouflage. A typical
inversion once again corresponds to deeper needs. Here is the
project, which is obviously also a dream:

> No law can in fact prevent individual artists from renting
> a house in a suitably prearranged complex, to live there
> according to their taste, to assemble periodically to talk
> of art or to pray, in short to live as they choose (. . .) .
> Their assembly thus belongs to the category of literary
> associations.

In this lay enclosure, which is to shelter a monk disguised as a
priest, the genuine cenobite to be protected against the law
turns out to be a mere adjunct. It is, to say the least, a strange
system of defense which utilizes a political contingency to
situate the esthete at the heart of an imaginary confinement.

Textually, the esthete is installed even more centrally
through pervasive images of immurement. Fictional techniques play on circumscription and de-finition. *Seul* (alone)
was the original title of Des Esseintes' story. *Soliloquy* is indeed its most consistent stylistic feature. Huysmans was fully
aware of the newness and pitfalls of a one-character novel centered on a dead-end, self-addressed discourse. A letter to
Théo Hannon announces "a very strange, vaguely clerical,
somewhat pederastic novel—a *novel with only one character.
. . .*" To Zola, he confesses his concern: "I really got myself into an awful tangle writing this novel *with only one character and
no dialogues.*"[38] Solipsism is of course a distinguishing characteristic of all Huysmans' fiction. His novels are dense with
monologuists' formulas. In *Là-Bas*: "Talking to himself in a
rambling manner. . . ," Durtal enjoys "discussing with himself daily." Only his cat overhears his "soliloquy" (xii, ii,
118, 122, 207). Free indirect discourse is exploited not in
order to penetrate from an outside into a relatively opaque interiority (as is the case with Flaubert) but to overhear oneself.

How did he return to catholicism, how had it come about?

And Durtal answered himself: I do not know; all I am aware of is that, after having been an unbeliever for many years, suddenly I have faith.

Let's see, he said to himself, let us nonetheless try to reason. . . .[39]

Such devices and structural elements are closely wedded to the basic themes. "One would have to know how to avoid discussing with oneself, he said to himself with distress." The connotation of an unavoidable necessity implies a chronic disease. This diagnosis is even clearer in the following self-observation: "Evidently, I am more affected [*atteint*] than I thought, he said to himself; here I dispute with myself like a casuist."[40]

Huysmans himself diagnosed the disease of thinking, evoking the "cerebral clinic" of the much-admired Poe, the terror of immured thought. Other writers could be invoked, specifically Andreyev, whose *Mysl* (*Thought*) depicts the isolation in the brain's trap, the confrontation with the self in the prison of thought, the dark internal castle into which no voice can penetrate to save him from himself. Huysmans' work must be read as part of a larger trend viewing the brain as the locus of a heroic sequestration. The hermeticism he advocated, his addiction to any artistic form inaccessible to the uninitiated, would justify this solipsism of the intellect. Promiscuity—if but promiscuity in admiration—he finds unbearable. Des Esseintes holds that the most beautiful painting and the most enchanting music become vulgar as soon as "the public" pollutes them with its enthusiasm (153).

This lack of aperture is confirmed at the stylistic level. Huysmans provides perhaps the best illustration of Valéry's paradox concerning the "precious" nature of realistic scripture—a scripture which, under pretext of objective distance, confers supreme value on the act of writing. Flaubert himself, though he proclaimed that "beautiful subjects" were almost an obstacle to beautiful works, felt that Huysmans had gone too far, and told him so. "The Ganges is not more poetic than the Bièvre, but the Bièvre is not more so either than the Ganges. Take heed not to relapse, as in the days of classical tragedy, into the aristocracy of subjects and into verbal preciosity."[41] The warning applies. Huysmans' delight in piquant juxtapositons irritated his earliest readers. Critics pointed to the combination of brutality and pretentiousness, accusing him of indulging in hyper-refined stylistic exercises on top of a dung heap (*marivaudage sur un tas de fumier*).[42] He eventually gave up the coarser subjects and the more sordid settings; but never freed himself from the *préciosité des mots* against which Flaubert had warned him. Stylistic games became in fact more ostentatious as the themes turned toward religiosity. There is talk of "delousing" the soul (*se dépouiller l'âme*), of priests who can be recognized by the "vaseline of their speech, the grease of their accent." The hero of *En Route*, suffering from spiritual dyspepsia (*dyspepsie d'âme*), is fearful of priests who will inflict on him their *pious veal bouillon* (3-4, 67, 71).

These stylistic mannerisms, together with all the techniques of circumscription, ultimately serve to confine the writer to his private stage. Similarly, the exchange system between esthetic and monastic concepts affirms the patient and autonomous elaboration of the text. For Des Esseintes, the great glory of medieval cloisters is a function of art and culture: "Latin saved . . ." (57), but saved so that new privileged enclosures can provide the luxury of artistic and cultural pleasures that will remain unshared. Is Des Esseintes a caricature? Hardly. For Huysmans too—his entire work ceaselessly proclaims it—withdrawal implies a specific notion of salvation. Only it is the poetic vision itself that becomes the redemptive enclosure, the *thébaïde raffinée*. And this vision, in spite of the author's conversion to religion, implies to the end an essentially private world.

III. The Ungraspable Camp

|| 10 ||

Servitude and Solidarity

. . . we need no drawings to imagine such places.
—Camus

After Huysmans, who modulates in his own key the romantic theme of the happy prison, one question emerges: how much longer could salvation be viewed in strictly private terms? In Proust's work, the room, the figuration of a precious inner world, remains the privileged locus of creative suffering and of redemption through art. But this metaphoric valorization of the private cell, this sanctification of the individual, were soon to appear difficult, if not downright outrageous. Two world wars, the spread of totalitarian regimes, the systematic political planning of human degradation and of genocide, were to thrust writers into the nightmare of history, compelling them, as Sartre put it, to practice a "literature of historicity."[1] Under these conditions, what was to become of the old dream of the cell?

It is true that Camus, only a few years ago, diagnosed the 20th-century addiction of what he termed *"lyrisme cellulaire."* But the expression, much like the entire texture of the novel *La Chute* in which it appears, is characteristically ambiguous. It can be read both as an expression of poetic nostalgia and of moral condemnation. Nostalgia? All of Camus' work is a plea for the rights of privacy. Meursault, the "stranger," no doubt a spiritual heir to Stendhal's Julien Sorel, discovers his authenticity and freedom in the alienating but protective prison cell. He too learns that the only trouble in jail is that one cannot lock one's door from the inside. Moral condemnation? While recognizing the lyrical potential of confinement, Camus evidently denounces the false prophet Jean-Baptiste Clamence, who locked himself up in the prison of the Amsterdam bar,

where he indulges in claustrophilic escapism. A prison within
a prison, this underworld bar is located in the heart of a city
whose concentric canals bring to mind the circles of Dante's
hell. Clamence, a suave voice in the desert of humanistic
smugness, an "empty" prophet himself guilty of the arrogance he denounces, ironizes on the lofty and individualistic
happy prison whose altitude and fine views supposedly encourage a sense of elevation and elation.

Instead of the happy prison, Clamence sarcastically proposes, as a symbol of our abjection and self-cultivated guilt,
the stinking underground cell known in medieval times as the
malconfort, or the more modern invention, the *cellule des
crachats*[2]—a fitting emblem of our supreme self-indulgence:
the luxury of a bad conscience. The denunciation of bad faith
is pushed to the limit by Camus. In this text that ironizes on
irony, the condemnation of a good conscience is in turn condemned. Clamence settled in the midst of the Jewish quarter
that had witnessed not too long ago one of the most hideous
crimes of history: 75,000 Jews deported or exterminated. But
indulging in a sense of guilt, private or collective, can be
another form of murder: the systematic undermining and ultimate negation of the image of man. By raising the possibility of this kind of spiritual genocide, Camus has written a
parable of the debate, crucial for our time, between humanism and anti-humanism.

The *lyrisme cellulaire* is not invoked by chance. This "lyricism" has a privileged status in the humanistic tradition. The
case of Flaubert, the "hermit" of Croisset, is exemplary.
Quite logically, his work leads up to the image of the two
clerks locking themselves up in order to continue copying.
The idea of the artist-monk had been thematized in works
overtly concerned with external "reality." Balzac's novels
provide ample illustrations of the temptation to refuse life in
order to seek fulfillment in monastic creativity. Raphaël de
Valentin settles in his garret (prison and ascetic enclosure: "a
cage worthy of the *Piombi* in Venice") which, through intel-

lectual labor, he metamorphoses into a *sépulcre aérien*, a super-terrestrial tomb, where he has hopes of being "re-born."[3]

The correlation writing (reading) = prison and the theme of the artist's beneficent immurement assume particularly complex forms in Proust. Recent criticism has shown how Proustian enclosures serve the de-realization of reality—hence the importance of the hypochondriacal aunt Léonie, the self-willed recluse. Serge Doubrovsky rightly refers to Proust's interest in partitions, to his "carceral phantasms" apparent even in his notion of the "binding" metaphor. In a rhetorical analysis of Proust's allegory of reading, Paul de Man also brings out the theme of enclosed space: though consciousness refuses imprisonment and seeks to escape toward the outside, the reading (= writing) process implies an interiority "that seeks to protect itself against the threats of an outside world."[4]

It is certainly not a coincidence that the poetic prestige of the prison image corresponds culturally to a period when art becomes increasingly the subject of art, and thought the subject of thought, as the writer indulges in his mirror disease. Retirement into an inner exile is a characteristic temptation of decadentism. The taste for hermetic, nocturnal existence and withdrawal to the protective hothouse go hand in hand with fear of life, of action, of commitment. The terror of open spaces, the Mallarmean hatred of the *bel azur*, suggest a fascination with sterility as well as a penchant for narcissism. Huysmans, as we have seen, conceives of a supremely comfortable "cell" where the esthete lives surrounded by mirrors. This kind of "cellular lyricism" was bound to provoke reactions. Perhaps Chekhov was thinking of Oblomov, in Goncharov's novel, who lives locked up in his room "like exotic fauna," dreaming of a lost paradise he attempts to recapture through death-in-life. Certainly Chekhov is sensitive both to the seductions of solitude and to its dangers. "True happiness was impossible without solitude. The Fallen Angel must have

betrayed God because he felt a desire for solitude, which the
angels know naught of."[5] Writers most drawn to seclusion
apparently begin to suffer from malaise. Thus Thomas Mann,
while suggesting that to become a poet one must probably
feel at home in some sort of jail, also gives the following
warning, not so far removed from the Satanic threat implicit
in Chekhov's commentary: "Solitude gives birth to the original in us, to beauty unfamiliar and perilous—to poetry. But
also, it gives birth to the opposite: to the perverse, the illicit,
the absurd."[6]

If our own period continues to elaborate prison metaphors,
it is in a spirit opposed neither to action nor to moral commitment. Malraux's work illustrates the counterpoint of solitude and solidarity, the confronting images of enclosure and
epic space. The opening signals of *La Condition humaine* pit
the cellular world of the hotel room (the death room with its
rectangle of electric light and its window bars) against the
"world of men," the world of the streets. The great scene of
the book, echoing (as does the title) Pascal's famous *pensée*,
describes the prisoners awaiting death. The autobiographical
Antimémoires, retrospectively glosses the novel: "In Pascal's
prison, man has succeeded in discovering in himself an answer that pervades, so to speak, with immortality those
worthy of it." From one text to another, Malraux remains
obsessed with the image of jail. It is an obsession with temporality and separation ("O prison, that place where time
stops—time which continues elsewhere . . ."), as well as with
solipsism (". . . to be compelled to seek refuge entirely in oneself is exhausting"). But carceral anguish allows one to trans-
cend the absurd: ". . . in this prison, we find in ourselves images powerful enough to negate our nothingness." According
to Malraux, the three great "novels of reconquest" were all
written by men who have known jail: Cervantes, Defoe,
Dostoevsky.[7] For Malraux was convinced that the experience
of incarceration provided the basic elements of any tragic

structure, as well as a lesson in freedom. He liked to quote Gandhi, who cabled his congratulations to followers of his who had been arrested, saying that freedom must often be sought within prison walls.[8]

Malraux no doubt felt that Pascal's vision of men in chains projects into our own era of concentration camps an emblematic image. Himself a prophetic witness at a time when most Europeans, suffering from the bad faith of the post-war years, refused to confront their own nightmare, Malraux understood that the private cell had become an anachronistic symbol. The catastrophic nature of the 20th century seemed to have cancelled out the possibility of dreaming in poetic privacy.

Collective penal servitude had replaced the cell of individualism. Chronologically speaking, one could say that the literary "figure" preceded the "reality" our own tortured era was destined to experience in the flesh. For side by side with the cellular lyricism so dear to the Romantic imagination, 19th-century literature is filled with visions of infernal horrors in the tradition of the *Dies irae*: poignant scenes of collective punishment, of dehumanizing penitentiaries. It is because Hugo and Dostoevsky felt convinced that individual salvation was not really possible, that they tended to glorify the criminal-convict, the *forçat*, and through him the figure of the "People," as a Promethean redeemer to be treated with almost sacred awe.

Art and reality periodically enter into a synchronic relation of exchange, a fecund shuttle between literary models and the conditions of a given society. Victor Serge's *Les Hommes dans la prison* is an excellent example of the merging of an old theme with a profoundly contemporary experience. Serge, a professional revolutionary who died in Mexico City in the late 1940's, personally knew and described the gloomy world of jails where he (like Malraux's fictional revolutionary Kyo) was thrown together with common criminals. His book is a semi-fictionalized autobiographic account ("All is fiction in this book, and all is true") that aims at transcending personal suffering to reach out to the larger community of pariahs in a world madder still than they are. Collective tragedy is conceived by him as an apprenticeship in solidarity. Victor Serge calls for a literature that will relate the individual destiny to that of the group. "I conceive literature only as a means of expression between human beings. . . . One must therefore be among those who struggle, suffer, fall, conquer." The prison, as a "lived" metaphor, lends itself to the fusion of documentary and thematic elements. The prisoners themselves, Serge observes, tend to universalize their experience. "There are so many prisons in the universe," says one of the old convicts, "every prison is a universe, every universe a prison." More significant still, the prison—myth and mechanized plant—looms as a life-crushing construct—the enemy of man. Serge explains: "There is no fictional hero in this novel, unless that terrible machine, *prison*, is its real hero."[9]

Repeatedly, Serge invokes the image of the machine. "Jail is a slow life-crushing machine." And again: "The crushing machine encloses me on all sides. . . ." This technical precision, linked to architectural efficiency unrelated to human needs and drives, unavoidably suggests the urban context. Speaking of jail, Serge writes: "In the modern city, I know only one irreproachable, perfect piece of architecture. . . ." The prison is in the image of the city. "Prison is . . . a bleak city besieged and dominated by the enemy it hems in."[10] But the terms of the metaphor remain reversible: the entire city appears as a huge jail.

Camus, in *La Peste*, suggests that the inhabitants of the plague-ridden city are all condemned, for an unknown crime, to an inconceivable condemnation—an *emprisonnement inimaginable*. Camus in fact originally planned to entitle his allegorical novel *Les Prisonniers*. The city of Oran, in the novel, is indeed immured by disease, segregated from the rest of the world, confined by the sudden collective awareness of its mortal condition. But Oran's epidemic is only a symptom of a worse calamity. The collective, dehumanizing threat of the modern *polis* is a greater threat than even contagious disease and physical corruption. A malevolent logic seems to threaten man's free spirit for the sake of a communal norm. The growth of the city myth in modern consciousness is no doubt related to the ominous threat of a pervasive, anonymous tyranny. Frightening utopias of an Orwellian type—as well as science fiction—announce an efficiency that also signifies the end of "humanistic" man. A model of the genre, Zamiatin's book, carrying as title the collective pronoun *We*, illustrates the logic of this repressive efficiency. Zamiatin, who probably influenced the author of *1984*, writes with the devil's logic: ". . . if human freedom is equal to zero man does not commit any crime [. . .]. The way to rid man of criminality is to rid him of freedom."[11]

Much could be said about these nightmare visions of the collective habitat, of the megalopolis as the modern penitentiary. Another Russian text, Briussov's *The Republic of the Southern Cross*, provides a prophetic description of a capital, the artificially lit Star City, whose windowless buildings are covered by an "impenetrable and opaque roof." Briussov's "modern" city ultimately appears like an immense, black, polluted coffer (or is it a coffin?), as a gigantic "insane asylum" filled with the stench of corpses. But the Russian work that develops in the most sustained manner the relation between bureaucratic planimetry and penitential anguish is Bely's novel *Petersburg*, with its disturbing perspectives, urban sense of emptiness, labyrinthine streets that seem the symbolic projection of the corridors of an oppressed mind. This cerebral and topophilic geometry, prefiguring the mental spaces of the Nouveau Roman, constitutes a figurative network: cubic houses, quadrangular partitions, perpendicular walls, parallelepipeds, cones, pyramids, trapezoids—all of them reflecting the specific torment within the "dark recess" of the compressed brain.[12]

The city looms as a jail in many a 19th-century novel. Houses in Balzac's Paris have a prison smell (*les murailles y sen-*

tent la prison). The gloomy streets of Dickens' London, in
their "penitential garb of soot," offer to the glance houses that
are jails, "old places of imprisonment." Melville, at the beginning of *Moby Dick*, before the grand departure, presents
the prison island of the Manhattoes through a series of carceral images: the city is "belted round" by wharfs; the inhabitants are "pent up" in lath and plaster, "tied" to counters,
"clinched" to desks, "nailed" to benches.[13] But no matter
how confining and oppressive the commercial megalopolis of
19th-century fiction may be, no matter how great the danger
of moral asphyxia, this is not yet the horror world of more
recent collective penitentiary nightmares or phantasms.

But are they mere nightmares and phantasms? Reality, alas,
caught up with, and even outdid, the most feverish fictional
constructs. When Walter Jens's *Nein. Die Welt der Angeklagten*
(*No. The World of the Accused*) appeared in the wake of World
War II, the over-intellectualized perspective on the intermi-
nable corridors bordered by torture chambers no longer was
able to account for a pervasive sense of fear. Jens's inquisito-
rial world, planned as though by a "textbook for concentration camp and prison wardens," in spite of scenes vaguely
reminiscent of Dostoevsky and Kafka, was bound to appear
somewhat pale and abstract beside a reality that refused to be
stylized.[14] The hard fact is that the era of concentration
camps, with its fundamental assault on the dignity of man,
brought about a radical change in the way imprisonment was
to be treated as a literary theme.

Could prison still serve as a poetic subject? Were not certain
horrors beyond artistic expression? Jean Cayrol, a former
camp inmate, stated this reticence which is very different
from silence. For the *concentrationnat*—as Cayrol puts it—
infiltrated daily life, contaminated all activities, created
around the survivors of the holocaust an "Ungraspable
Camp." The opening of his essay *Pour un Romanesque Laza-
réen* deserves to be quoted:

> There is nothing to explain. Concentration camps have
> been experienced differently by their victims. Some died

of them; others die of them slowly, cut off from a return, growing old in the larval form of a half-forgotten terror. Many live of them, trying to force their way through this Ungraspable Camp which, once again, surrounds them, casts a spell on them, confuses them.[15]

The image of the "Ungraspable Camp" (*Insaisissable Camp*) accounts for the *displacement* of the subject. The concentration camp terror could not be contained in a privileged space.

The most diverse documents on concentration camps bear witness to the non-assimilable nature of the experience in literary terms. The act of writing was never an end, but a means of survival. One of the most moving texts to emerge from the Nazi mass exterminations is a study of writings by doomed ghetto and extermination camp inmates who tried desperately, in the face of imminent annihilation, to communicate their testimony in a last-minute, almost from-beyond-the-mass-grave message of fraternity. Michel Borvicz has piously collected and analyzed these heart-rending scribblings, calling them the *contre-poison de la mort*—the antidote of death. He quotes Nico Rost—his notebooks were posthumously published under the title *Goethe in Dachau*—for whom writing and note-taking were the daily "vitamins L and V" (*Lernen und Zukunft*: Study and Future). Quite significantly, however, Borvicz concludes his *Ecrits des Condamnés à mort sous l'occupation allemande* with a sharp distinction between the experience of prison (where inmates reaffirm beliefs that predate their incarceration) and the radically alienating experience of camps:

> . . . a prison (with all the suffering that awaits the victims) did not present an essentially new aspect. Extermination camps, on the other hand, daily forced human beings to face conditions heretofore unthinkable, bringing them in contact with problems of existence, of the human body, of its place in the order of the universe.[16]

David Rousset's *L'Univers concentrationnaire*, also the book of a "witness," makes a similar point, stressing the uniqueness

of the experience, its fundamental inaccessibility to those who
were not exposed to it. "It is a world apart, totally closed on
itself; it is the strange realm of a special *fatum*. The fathom-
lessness of camps."[17]

Yet cultural traditions and models remain binding. The references serving to define this esthetically unassimilable experience are strangely literary. A chapter of Borvicz's book is
entitled "Recourse to Heritage" (*Recours au patrimoine*). In
part, it is a matter of survival: the doomed inmates learn
poetry by heart, thus providing themselves with a "living an-
thology." But the paradox calls for another explanation. The
mediation of culture becomes necessary because words are
not adequate to the experience. Literature is thus made to
function as the mediator to a meaning it cannot itself carry.
Victor Serge, in order to describe a non-fictional experience
of the penitentiary, quotes Verlaine and Mallarmé, refers to
Dostoevsky's *House of the Dead*, invokes Alexandre Dumas,
recalls Hugo's *Les Misérables*. This referential system is particularly appropriate in this case, since Serge remains deeply
attached to the traditional prison theme: he extols prison introspection ("Introspection reveals the endless perspectives of
the inner life") as well as man's victory over the world of bars
("Victory over jail is a great victory . . .").[18] But the same
priority of literature and of literary themes is to be found in
Rousset's *L'Univers concentrationnaire*: references to the tragic
buffoonery of Jarry's *Ubu Roi*, to the mad logic of Kafka's
novels, to the underworld of Dante, to Céline's haunted
pages. Similarly, Jean Cayrol, remembering the world of
concentration camps, refers to Joseph K. in *The Trial*, quotes
a sentence by Pierre-Jean Jouve, makes passing mention of
Swift, Balzac, and Nerval.[19]

This persistence of the literary image, this survival of the
bookish referent, imply a relationship between stereotype and
mediation. The ceaseless shuttle between "life" and "art" illustrates the inadequacy of the mimetic concept; but it also illustrates the inadequacy of a theory hostile to representation.
If the prison theme has evolved, it is largely because totalitar-

ian ideologies have relegated the happy cell of humanistic individualism and poetic reverie to the status of a reactionary
anachronism. Private salvation, much like private happiness,
almost came to appear as morally offensive. Stendhal's *chasse
au bonheur*, even if such a pursuit of felicity led to the Farnese
dungeon or to the charterhouse, was no longer conceivable
without a sense of guilt. A character in Camus' *La Peste* sums
up this malaise of individualism: ". . . there may be something shameful in being happy alone."[20]

It is easy to understand by what logic the Revolutionary
consciousness rejects a literature of individual destinies. Victor Serge writes: "It seems to me indeed that time has come at
last for a literature that discovers the masses, as well as the
link between the individual and his fellow men, and will pose
the problems of individual destiny only in terms of a common
fate." But if Serge is so engaging, it is because he finds it hard,
all the same, to slough off his "romantic" heritage. Not only
does the "monastic cell" appear in his work, but the notion
of the spiritually "free" captive as well. The prisoner, in
his "numbered tomb," surprises the jailor because of his
"radiant" face and triumphant silence.[21]

But there was a new handwriting on the wall. The Existentialist generation challenged the glorification of the private
cell, even in texts that resorted to a prison setting. Malraux, in
the preface to *Le Temps du mépris*, a novel that deals with the
incarceration and torture of a Communist leader in a Nazi jail,
specifically repudiates the "unformulated individualism" of
19th-century literature which safeguards and justifies the so-
called "inner world," and by so doing ultimately betrays
man's commitment to solidarity. Jean-Paul Sartre, several
years later, was to be even more categorical in condemning
bourgeois humanism, as he called for the death of analytical,
and above all self-analytical, writing. In the manifesto-preface
to the first issue of *Les Temps Modernes*, he plainly stated: "We
are convinced that the spirit of analysis has outlived itself, and
that its only function today is that of disturbing the revolutionary consciousness and of isolating human beings. . . ."[22]

Solidarity is the prime virtue for the Existentialist generation. Significantly, one of Camus' early ventures was a theatrical adaptation of Malraux's novel *Le Temps du mépris*. To be
sure, Camus' voice has none of the stridence of Malraux's.
Nor is his a call to physical courage. In fact, heroism is not
highest on his scale. First comes the *exigence généreuse du
bonheur*—man's birthright to happiness. And there is little
doubt that Camus remains somewhat skeptical, at times
frankly pessimistic, about man's ability to step out of his solitude. *Jonas* ends with the undecidable deciphering of characters inscribed on a white cloth: ". . . it was not clear whether
one should read *solitary* or *solidary*." The parable *Le Renégat*,
one of Camus' most powerful stories, confirms this note of
pessimism or doubt. The missionary who sets out to convert
the inhuman "closed city" becomes entrapped in the evil
sanctuary, and is ultimately converted to the cruel practices of
his tormentors. Nonetheless Camus' "message" remains one
of brotherhood, as exemplified by the imprisoned inhabitants
of the city of Oran, in *La Peste*, who discover, beyond the
surface temptations of selfishness, a need and a potential for
collective responsibility. The narrator in the novel explains:
". . . the plague had overrun everything. There were no
longer any individual destinies, there was only a collective
history. . . ."[23]

If engagé writers experienced some difficulty in neatly di-
viding the world between the forces of good and evil, hope
and negation, fraternity and solipsism, this may well be because the "existentialist" perspective implied both an ethics of
will and human freedom (choice and action) as well as a "psychology" which diagnosed man's otherness and irremediable
solitude. Prison, in this key, remained a privileged image.
The case of Sartre, as we shall see, is exemplary.

‖ II ‖

Sartre and
the Drama of Ensnarement

All is a trap . . .—Huis-Clos

*If you claim to be free, then you must praise the freedom of
the prisoner . . .*—Les Mouches

"WE ARE CORNERED . . ."

Sartre, whose central concern is man's freedom, seems almost
obsessively drawn to the prison metaphor. The painful secret
of the gods—a secret Orestes shares with Zeus in *Les
Mouches*—is that man is free. The function of the writer,
much like Orestes' compulsion in the play, is to proclaim this
terrifying and exhilarating truth. In the essay *What Is Literature?* Sartre sets forth this function in explicit terms: "The
writer, a free man writing for free men, has only one subject:
freedom." But such a revelation requires a literature of *situations*. The truth of freedom can be conceived only from
within entrapment. "Each situation is a trap, there are walls
everywhere."[1] The titles themselves suggest images of confinement, enclosure and immurement: *Le Mur* (The Wall),
Huis-Clos (No Exit), *La Chambre*, *Les Séquestrés d'Altona*, *Intimité*, *Le Séquestré de Venise*. They communicate a sense of the
walled-in quality of human consciousness and human existence. Bounded by external contingencies and the imperatives
of a dilemma, the Sartrean hero appears inextricably
jammed-in.

Literal prisons, or places of detention, are frequently the
setting. The cell-like room in *Huis-Clos* is the symbol of the
living hell of guilt and ceaseless judgment. In this peculiar torture chamber there are no racks; the conventional torture instruments are absent. But there are the atrocious tortures of

the mind as it is ensnared by itself and by the relentless glance of "the other"—tortures symbolized by permanent exposure to light, absence of sleep, and eternal cohabitation with inmates who turn out to be the tormentors. *Fait comme un rat* (trapped like a rat), concludes one of the characters. On one level, the trap is the prison of a past life that now, having been completely lived out, rigidly immobilizes the characters. In *Morts sans sépulture*, the action takes place in a room where Resistance fighters, while listening to the cries of their comrades, wait for their turn to be tortured. Fear and pride, as well as the distance separating those who have been tortured from those who have been spared, here create prisons within a prison. In *Le Mur*, we witness the anguished night of a political prisoner, during the Spanish Civil War, waiting for dawn and the moment of execution. The cruel tricks of the imagination, the hallucinations and visceral reactions produced by fear, the sense of rift and absurdity as the proximity of death already separates man from his life, have perhaps never been treated more vividly—not even by Leonid Andreyev, whose *The Seven Who Were Hanged* may well have inspired Sartre.

Even when the setting is not a jail, confinement remains a basic metaphor. Hugo, the young revolutionary intellectual in *Les Mains sales*, seeks refuge with Olga and remains throughout the play, until his final choice, in what could be called protective custody. The prostitute's room in *La Putain respectueuse*, is also—for a while at least—an asylum for the hunted Negro. Often enclosure is self-imposed. Frantz von Gerlach, the guilt-ridden former German officer in *Les Séquestrés d'Altona*, withdraws into self-inflicted confinement, complicated by an incestuous relationship with his sister that further entraps him. The bolted door and the walled-up window are symbols of a refusal of life and truth, of a fruitless effort to escape from bad conscience. Frantz eventually immures himself in his own delirium. For madness can be a trap as well as an impenetrable wall. In *La Chambre*, Eve has voluntarily locked herself up with her mentally sick husband, who gradually sinks into total insanity. It is in fact another prison within a prison, as Eve tries in vain to reach her husband beyond the steadily thickening wall of his madness.

Sometimes, notably in the plays, the dramatic structure locks the situation within itself, apparently allowing the protagonist no escape whatsoever. Hugo, in *Les Mains sales*, who has just been released from jail, is seen in a closed room where he must explain the motives of his past "political" act. The major part of the play is thus encased, by means of a flashback between a committed murder and an outcome (life or death) that will entirely depend on the answer this retrospective interpretation of motives will provide. It is difficult to conceive a more immobilizing situation than the one achieved through this dramatic compression of time and irrevocable action within a "theatrical" time (from 9 p.m. to midnight) that barely exceeds the actual time of the performance.

The theater lends itself to the prison image. The epic tradition calls for movement in time and space. Tragedy, especially in the French tradition, with its insistence on the "unities," most often focuses on a crisis in which the protagonists have reached a seeming impasse. Racine's antechambers are not so different from Sartre's cell, where characters are locked together in a death dance. Greek tragedy is filled with images of restriction and entanglement: the chains of Prometheus, the fatal webs and nets in *Agamemnon*, the meshes of fate and the trap of intellect in *Oedipus*. The conventional modern stage, with its three walls—the fourth wall being the inexorable eye of the public—may be said to symbolize an issueless situation.

These are presumably permanent features of the tragic theater. But in Sartre's plays, the prison motif is bound up with psychological obsessions as well as with philosophical themes. At first glance, the flashback in *Les Mains sales* seems to immobilize a past that cannot be altered. Yet this is a misreading of the play. The real suspense is not to be summed up by the question: What will happen to Hugo?—but by the far more important one, referring to volition and creation: What meaning will he choose to give his past act? For it is up to him

to bestow a meaning upon his past. The flashback thus leads
not to sterile investigation, but to a choice and consequently
to an act *in the present*. The element of surprise—for there is a
coup de théâtre—is not at all related to Hugo's fate (political
liquidation or survival) but to his will and to his decision. Or
rather: the *coup de théâtre* is the hero's breaking out from what
appears like a set, predetermined order.[2] The philosophical
implications are clear. The significance of a human act must
not be sought in motivation, which is always muddled, nor in
the prison of a given psychology, but in the allegiance to the
act itself—for man *is* his acts—and in its relation to a given
situation. Every heartbeat thrusts into the world a decision
through which we reinvent ourselves. When Hugo, at the end
of the play, kicks open the door so his murderers can come in,
he paradoxically escapes to an authentic freedom.

Man's distinguishing feature, Sartre explains in pages devoted to the progressive-regressive method, is his ability to
"go beyond a situation." Sartre's psychoanalytic interests
focus less on the determining trauma than on the original *project*: we all live our situation as our *future*. Man defines himself
through what he does with "what was made of him."[3] But at
the beginning, every situation is a trap. Sartre's favorite
haunts, as well as the *luoghi ameni* of his fictional world, are
most often both anonymous and walled-in: hotel rooms,
dimly lit cafés, night clubs (the French *boîte de nuit* connotes
the sealed-in atmosphere), reading rooms in public libraries
—all suggest airlessness and reclusion. Camus' work also
provides illustrations of symbolic enclosures, though in
another key: the stranger Meursault in his North African jail;
the renegade-missionary in the ghastly chambers of the city of
salt; Clamence sitting out his life in the dingy bar at the dead
center of the last circle of Amsterdam's canals; an entire city in
La Peste, locked in and isolated. For Cripure, the crippled
giant-philosopher in Louis Guilloux's *Le Sang noir*, the entire
"sublunar" world is a prison. Modern literature, from Dostoevsky's underground man to Beckett's pariahs, is filled with
aggressively lonely, hedged-in figures. It is also filled, since
The House of the Dead, with penal colonies.

Yet Sartre hardly indulges in cellular lyricism. His is rather the drama of an isolated consciousness as it faces the collective political and ideological tragedy of our time. Sartre himself made it clear that his generation was brutally thrust into the nightmare of history. "We were driven to create a literature of historicity," he explains in an essay on the function of literature. He admires the writers of the 18th century because they apprehended in its purity "a new dimension of temporality: the Present."[4] This is indeed the aim he sets for himself in the opening statement of the first issue of *Les Temps Modernes*: not to miss out on anything in one's time. His generation, he kept reminding his readers, had indeed learned that this was no longer a time to play with esthetic problems or to seek private salvation through art; that private salvation was in fact no longer admissible, and the meaning of traditional humanism had to be challenged.

The era of concentration camps (*l'ère concentrationnaire*, as it came to be called) meant for Sartre the reign of torture, as well as the unmedicable guilt of not having been himself tortured. He explains in what sense his generation felt historically *situated*: ". . . we lived at a time when torture was a daily occurrence." And torture, for Sartre as well as for Malraux, is evil without remission: a permanently celebrated black mass which became the haunting daily reality under the Occupation. "We knew that it was celebrated in all parts of Paris while we were eating, sleeping, or making love. . . ." It was a lesson in exclusion and solidarity which only a "literature of extreme situations" could account for.[5] In the face of deportation and extermination camps, moral problems could no longer be comfortably relegated to the classroom; they had to be faced, here and now, leaving little room for theorizing or for cozy innocence. It is significant that the most haunting memory associated with the guilty past of Frantz, in *Les Séquestrés d'Altona*, is the construction of a concentration camp on family land sold by his father to Himmler.

This fear of a complicity with evil helps to explain why Sartre seeks a complicity with the victims. To be *dans le coup*, to be *dans le bain*, are typical expressions of Sartrean solidar-

ity, pointing to involvement and entrapment with others.
They are the social and political equivalent of the metaphysical *nous sommes embarqués* of Pascal. This urge to "be with,"
this compulsion to enter into a collective prison, has been
given articulate allegorical form in *Les Mouches*. The inhabitants of Argos are seen as the prisoners of a tyrannized city—
prisoners who are, however, willfully blind to their servitude, as well as to their bad faith. It will be Orestes' mission
to reveal this blindness to them, and thus acquaint them with
their own feared freedom. This, however, he will not be able
to do until, by committing a crime, he himself becomes a
member of the imprisoned community.

The contradictions are apparent enough. How is one to
reconcile self-willed immurement with the shame of the private cell and the urge to enter into a collective imprisonment—and eventually a collective liberation? In *Qu'est-ce que
la littérature?*, Sartre proposes the following formula: "My
freedom is indissolubly linked to that of the others."[6] But in
Sartrean terms, this proposition could be inverted: my servitude is indissolubly linked. . . . The point is that, whether
for freedom or for servitude, the prison theme implies for
Sartre the relation of the self to *the other*.

THE SIN OF OTHERNESS

Huis-Clos provides a dramatic illustration of man's double
imprisonment: in the self, and through the presence of others.
The play is based entirely on a reversed metaphor: it is not
hell that is described as a condemnation to the self under the
judging eye of another consciousness, but life-in-the-self and
in the presence of others that is hell. The play provides a figuration of man's solipsistic, yet interdependent, condition.
"*L'Enfer c'est les autres*" (Hell is the others), concludes one of
the characters. (*Les Autres* was the original title of the play.)
Every character in *Huis-Clos* is trapped in a private world of
guilt and shame: the infanticide, the sexual pervert, the cow-
ard. In the mirrorless room, they turn to "the others" as to

consoling or flattering mirrors, only to come face to face with their severe glance and confining judgment. There is no exit. Through what amounts to psychological *voyeurism*, the other becomes at the same time accomplice, witness, and judge, as mutual confessions turn out to be exercises in bad faith. The eye of the other is woefully needed, but also feared. The sense of identity depends on the availability of the mirror. But the mirror allows for no escape (". . . I am a trap, a trap for her"). The search for an exit seems doomed from the outset: one cannot break through a mirror. The protagonists are thrown back within their own limits. What salvation in this hellish trap? "To look into oneself," proposes Garcin. But this escape toward a hidden inner self is equally impossible. For we necessarily recreate within ourselves a glance that substitutes the glance of the others; we internalize a judgment which will play out within us the judgment of another consciousness. Man is caught, trapped: *Fait comme un rat*. The play symbolically comes to an end with an attempt at an impossible murder. We cannot eliminate our witness.

Man is thus, in the Sartrean context, caught in an inalienable subjectivity from which he cannot extricate himself. Contingent and superfluous, his existence is described through images suggesting viscous, gummous, sticky sensations: *glu* and *englué* are favorite terms in Sartre's vocabulary. This adhesion to the self, this awareness of one's own insipid taste, is also a fundamental source of anguish. Dereliction, Sartre explains in one of his essays, begins when man no longer has any witness but himself. "Then he must drink the bitter cup to the dregs, and experience fully his human condition."[7] For existence itself is perceived as guilt: the original guilt of being. This "sin of existing" experienced by Roquentin in *La Nausée*, is shared by almost all of Sartre's characters. Brunet, like Mathieu in *L'Age de raison*, feels "vaguely guilty"—"guilty of being alone, guilty of thinking and of living. Guilty of not being dead."[8]

This psychological rift within the prison of self has its counterpart in Sartre's notion of the irreconcilable, yet inter-

dependent, relationship of the *en-soi* and the *pour-soi*. Discussing the "stumbling block of solipsism," in *L'Etre et le Néant*,
he stresses the double alienation of man, in relation to the
other and in relation to himself.[9] The Sartrean hero is thus
subjected to a double glance: the glance of the other, the
glance of his *pour-soi*. Stendhal wistfully complained that the
eye cannot see itself. This is a blessing Sartre does not grant
his characters. It would seem that they are endowed with precisely such an introverted vision. "Mathieu . . . *saw himself*
think; he was horrified by himself. . . ."[10]

The self-torturing potential of the mind, the self-punishing
workings of the intellect, are permanent themes in Sartre's
work. Garcin, in *Huis-Clos*, cries out: "Give me rather a
hundred burns and flayings than this agony of mind."
Mathieu, in *L'Age de raison*, sees himself rotten to the core:
"Thoughts, thoughts on thoughts, thoughts on thoughts of
thoughts; he was transparent and rotten to infinity."[11] Hugo,
the young bourgeois intellectual who has joined the revolu-
tionaries in *Les Mains sales*, knows that he remains trapped
and paralyzed by his intellect. He has chosen Raskolnikov as a
battle name. The choice is symbolic: the name, in Russian,
implies a rift. All of Sartre's intellectuals—and who in his
work is not an intellectual?—are compulsive thinkers suffering from the mirror-disease of thought. Lucidity does in fact
appear as third-degree torture: the electric light in *Huis-Clos*,
condemning the inmates to live with their eyes wide open; in
L'Age de raison, the relentless sun in the "lucid sky," dazzling
Mathieu and forcing him to blink.[12] Sartre's characters not
only think, they watch themselves think. Their thoughts
are reflected and indefinitely multiplied in a looking-glass
that turns into a sophisticated instrument of self-torture.
"Nausea," among other things, is the loathsome weariness
that accompanies this pathological cerebration. Consciousness can find no escape from itself. One is reminded of
Baudelaire's self-torturer, L'Héautontimorouménos.[13]

But the immurement in the self allows for no respite.
Sartre's protagonists are prisoners without privacy. They are

caught in a dilemma: they need and they fear the judging eye. Johanna, in *Les Séquestrés d'Altona*, sees all the members of the family as "jailor-slaves." And Frantz, who at one point says to Johanna: "I won't let myself be judged by my younger brother's wife," later pleads with her to judge him. The novels are crowded with characters fenced about by another consciousness at the very moment they seem most withdrawn in themselves. Mathieu, walking through the streets of Paris, suddenly stops aghast, realizing that he is not alone: in her "shell-like room," Marcelle continues to hold him. "Marcelle had not let him go. She was thinking of him. She was thinking: dirty bastard. . . . The consciousness of Marcelle remained somewhere out there. . . . It was unbearable to be thus judged, hated." But a consciousness that holds captive can also reject. Hence this other moment of panic: "Behind him, in a green room, a little consciousness filled with hatred was rejecting him. . . ."[14] The desire to break through this immurement can become only more intense with time.

For almost as persistent as the guilt of *being* is the sin of *being another*. Goetz's complaint in *Le Diable et le bon Dieu* ("You are not me, it is unbearable") echoes throughout Sartre's writings. This tragic awareness of otherness is intimately wedded to a guilt of class consciousness, the shame of being a *fils de bourgeois* which has afflicted French intellectuals ever since the middle of the 19th century. Hence the dream of a downward *déclassement* toward the proletariat, the breaking into the prison of another class. But this dream appears doomed. "They will never accept me." Hugo's despondency has much to do with his conviction that he cannot escape his class. It is indeed noteworthy how often Sartre refers to the condition of the bourgeois as a form of imprisonment. In *Situations II*, he explains that the bourgeois writers are trapped: "Born of bourgeois parents, read and paid by the bourgeoisie, they must remain bourgeois, for the bourgeoisie, like a prison, has sealed them in." The proletariat is doubly inaccessible to the bourgeois revolutionary who yearns to reach out to it and be accepted, for it too is trapped in its own class

consciousness (". . . an iron curtain separates us from these
men . . ."); as a class, it is "encircled by a propaganda which
isolates it, it is like a secret society without doors or windows."[15]

Ashamed of his own class, Sartre comes to envy those
who, according to him, were born prisoners of a more enviable class. How many of his protagonists share this sense of
alienation and this envy! Hugo is a typical *déclassé* who cannot
cast off his *peau de bourgeois*. Goetz's situation, in *Le Diable et
le bon Dieu*, is even more exemplary: a bastard nobleman who
cannot become a plebeian. Nasty, the leader of the mob, explains that Goetz cannot save the poor, only corrupt them.
And when Goetz affirms his solidarity ("I am one of you"),
Nasty replies with a flat "No." What right has Nasty to speak
on behalf of the peasants? The answer is clear: "I am one of
them." And Goetz will never be.

But "they" signifies more than a social group or a political
party. "They" are all those who have undergone what I did
not undergo, all those who have suffered what I have not suffered. Between their suffering and myself lies an unbreachable
distance. Their very imprisonment confines me and excludes
me. This separation created by suffering is perhaps the most
important tragic theme in Sartre's work. It is at the core, for
instance, of *Morts sans sépulture*, a play that is far more than a
rough topical treatment of the torture of captured Resistance
fighters. It is a series of variations on the intolerable divorce
created by the presence of pain. Not only is each character
confined to his terror, to his torment, to his humiliation and
pride, but the glance of the one who has undergone torture
becomes unbearable to the one who has been spared. Even
worse: how is one to bear the glance of someone who has
been tortured for our sake? "Must I have my nails torn out to
become your friend again?" cries out one of the characters.
The Sartrean hero develops a morbid jealousy of the victim, a
yearning for pain as an initiation into a forbidden brotherhood. Hugo knows that his new comrades would never forgive him for having been a well-fed child. "They will never

accept me," he moans. There is the same feeling of rejection in *Le Diable et le bon Dieu*. Goetz tries in vain to take upon himself the suffering of his dying mistress, as he tries in vain to share the agony of the peasants. The Worms priest sums up this bitter sense of isolation: "It's always the others who suffer, not I. . . . Why do they always suffer so much more than I. . . ?" The determination to break into the prison of the other is exacerbated by frustration. As early as in *La Chambre*, the desire to "break into" assumes an obsessive quality. Only here the compulsion has not yet taken on social and political overtones. Eve feels excluded from her husband's insanity. But she is determined to join him behind his wall. That, of course, is the meaning of her willful confinement to the sick man's room.

The dialectic of enclosure and escape can be traced throughout Sartre's work. The Sartrean protagonist seeks to leave his private cell, only to break into the cell of the other, and ultimately into the collective prison of a given group. This attempt to penetrate, violently if need be, into an imprisoned collectivity is the subject of *Les Mouches*, a play written and performed during the German occupation, at a time when the words "prison" and "freedom" were tragically loaded. It was impossible not to perceive a parallel between Sartre's city of Argos and the France of Vichy, defeated, guilt-ridden, degradingly submissive. The play is studded with topical allusions. Orestes returns on a national holiday designed by the rulers to keep collective remorse alive. Aegisthus, like Pétain, is a collaborator; the one collaborates with Nazi ideology, the other with the tyranny of Zeus. The flies are the symbol of moral decay. But, characteristically, the inhabitants are fond of their flies. The little idiot boy whose eyes are literally covered with flies smiles contentedly. For the flies, like sterile remorse, can give comfort. The people of Argos, in Sartre's play, indeed like their running sores so much that they scratch them with their dirty nails to keep them festering. The city of Argos thus appears as the sordid city of *non-freedom* and *non-responsibility*. It is also the city of guilt. And Zeus the tyrant, whose nostrils are tickled by the stench of carrions, relishes the odor of guilt—for guilt and shame that blind men to the possibility of their responsible action are the god's only hope of repressing man's freedom.

Orestes' desire to win the name of guilt-stealer (*voleur de remords*) marks his attempt to enter into the prison of the collectivity, first to save himself from his own negative freedom, but ultimately, having found his roots, in order to rediscover, and reveal to others, the meaning of authentic freedom. To achieve this, he must first commit an irrevocable act: the murder of his mother. What matters is thus not the avenging of past crimes, as in Aeschylus' tragedy, but a binding and at the same time liberating enterprise which Sartre conveys through a series of prison images.

At the beginning of the play, Orestes' "innocence" is like a wide moat separating him from the people of Argos. He stands, figuratively, *outside*. The city excludes him: "It fends me off with all its walls, with all its roofs, with all its locked doors." This hostile entity he wishes to "seize"; or better, to settle in it, to make it into a protective enclosure. He wants to draw the city around him like a thick blanket and curl himself up in it (. . . *je veux tirer la ville autour de moi et m'y enrouler comme dans une couverture*). Elsewhere, he says to Electra, who has just warned him that even if he stayed a hundred years, he would still be a stranger: "I must go down into the depths, among you. For you are all living at the very bottom of a pit." Ultimately, the breaking-into-the-prison is expressed in a language of violence: "I'll turn into an ax and hew these obstinate walls asunder; I'll rip open the bellies of those bigoted houses. . . . I'll be a wedge driving into the heart of the city, like a wedge rammed into the core of an oak tree." The simple but perhaps unattainable aim is to achieve a human solidarity which would liberate the individual from his false freedom and bind him to the freedom of a solidary group: "To become a man among men." It is significant that Goetz, in *Le Diable et le bon Dieu*, repeats Orestes' wish word for word: *Je veux être un homme parmi les hommes.*

TO INVENT AN EXIT

The prison metaphor relates to the intentionality of Sartre's texts. For literature, according to Sartre, is a *project* in search of a meaning that was not there at the outset. He himself stated in an interview that he discovered and developed his concept of freedom in the process of writing *Les Mouches*. The exploratory exercise of writing does not uncover a meaning, it *is* the meaning. In Sartrean terms, literature does not describe a "situation," it *is* the "situation." And, of course, every situation is a trap.

To begin with, there is existence itself. The raw experience of *Dasein*, of "being there," is that never-ending ensnarement in a perpetual present that Sartre describes so well in *La Nausée*. By means of a diary method that adheres to the banal, fragmented, and essentially undramatic experience of unfiltered, uninterpreted reality, Sartre shows how Roquentin lives each moment as it weighs on him, in an opaque immediacy, caught in a permanent indetermination. The diary form functions as an exercise in discontinuity as narrator and reader become prisoners of the present indicative. Pure existence is thereby shown as innocent of meaning. But the imprisonment in the here and the now also turns out to be a revelation.

This revelation, this nausea comparable to an ecstasy of horror, is an apprenticeship in freedom. Roquentin discovers that existence is original contingency, that life is not justifiable in its essence, that man is condemned to be free. He does not have but *is* his freedom. It is a bitter and uncomfortable lesson: man cannot delegate a responsibility that he, and he alone, must bear. This relation between freedom and responsibility is the cornerstone of Sartre's ethical project. Like Heidegger, Sartre stresses the "intentional structure" of human awareness, though he does not understand the notion of ecstasy in the Heideggerian sense. In a key passage of *L'Etre et le Néant*, entitled "Freedom and Responsibility," Sartre writes that "Man, condemned to be free, carries the weight of the whole world on his shoulders."[16] Subjectivity and alienation, according to him, are the conditions of man's entrapment as well as of his creative role.

The image of the trap (*tout est piège*) is thus potentially dynamic, insofar as man is condemned to seek an exit. *"Nous sommes drôlement coincés"* (Are we trapped!), says Frantz in *Les Séquestrés d'Altona*. But immediately he adds: "There must be an exit"—and he repeats this twice. Sartre himself, in his essay on the function of literature, asseverates that it is the writer's duty to unveil to man, in each concrete situation, his potential for action; that he must measure man's servitude only to help him break out of it.[17]

This view of "man-in-situation" is reflected in Sartre's literary precepts as well as in his practice, particularly his dramaturgy. In the same passage that welcomes the new theater of entrapment, Sartre also calls for the demise of the traditional theater of "characters." "No more characters: protagonists are entrapped freedoms, like the rest of us. What exits are there? Each personage will be nothing but a choice of an exit and will be worth exactly the exit he chose." It is, however, less a choice than an invention. The prisoner does not find the hole, he makes it. In the passage quoted earlier ("each situation is a trap, there are walls everywhere"), Sartre adds: "I have expressed myself badly: there are no exits to *choose*. An exit has to be invented."[18] And to invent an exit is to invent oneself.

In literary terms, this means that the playright as well as the novelist must turn away from conventional studies of "inner life." Malraux had taken the bourgeois novelists to task for concerning themselves exclusively with private "psychologies." Sartre, in his introductory essay for *Les Temps Modernes*, also proclaimed the death of the spirit of analysis which stresses "differences" and immobilizes human beings in their pseudo-essences.[19] For Sartre, just as for Malraux, man is not what he hides but what he does. He is the sum total of his acts. By his acts he creates himself. Neither subject nor object, man is an eternal project. Sartre scorns the omniscient type of novelist who assumes a god-like privilege of dissecting, explaining, and predicting his characters. His protagonists may find themselves in a trap, but it is not the trap of their psychology. Their actions are not the expression of what they are, but the means by which they become what they are not yet. A literature of *praxis*, Sartre called it; one that does not describe or explain, but brings man face to face with his latest dilemma.

Sartre himself is temperamentally drawn to "impossible" situations, as shown by the permanent conflict between his philosophical tenets and his political sympathies. Replying to objections formulated by Georg Lukács in *Existentialisme ou Marxisme*, Sartre comments on the precise nature of this dilemma:

> We were convinced *simultaneously* that historical materialism supplied the only valid interpretation of history and that existentialism remained the only concrete approach to reality. I do not pretend to deny the contradictions in this attitude. . . . Many intellectuals, many students have experienced and are still experiencing the tension of this double exigency.[20]

Honesty lies in the refusal to juggle away a difficulty or a contradiction. Sartre welcomes the trap of any dilemma because in it alone man can take the full measure of his inventive, self-liberating potential. For he believes that, faced with the alternatives of any dilemma, man will of a sudden discover a third possibility—a discovery that amounts to an act of creation. Exploiting in his own manner the dialectics of necessity and freedom, Sartre, too, endows the prison metaphor with salvational virtues.

||12||
Epilogue:
The Borderline Zone

*In this borderline zone, between solitude and commu-
nity . . .—*Kafka

Sartre is not the only writer of his generation to have strug-
gled with a double postulate. The title of Simone de
Beauvoir's novel *Le Sang des autres* (The Blood of the Others),
sums up the tension between the themes of communion and
of otherness. The epigraph of the novel is taken from Dostoevsky: "Everyone is responsible to everybody for everything." On the surface, this novel about the French Resistance
appears to illustrate the dictum. Yet the characters experience
from beginning to end what Simone de Beauvoir calls "the
crime of existing," the "curse of being another," the walled-
in quality of human experience. Sartrean formulas stud the
text: ". . . I was at fault forever . . ."; ". . . I never have been
one of them . . ."; ". . . everyone himself only for himself,
existing next to others, forever separated from them:
another." Ensnared in their otherness and in their bad conscience, the existential protagonists live out a condition of
tragic freedom within cellular confinement.[1]

This specific relation of freedom to a sense of condemnation is a redundant theme for the Existentialist generation.
Solipsism and solidarity confirm each other, while cancelling
each other out. If Jean Cau's *La Pitié de Dieu* (1961) com-
manded attention at the time, it is not because of virtuosistic
skill, but because it illustrates, very much like *Huis-Clos*,
where hell turns out to be "the others," the fusion of private
and collective imprisonment. Jean Cau imagines four prisoners in a cell, all presumably there on murder charges, who indulge in orgies of mutual confessions. Seeking for reasons to

believe in their own innocence, they become willing accomplices in self-delusion. This confessional game, a pretext for dishonesty and self-indulgence, also reveals to what extent the fellow prisoners depend on each other. Individual memories merge into a collective memory. The shared cell suggests an extension, a release from privacy.

But this release provides no guarantee. The effort at transcending through depersonalization, whether in joint action or joint suffering, fails to exorcise the sense of dereliction. Malraux, who tirelessly professed "virile fraternity," remained nonetheless haunted by the unbreachable immurement in the self. Kyo, in *La Condition humaine*, may console himself at the thought that it is easy to die if one does not die alone; but not everyone lives and dies in such a heroic register. For Ch'en, the terrorist, Revolution itself is essentially a solitary exercise. What fascinates him is "the complete possession of himself." Clappique also knows the morbid need to "embrace" (*étreindre*) his own fate, to "possess himself." And the prison experience is far from being always viewed as an apprenticeship in communion. Moreno, in *L'Espoir*, remarks that the two worlds—the inside and the outside—"do not communicate." Worse still, interiority inhibits transcendence. "They say that to be blind is a world of its own. To be alone also is. . . ." An ambivalent sentence, to be sure: the "world" in question ultimately signals a vast solitude.[2] Even fellow imprisonment remains problematic in prison literature, especially when stripped of mythic or propagandistic elements. Dostoevsky, in whose work documentation and myth-making compete, writing in *The House of the Dead* about the "compulsory communism" of jails, observed that prisoners hate one another more readily than people living in freedom.

Rejecting the myth of the happy prison does not necessarily imply an ethics of solidarity. Two writers played a paradigmatic role in determining the modern perspective on the cell. First Dostoevsky, whose "paradoxalist" and egocentric hero of *Notes from Underground* defines himself as an "anti-hero," and describes his withdrawal to his "shell." The word "shell"

(*škorlupá*) is significantly surrounded by other terms of confinement: *ocobnak* (isolated apartment, with the stress on the
apartness) and *futlar* (case, box or sheath)—both of them con-
firming the notion of a defensive seclusion (chap. 8). The narrator explains: the shell-étui serves to hide from his fellow
men.

The other "model," enigmatic and ambivalent, is that of
Kafka. "Everyone carries a room in him" (*Jeder Mensch trägt
ein Zimmer in sich*): the human condition implies for him interiorization of cellular punishment. Kafka is obsessed by the
image of the cage. The private notebooks published under the
title *Er* (He) elaborate the old image of the brain-as-dungeon,
but with clinical undertones of an obstruction. "The bony
structure of his own forehead blocks his way. He batters himself bloody against his own forehead." Such blockage is the
harsh reality (*grobe Tatsache*) of being-in-jail (*Gefangenseins*).
This confined status of man is hardly viewed as beneficent. It
is repressive and oppressive—yet also strangely desirable.
Jean Starobinski astutely remarks that from inside his ghetto-
like private universe Kafka dreams of being "admitted to the
world."[3] But the "world" excludes, denying all security—
hence the obstinate dream of a refuge. Kafka's fear of confinement is steadily counteracted by the desire to break into
the castle, to seek asylum in a symbolic prison-fortress. "My
cell—my fortress," reads one of his terse entries. He would
like to convert the painful affect into a happy one. In the *Letter
to the Father*, the revealing metaphor is precisely that of reconstruction (*umbauen*). He would like to transform his oppressive abode into a pleasure castle. "It is as though one were
prisoner and intended, not to escape, which would perhaps be
possible, but rather—and simultaneously—to rebuild the
prison into a pleasure castle [*Lustschloss*]." But here is the rub:
if he escapes, he cannot rebuild; if he rebuilds, he cannot escape.[4] It is a double discontent, for the prison itself is in-
adequate to its function, and the prisoner afraid of his freedom. "He could have resigned himself to a prison [. . . .] But
it was a barred cage he was in. Calmly and insolently, as if at

home, the din of the world streamed out and in through the bars, the prisoner was really free [. . . .] He could simply have left the cage. The bars were yards apart, he was not even a prisoner." The bitter remark (he was not even a prisoner!) must be read against the expressed yearning for the cell ("To end up as a prisoner, that might be the aim of a life")—a yearning that justifies the surrealistic image of a cage gone "in search of a bird." But this carceral vocation is thwarted by the condemnation to live in a "borderline zone, between solitude and community. . . ."[5]

This borderline zone is of course not Kafka's exclusive domain. Russian literature, in the Dostoevskyan tradition of mental anguish and guilt, frequently locates the "action" in this in-between, twilight region. Leonid Andreyev, in a text entitled *Thought* (*Mysl*), depicts the trap of intellect, and the mental mechanisms that immure the self in the prison of the mind. With him also prison and private castle become interchangeable. "My castle became my prison," complains the victim of compulsive cogitation. "In the inaccessibility of the castle, in the thickness of its walls, lay my perdition." More ambivalently still, Vyacheslav Ivanov, in *Freedom and the Tragic Life*, comments on the typically Russian nostalgia for the "inward cell," for "holy" seclusion. He quotes Maria Timofeyevna's song in Dostoevsky's *The Possessed*:

> This tiny cell suffices me;
> There will I dwell my soul to save . . .

Yet he denounces Raskolnikov, the "magician of self-incarceration" as an alien of God, and considers Kirilov, a self-absorbed "hermit of the spirit," as exiled to inauthenticity. According to Ivanov, Dostoevsky's revelation is that self-enclosure in solitude leads to a disastrous mystique of guilt.[6]

The Existentialist and post-Existentialist writers also haunted the borderline zone in almost all their works. Sartre and Simone de Beauvoir, though seemingly extolling choice, action, and social responsibility, indulged, as we have seen, in

images of self-alienation, in the double trap of guilt and
otherness. The seduction of this trap appears even more powerful in the so-called Nouveau Roman: man is seen as
bounded by his own horizon, hemmed-in within strictest
limits—if he is not downright negated to the extent that this
type of writing tends to be a radical critique of the transcendental signified. The discrediting of anthropocentric and
logocentric views of the world signals a crisis. Not only does
the concept of heroism seem dead, but the notion of "hero" as
central character is steadily subverted. Under these circum-
stances, the meaning of imprisonment itself turns out to be
problematic.

Thus Nathalie Sarraute, in her essay *L'Ere du soupçon*, proclaimed the death of the "personage." Her own novels are an
extreme illustration of the borderline zone: they provide
neither an "outside" nor an "inside." The reader moves
through an indifferentiated verbal space where the tiniest
tremor, vibration, fluttering, variation in current and sub-
current, is magnified into the ominous reverberation of a vast
echo chamber. All lines of demarcation seem to be abolished.
Yet this echo chamber remains essentially that of a locked-in
subjectivity. The verbal space is airless. The multiple inner
monologues, while denying the traditional notion of character viewable from the outside (and therefore reassuringly
identifiable), in fact stress the essential innerness and incommunicability of all experience. Sarraute's fictions deal with
the terror of all contact, the love-hate of the protective shell,
the confining and deadly aloneness. In thematic terms, *Le
Planétarium* remains her most representative work. The title
suggests that "the other" is a million light years away, in fact
something of a petrified geography, a dead star. If he comes
close enough, it is to constitute a threat. Encirclement, entrapment, encagement, immurement, are the key images of
Sarraute's world. "They are on him. They encircle him. No
exit. He is caught, locked in." Or again: "Order is reestab-
lished. Back to your cages, back to your cells. . . ." Prison
doors never open; escape is not thinkable. It is literally an is-

sueless world: ". . . a strange sensation of choking. . . . Something heavy fell back on him, a tombstone, the door to a vault, they are locked in. . . ." And elsewhere: "Caught in the meshes. Squirrels turning in their gilded cage. Probably making now and then a pathetic effort to escape. But too weak to break the bars."[7]

Alain Robbe-Grillet, in quite a different register, also subverts through his fictional constructs the possibility of interpreting a given "psychology," while confining the seeing consciousness within untransgressible limits. His theoretical pronouncements cast light on this no-man's-land: breakdown of essentialist concepts, discrediting of outworn myths of psychological depth, call for a literary language that would cope strictly and accurately with the world of surfaces. What is at issue is the hypothetical absence of a privileged point of view, the creation of a narrow fictional perspective without recourse to what lies beyond the vision of a single consciousness. Robbe-Grillet favors cyclical structures, the use of the restrictive present indicative, the oppressive repetition of geometric patterns, the anonymity of characters known to us only by their initials or serial numbers. He is fond of detective story devices (but here the seeker and the sought merge), as well as of the labyrinthine riddle of the modern city. Circular deambulation is the most common activity in this fantasy world; it implies that the end is in the beginning, that the mystery remains unsolved.

The seduction of confinement may well be symptomatic of a basic fear of change, of instability, of turbulence. It is surely not a coincidence that some of the most anguished or "unstable" writers of our time rediscovered the Romantic prison metaphor. Jean Genet, for whom the prison cell was not exactly a poetic figure at the outset, but a live experience, sings with arresting syntax of the consolatory beauty of cellular confinement: ". . . the prison cell, which I now love like a vice, brought consolation of myself by oneself" (. . . *m'apporta la consolation de moi-même par soi-même*). It is for him an almost sacred world of security that allows for the stripping of all vain lendings—a place where one can return to the self's center. "The sweet prison cell"—Genet seems to yearn as for a maternal womb. In his work we find, transposed, some of the great prison themes. *The prison haven*: "Prison offered me the first consolation, the first peace . . ."—"Prison offers the prisoner the same feeling of security a royal palace offers the king's guest." *The place of dreams*: in jail, one can "feed on dreams"; ". . . dreams are cultivated in the dark"; jail is the place "where dreams are shaped. . . ." *The locus of myth*: prison is a "fabulous world." Genet himself hesitates to inquire into the precise cause of his prison-nostalgia: "I do not care to know if it is to expiate a crime unknown to me. . . ." What he does know, is that he yearns for the penitentiary: ". . . My nostalgia is so great that they'll have to take me there."[8]

For Samuel Beckett, the inner experience is neither exalting nor exalted. Yet the art of "croaking" (*savoir-crever*) goes hand in hand with a search for a privileged enclosure. The fascination with double incarceration—in the world and in the self—takes on various forms, including the trash-cans that bury alive. The voice in *L'Innommable* (The Unnamable), pondering on the symbolic "enormous prison" in which no human relation is possible, calls for a simple "cell," the wished-for comfortable cell of self-confinement and of an identity that remains until the end problematic: ". . . I'm not outside, I'm inside, I'm in something, I'm shut up [. . .] no need of walls, yes we must have walls, I need walls, good and thick, I need a prison, I was right, for me alone, I'll go there now, I'll put me in it, I'm there already, I'll start looking for me. . . ."[9]

Such a conception of the private cell, no longer viewed as a privileged space for romantic reverie but as the locus of a dark truth, no doubt dramatizes the destitution of modern man whom the pervasive concentration camp experience and threat of mass extinction deprived of even the grim sense of penal solidarity. Neither solitary, nor solidary—that seems to be the harsh conclusion of those who experienced camps. "Solitude was precisely what was lacking in the *sharashka*, as it was in every camp," observes Solzhenitsyn.[10] Nonetheless, the prison image continues to evoke the lonely persona of the writer, though no longer as a glorious Promethean visionary glimpsing the light from his narrow dungeon, but as a hermetic, futile, guilt-ridden figure dreaming, *incommunicado*, of a mandate of redemption that was not conferred upon him. This alienation of the writer is made ironically explicit in Sartre's autobiography *Les Mots*: "I indulged in my darkness, I wished to prolong it, to make a virtue of it. I envied the famous prisoners who in their cells wrote on candle paper. They had kept the obligation to redeem their contemporaries, and lost that of frequenting them."[11]

The conjugation of the redemptive note and the sense of an unviolable solitude confirm the equivocal status of the prison image in the Western tradition. Symbol of incommunicability, it also functions within a soteriological scheme. This basic ambivalence lends itself to other ambiguities, as well as to dialectical structures: on the one hand, inflicted or self-willed sequestration converted into spiritual liberation; on the other, "communication," implying responsible action, but possibly also a denial of the inward life. The modalities of this dialectic, the specific uses made of the symbol, cast light on the concept of man formulated by individual writers and by successive generations. The literature of action and of commitment, in the 1930's and 1940's, rejected a certain type of *lyrisme cellulaire*, and seemed thereby to challenge humanist individualism. A reaction against this literary activism was bound to occur. The 1950's marked a return to a literature of introversion (though not of introspection), a literature of fragmented vision. But this return to images of separation and solitary confinement neither reaffirmed the romantic prestige of individualism nor the prerogatives of the private dream. It embedded writer and reader alike in their bad faith and their bad conscience.

Perhaps it is Camus who most keenly drew the lesson of the specific duplicity and the specific threat involved in this assault on humanistic values. Jean-Baptiste Clamence, the penitent-judge in *La Chute*, takes masochistic delight in debunking his own brand of arrogant liberalism. But the strategy of his "oriented speech" (*discours orienté*), his cunning efforts to draw the invisible listener into an aggressive complicity, make it clear that it is not the spirit of humility that moves him. For he assumes the right to deny innocence to man. If he judges himself severely, it is to be able to judge others—to judge without charity, without redemptive intention. To judge, so as to excel in contempt. "Every man testifies to the crime of all the others. That is my faith and my hope." The aim is an epidemic of guilt. "No excuse ever, for anyone, that is my principle from the outset." And again: "One must begin by extending condemnation to everyone, without discrimination. . . ." The voice of the prophet turns out to be diabolic in its negativity. "I deny good intentions. . . ." But to extend condemnation indiscriminately ("When we will all be guilty, it will be democracy") is to negate the dignity of man.[12]

It is precisely Clamence, the false prophet of a "locked-in little universe," who from within his private hell denounces the *lyrisme cellulaire*. Are we not to understand that for Camus the old dream of the happy prison is infinitely less immoral than this levelling in emptiness, this willing submission to the collective penitentiary? It is the measure of Camus' intellectual honesty and sensitivity to the troubling issues of our age that he was able to deplore the self-centeredness associated with the happy prison, yet also to suggest how much poorer man could be if deprived of the lyrical and spiritual potential symbolized by the private cell. Jean Cayrol, meditating on concentration camps and on the prisoner's dreams, looks ahead with dread to the future: "I think with horror of the refinements that will be introduced into tomorrow's concentration camps, of their even more extraordinary nature, where *man will be deprived even of the gift of suffering*."[13] Maybe it is this that ultimately separates us most sharply from our Romantic heritage: the dream of a happy prison has become hard to entertain in a world of penal colonies and extermination camps, in a world which makes us fear that somehow even our suffering can no longer be our refuge.

Notes

1

1. In *Surveiller et punir. Naissance de la prison* (Gallimard, 1975), Michel Foucault has analyzed the strategy of punishment and the "politics of coercion" in modern society. See also "Les Intellectuels et le pouvoir," entretien Michel Foucault-Gilles Deleuze, *L'Arc*, 49, 1972, p. 6. Chekhov, in one of his most interesting short stories, had already suggested that society affirms itself through enclosure. ("Ward No. 6," in *The Portable Russian Reader*, ed. Bernard Guilbert Guerney, N.Y., The Viking Press, 1947, pp. 244-320.)

2. "Les Poètes et la prison," in *Création et Destinée*, A la Baconnière, Neuchâtel, 1973, pp. 145-146. This article first appeared in *Labyrinthe*, Geneva, 15 October 1945.

3. "Quelques recherches sur l'emploi du temps dans les Prisons d'Etat," préface to *Picciola*, Boston, Otis, Broaders and Company, 1845, pp. 3-38.

4. See the account of the penological polemics in P. Savey-Casard, *Le Crime et la Peine dans l'oeuvre de Victor Hugo*, Presses Universitaires de France, 1956.

5. See Jacques Leauté, *Les Prisons*, Presses Universitaires de France, 1968, pp. 9-12. Michel Foucault rightly insists on the techniques of "Christian monasticism" and the "myths of resurrection." (*Surveiller et punir*, Gallimard, 1975, pp. 125, 242.)

6. *Le G.I.P. enquête dans une Prison modèle: Fleury Mérogis*, 1971, p. 11.

7. Pierre Le Moyne, *Devises héroïques et morales*, Paris, A. Courbé, 1649.

8. Gustave Geffroy, *L'Enfermé* (1897), Fasquelle, 1919, pp. 111, 124, 145, 268.

9. Maurice Lévy, *Le Roman "Gothique" anglais 1764-1824*, Toulouse, Imprimerie M. Espic, 1968, pp. 622-634. Concerning the "anguish of imprisoned space" in Piranesi's work, Marguerite Yourcenar believes that the image of dream structures precedes the "image of real structures." ("Les prisons imaginaires de Piranèse," in *Nouvelle Revue Française*, 97, January 1961, pp. 63-78.)

10. See the remarkable pages by Jean Starobinski in *L'Invention de la liberté*, Skira, 1964, pp. 197-203.

11. Casanova, *Mémoires*, Livre de Poche, 1969, iv, p. 314.

12. Gaston Bachelard, *La Poétique de l'espace*, Presses Universitaires de France, 1957, p. 79.

13. See Albert Béguin's development about Novalis in *L'Ame romantique et le rêve*, J. Corti, 1939, pp. 204-213.

14. Victor Hugo, *Œuvres complètes*, Le Club Français du Livre, xi, pp. 114, 587, 691.

15. Daniel Defoe, *Robinson Crusoe*, Signet-New American Library, 1961, pp. 146-147.

16. Simone Weil, *La Pesanteur et la grâce*, Plon, 1948, pp. 112-113, 146.

17. Villiers de L'Isle-Adam, *Axël*, Les Maitres du Livre, 1912, p. 224.

18. Solzhenitsyn, *The Gulag Archipelago*, Harper & Row, vol. 2, 1974, pp. 604-616.

19. "Dialogo di Torquato Tasso e del suo genio familiare," in *Poesie e prose*, Mondadori, 1949, pp. 874-881.

20. *Libertà—A la Cellule IV bis (prison royale de Gênes)*.

21. *Les Plaisirs et les jours*, Gallimard, 1924, p. 13.

2

1. *Lettres philosophiques*, xxv.

2. *Supplément au Voyage de Bougainville*, ed. Herbert Dieckmann, Librairie Droz, 1955, p. 48.

3. Edmond Estève quotes these lines in "Le 'théâtre monacal' sous la Révolution," in *Etudes de Littérature préromantique*, Champion, 1923, pp. 83-137.

4. The numbers in parentheses after the quotations from the *Pensées* refer to the numbering in the Brunschvicg edition, Hachette, 1909.

5. "Sur la Mort" and "Pour la Profession de Mademoiselle de La Vallière," in *Sermons choisis*, Hachette, 1929, pp. 295, 425.

6. "Pascal," in *Les Métamorphoses du cercle*, Plon, 1961, pp. 50-51.

7. See the year 1832 in *Journal d'un poète*. See also Catharine Savage, "Cette prison nommée la vie: Vigny's Prison Metaphor," in *Studies in Romanticism*, ix, 1970, pp. 99-113. .

8. On the tradition of the body-prison, see Pierre Courcelle, "Tradition Platonicienne et traditions chrétiennes du corps-prison," in *Revue des Etudes Latines*, 43, 1965, t. xliii, pp. 406-443.

9. *Lettres chrétiennes et spirituelles*, 1645-1647, t. ii, p. 33. Quoted by Michel Le Guern, in *L'Image dans l'œuvre de Pascal*, A. Colin, 1969, p. 176.

10. "Pour la Profession de Mademoiselle de la Vallière," "Sur la Mort," in *Sermons choisis*, Hachette, 1929, 419, 421, 299, 305.

11. Cardinal de Bérulle, "Œuvres de piété," lxxviii, cxx, cxciv, in *Œuvres complètes*, J. P. Migne, 1856, pp. 1053-1054, 1145, 1277.

12. Pierre Courcelle, *art. cit.*, pp. 404-443.

13. For a useful discussion of this question, see the article by J. Bainval on the "soul," in *Dictionnaire de théologie catholique*, Letouzey et Ané, 1909.

14. *Pensées et Opuscules*, Hachette, 1909, p. 89. The image of man-the-criminal in prison, waiting for execution in God's cell, is already developed by Saint Thomas More (*A Dialogue of Comfort Against Tribulation*, ed. Leland Miles, Indiana University Press, Bloomington, 1965, III, chap. xx). This text was in fact written in jail.

15. *Œuvres complètes*, Pléiade, 1961, p. 1284.

16. *Le Génie de Pascal*, Hachette, 1924, pp. 192-193.

17. *Pensées et Opuscules*, Hachette, 1909, p. 58.

18. *Le Mie Prigioni*, Ulrico Hoepli, 1932, p. 198. The sentence is attributed to the old priest Giordano, who encouraged him, after his liberation, to write this book.

19. *Le Dieu caché*, Gallimard, 1955, p. 229. *Pascal et son temps*, Plon-Nourrit, 1907, III, p. 411.

20. *Œuvres complètes, op. cit.*, p. 573.

21. "Pascal" in *Les Métamorphoses du cercle*, Plon, 1961, p. 64.

22. *Pensées et Opuscules*, Hachette, 1909, p. 183.

23. Gaston Bachelard, *La Poétique de l'espace*, Presses Universitaires de France, 1957, p. 169.

24. *Essais*, II, 18.

25. J. G. Zimmerman, *Solitude*, London, 1799, pp. 10, 12, 41, 50, 134, 200.

26. *Cinquième promenade*.

3

1. *Ange Pitou*, Nelson, I, 236. *Madame Putiphar*, Léon Willem, 1877, II, 268-269.

2. *Histoire de la Révolution Française*, Œuvres complètes, E. Flammarion, I, 239, 45-46, 7-8.

3. *Ibid.*, I, 241.

4. *Op. cit.*, I, 280.

5. *Op. cit.*, I, 129, 123.

6. *La France Libre*, 2ᵉ édition, 1789, 72.

7. *Apologie de la Bastille, Pour servir de réponse aux Mémoires de M. Linguet sur la Bastille . . . par un homme en pleine campagne*, Kehl et Lausanne, François Lacombe, 1784, p. 71.

8. *Mémoires Historiques et Authentiques sur la Bastille*, London, 2

vols., 1789, ɪ, vii, ix. On the Bastille legend see also A. Arnould et Alboize du Pujol, *Histoire de la Bastille*, Administration de Librairie, 1844, 6 vols.

9. *Ange Pitou*, ɪ, 236 ff. Pétrus Borel, *Madame Putiphar*, Léon Willem, 1877, ɪɪ, 268-269. *Histoire de la Révolution Française*, E. Flammarion, ɪ, 122.

10. See Jean Mistler, *Le 14 Juillet*, Hachette, 1963, 80.

11. See Frantz Funck-Brentano, *Légendes et Archives de la Bastille*, Hachette, 1902, p. 44.

12. *Mémoires Historiques et Authentiques sur la Bastille*, London, 1789.

13. *Les Lettres de cachet*, Hachette, 1926, 239.

14. J. Dussaulx, *Observations sur l'Histoire de la Bastille publiée par Monsieur Linguet*, London, 1783, pp. 5, 36, 109.

15. *Archives de la Bastille*, A. Durand et Pedone-Lauriel, 1866, xxvɪɪ-xxvɪɪɪ. More recently, Jacques Godechot (*La Prise de la Bastille*, Gallimard, 1965, p. 122) maintained that the prisoners were well treated, that they could take walks and play games.

16. *La Bastille au Diable*, chez Laurens, 1790, p. 33.

17. *Les Martyrs vengés*, Calmann Lévy, 1890. Other novels of the same author are: *Le Baron de Trenck*, *Les Martyrs de la Prison*, *Les Mystères de la Bastille*. The latter describes an episode that precedes *Les Martyrs vengés*.

18. That is the case of *Récit Historique de ce qui s'est passé dans la ville de Paris, depuis le commencement de Juillet, jusqu'au 13, 14, 15 et 16 du même mois de l'anée 1789*, De l'Imprimerie de Valleyre, s.d.; and of *La France régénérée ou les traîtres punis*, s.l.n.d.

19. *Le Cachot de Beauvais*, à Aix, chez Gibelin-David et Emaric-David, L'An second de la République française, p. 8. Other texts have telling titles: *Récit des malheurs, peines et souffrances, qu'éprouvaient les prisonniers enfermés à la Bastille. Par un d'eux détenu pendant 50 ans dans cette prison*, Paris, chez Cailleau fils, s.d.; *Lettre d'un ancien prisonnier de la Bastille*, 1790; *Remarques et anecdotes sur le château de la Bastille*, Goujon, 1789; *Particularités concernant la Bastille*, Paris, Volland, s.d.; *Recueil fidèle de plusieurs manuscrits trouvés à la Bastille*, Paris, Girardin, 1789; *Lettre d'un ancien prisonnier de la Bastille*, 1790. The preceding is only a sampling.

20. See *L'Histoire du sieur Abbé-Comte de Bucquoy, singulièrement son évasion du For-L'Evêque et de la Bastille*, Paris, R. Pincebourde, 1866; *L'Inquisition Françoise ou l'Histoire de la Bastille*, Amsterdam, Balthazar Lakeman, 1724, 5 vols.

21. *Dialogue entre le Donjon de Vincennes et la Bastille* (l.l.n.d.), pp. 5, 16. Linguet, *Mémoires sur la Bastille*, London, Thomas Spilsbury, 1783, pp. 4-5. Constantin de Renneville, *L'Inquisition Françoise ou*

l'Histoire de la Bastille, Amsterdam, Balthazar Lakeman, 1724, 5 vols., II, xiv. See also Jean Mistler, *Le 14 Juillet*, Hachette, 1963, p. 70.

22. *Les Oubliettes retrouvées dans les souterrains de la Bastille*, Grangé, s.d.; *Mémoires Historiques et Authentiques sur la Bastille*, v; *Histoire de la Révolution Française*, Pagnerre, Furne et Cie, 1869, II, 371-372; Mirabeau, *Des Lettres de Cachet et des Prisons d'Etat*, Hamburg, 1782, pp. 17-20.

23. Mirabeau, *ibid.*, I, 94; II, 25, 39.

24. Emile Hamont, *Prise de la Bastille, Poème National par le Peuple, Le 14 juillet 1789*, Challamel Ainé, 1881, p. 6.

25. Cesare Beccaria, *Dei Delitti e delle pene*, Florence, Felice le Monnier, 1950, chapter 1, p. ix.

26. *Des Lettres de Cachet et des Prisons d'Etat*, Hamburg, 1782, I, vii, 47, 91, 93-97, 256, 260-261; II, 5, 9, 42, 67.

27. Victorien Sardou, Preface to *Légendes et Archives de la Bastille*, XVI, XXII. Frantz Funck-Brentano, *ibid.*, p. 156.

28. See *Mémoires de Linguet et de Latude suivis de Documents divers sur la Bastille et de fragments concernant la captivité du Baron de Trenck*, Firmin Didot, 1866, pp. 243-248, and also a more piquant version: *Histoire d'une détention de trente-neuf ans dans les prisons d'Etat*, Amsterdam, 1787. Concerning the pride in the escape exploit, Casanova writes in an exemplary fashion: "Thus Providence helped me in the preliminaries to an escape that was to be admirable, if not prodigious. I confess my pride; but this pride does not come from success, since good fortune played a considerable role; it comes from the fact that I considered the exploit feasible and that I had the courage to undertake it." (*Mémoires*, Le Livre de Poche, 1969, IV, 286.)

29. *Mélanges de Littérature*, Le Divan, 1933, II, 265-266.

30. *Légendes et Archives de la Bastille*, pp. 225-227.

31. *Le Comte de Monte-Cristo*, Le Livre de Poche, 1973, I, 206.

32. *Madame Putiphar*, Léon Willem, 1877, pp. 266-267.

33. *L'Inquisition Françoise ou L'Histoire de la Bastille*, Amsterdam, Balthazar Lakeman, 1724, I, 53.

34. *Ange Pitou*, Nelson, I, 236. Elsewhere, he writes concerning the Bastille: "The people hated it as a living thing; it had made of it one of the huge Tarasques, one of these Gévaudan animals that ruthlessly devour human beings" (I, 214).

35. *Dialogue entre le Donjon de Vincennes et la Bastille*, l.l.n.d., pp. 3, 5.

36. *Die so gennante Hölle der Lebendigen das ist die Weltberuffne Bastille zu Paris*, 1719. This German version of the "living hell" tells the escape of the abbé de Bucquoy.

37. Modern society's technology of coercion has been amply dis-

cussed in Michel Foucault's work, in particular in *Surveiller et punir*, Gallimard, 1975.

4

1. Baudelaire, "Pétrus Borel," in *Œuvres Complètes*, Pléiade, 1961, 724-727. Enid Starkie, *Petrus Borel—The Lycanthrope*, London, Faber and Faber, 1954, p. 91.

2. Flaubert, *Correspondance*, Conard, 1926-1933, IV, 454-455.

3. The pages quoted in parentheses refer to the Léon Willem edition, 1877. There is also a recent edition of the novel (Régine Deforges, 1972), with an interesting introduction by Béatrice Didier, " 'Madame Putiphar,' roman sadien?"

4. Baudelaire, "Pétrus Borel," in *Œuvres Complètes*, Pléiade, 1961, pp. 724-727.

5. Some readers have questioned the relation between the prologue and the plot of the novel. Thus Enid Starkie writes: "One wonders why this poem was placed here for it has no connection with the novel . . ." (*op. cit.*, p. 139).

6. Baudelaire, *op. cit.*, p. 725.

7. Janin's article appeared in the *Journal des Débats*, June 3, 1839. For Janin's own parody of prison-hell, see *L'Ane mort* (Ernest Bourdin, 1832), p. 217. This edition has interesting illustrations by Tony Johannot.

8. Eino Railo, *The Haunted Castle*, London, George Routledge, 1927.

9. Maurice Lévy, *Le Roman "Gothique" anglais* (1764-1824), Toulouse, Imprimerie M. Espic, 1968. See also R. Virolle, "Vie et survie du roman noir," in *Manuel d'Histoire Littéraire de la France*, Editions Sociales, 1972, IV, 138-147.

10. *Melmoth the Wanderer*, Boston, Wells and Lilly, 1821, 4 vols., II, 103, 106, 128, 135, 25.

11. *Des Lettres de Cachet et des Prisons d'Etat*, Hamburg, 1782, II, 25, 39. The lines evoked by the expression *le cachot de la faim* are: "*Breve pertugio dentro della muda, / La qual per me ha'l titol de la fame.*"

12. *Notre-Dame de Paris*, Œuvres Complètes, Club Français du Livre, 1967, IV, 116, 118-119.

13. See Edmond Estève, "Le 'théâtre monacal' sous la Révolution," in *Etudes de Littérature Préromantique*, Paris, Champion, 1923, pp. 83-137.

14. See Enid Starkie, *Petrus Borel—The Lycanthrope*, London, Faber and Faber, 1964, p. 98.

15. Mirabeau, *op. cit.*, p. 93.

16. Baudelaire, *op. cit.*, pp. 725-726.

17. *La Nouvelle Justine ou les Malheurs de la Vertu*, Au Cercle du Livre Précieux, 1963, I, 297.

18. Freud, *A General Introduction to Psychoanalysis*, Garden City Publishing Company, 1943, p. 121. The motif of the chink, in relation to the dream of liberation, is typical. Gaston Bachelard, discussing a text of Hermann Hesse which describes a prisoner who painted on his wall a train entering into a tunnel: "... painting his dream, he has escaped through a chink in the wall." (*La Poétique de l'espace*, Presses Universitaires de France, 1957, pp. 141-142.)

5

1. The numerical references after quotations from Stendhal's novels and autobiographical writings are to the Pléiade edition. For all other texts, the Divan edition has been used.

2. For an enlightening discussion of the sources and models of the Farnese Tower, see Harry Levin's "La Citadelle de Parme," *Revue de Littérature Comparée*, 1938, pp. 346-350.

3. For a detailed study of the structural relations between these scenes, see Stephen Gilman, *The Tower as Emblem*, Vittorio Klosterman, Frankfort, 1967, pp. 41-46.

4. Proust very aptly characterized the Stendhalian vision as "*sentiment de l'altitude se liant à la vie spirituelle*" (*A la Recherche du Temps perdu*, Pléiade, 1964, III, 377).

5. *Œuvres intimes*, Pléiade, 1966, p. 373. For a study of Stendhal's affinities with Rousseau, see my article "Stendhal lecteur de Rousseau," in *Revue des Sciences Humaines*, octobre-décembre, 1968, pp. 463-482.

6. An interesting development concerning this tradition can be found in Stephen Gilman, *op. cit.*

7. X. B. Saintine, *Picciola*, J. Hetzel, s.t., p. 28. In a footnote to his edition of *La Chartreuse de Parme* (Garnier, 1942, p. 640), Henri Martineau points out this analogy.

8. This image of the writer's elevated quarters occurs in various contexts. About *Promenades dans Rome*: "... *que je serais heureux à un quatrième étage, en en faisant un pareil* ..." (*Corr.*, VIII, 347). In *Vie de Henry Brulard*: "... *depuis quarante-six ans, mon idéal est de vivre à Paris, dans un quatrième étage, écrivant un drame ou un livre*" (p. 261).

9. Jean Pierre Richard has beautiful developments on the Stendhalian glance dominating landscapes "*nettoyés de toute incertitude,*" and the shadow that protects that glance (*Littérature et Sensation*, Seuil, 1954, pp. 33, 51). See also Jean Starobinski's remarkable pages

on the need to hide and the pleasure of masquerades in "Stendhal pseudonyme," *L'Œil vivant*, Gallimard, 1961, pp. 193-244.

10. The already mentioned passage in *Le Rose et le Vert* also stresses the delights of "being seen." But, in that case, the one who knows himself to be seen does not see. In any case, the metallic sheets provide a separation. One should also recall the game of glances, in *Lucien Leuwen*, between the young lieutenant and Mme de Chasteller, who is protected by her blinds.

11. *Le Décor mythique de la Chartreuse de Parme*, Corti, 1961, p. 162.

12. *Pensées. Filosofia Nova*, I, 153.

13. See Gérard Genette, "Stendhal," in *Figures II*, Seuil, 1969, pp. 155-193; also, for an interesting analysis of the relation of language to silence, Shoshana Felman's discussion of *Armance*, in *La "Folie" dans l'œuvre romanesque de Stendhal*, Corti, 1971, pp. 176, 179, 200.

14. *Pensées. Filosofia Nova*, I, 261, 258-260.

15. *Souvenirs d'Egotisme*, p. 1472. *Prison de soie* can also be read as a pun on *prison de soi* (prison of self).

6

1. The numbers in parentheses refer to Victor Hugo, *Œuvres complètes*, edition Jean Massin, Le Club Français du Livre, 1967-1970, 18 volumes. For *Dieu*, I have utilized the critical editions of René Journet and Guy Robert, *Le Seuil du Gouffre*, Nizet, 1961, and *L'Océan d'en haut*, Nizet, 1960, to which correspond the abbreviations *S.G.* and *O.H.* My friend Joseph Frank drew my attention to the allusion in Dostoevsky's letter.

2. Such a density was denied by Jules Janin (see chapter XXV of *L'Ane mort et la Femme guillotinée*, and Nodier's article in *Journal des Débats*, 26 February 1829.)

3. *Œuvres complètes*, Le Club Français du livre, 1967, III, 616.

4. See Yves Gohin, "Les réalités du crime et de la justice pour Victor Hugo avant 1829," *ibid.*, p. xi.

5. "Actes et Paroles, II." *Œuvres complètes*, Le Club Français du Livre, XII, 866.

6. See Gustave Charlier's article, "Comment fut écrit 'Le Dernier jour d'un condamné,' " in *Revue d'Histoire Littéraire de la France*, 22, 1915, pp. 321-360.

7. *Œuvres complètes*, Le Club Français du Livre, III, 1153, 1199, 1196, 1195.

8. *Ibid.*, IV, 154, 233.

9. *Ibid.*, XI, 361; IX, 292, 358.

10. *Ibid.*, XV, 504-505.

11. *La Terre et les rêveries du repos*, J. Corti, 1948, p. 226.

12. "Les Poètes et la prison," in *Création et destinée*, A la Bacon-nière, Neuchâtel, 1973, p. 145.

13. *Carnets intimes*, Gallimard, 1953, p. 221.

14. "Hugo," in *La Distance intérieure*, Plon, 1962, p. 208.

15. The psychoanalytic criticism of Charles Baudoin (*Psychanalyse de Victor Hugo*, Editions du Mont-Blanc, Geneva, 1943) takes as its point of departure the poem "La Conscience" and stresses the motif of the brother-hatred.

16. The name of Piranesi appears frequently. In "Puits de l'Inde!" it is associated with the *"effrayantes Babels."* In *William Shakespeare*, his *"vertige tragique"* is evoked. In *Dieu*, he is called *"maçon d'apocalypses."* It is moreover interesting that in *Les Contemplations*, Hugo not only associates Piranesi's *"noir cerveau"* to the image of the tower of Babel, but that he counts him among the *"Mages."* On Pi-ranesi and French Romanticism, see Georges Poulet, "Piranèse et les poètes romantiques français," in *Nouvelle Revue Française*, pp. 160 and 161, April and May 1966, pp. 660-671, 849-862; and Luzius Kel-ler, *Piranèse et les Romantiques français*, J. Corti, 1966.

17. Charles Baudoin (*op. cit.*) sees in this motif of the Iron Mask the double symbolism of the sacrificed brother and the guilty brother. In "A Eugène Vicomte H.," the brother who has just died appears in his *cage charnelle*. God has "compressed" his head.

18. *Les Burgraves* also seem composed under the sign of immure-ment. The exposition of the play is done by a choir of captives; the first character to appear is Guanhunara, the chained symbolic figure of slave-hatred.

19. *Les Misérables* (XI, 64).

20. On Hugo's inquiries into prison, see P. Savey-Casard, *Le Crime et la peine dans l'oeuvre de Victor Hugo*, Presses Universitaires de France, 1956.

21. It is not impossible that his curiosity was awakened, during his childhood, through the proximity of his school, the pension Cor-dier, to the prison of the Abbaye. See *Victor Hugo raconté par un té-moin de sa vie*, I, 952.

22. On the structural relationship of Javert to Jean Valjean, see Jean-Pierre Richard's excellent article "Petite lecture de Javert," in *Revue des Sciences Humaines*, 156, 1974, pp. 597-611.

23. In *Les Contemplations* (IX, 149), Dante was first a mountain, then an oak, finally a man and a poet. On death as liberation and as prison, see *Œuvres complètes*, IX, 335-336, 274.

24. Michael Riffaterre has some suggestive observations on the in-finite within the poet's mind in "La poésie métaphysique de Victor Hugo. Style, symboles et thèmes de *Dieu*," in *Romanic Review*, De-cember 1960, pp. 268-276.

25. *Les Misérables*, éd. Garnier, 1957, II, 823.

26. *Ibid.*, ii, 837.

27. According to Enjolras, in *Les Misérables* (xi, 785): *"Comme il n'y aura plus de Satan, il n'y aura plus de Michel."*

7

1. Gianni Mombello, speaking of a literary tradition parallel to the one that was inaugurated by Silvio Pellico's *Le Mie Prigioni*, points out the metrical resemblance of certain poems by Musset, Nerval, and Verlaine. ("Breve nota su 'Mes Prisons' de Verlaine," in *Studi Francesi*, 17, May–August 1962, pp. 292-293.)

2. Gerard de Nerval, *Œuvres*, Pléiade, 1956, i, 85.

3. *Ibid.*, i, 513.

4. The numbers in parentheses refer to the Garnier edition of Nervals *Œuvres* (ed. H. Lemaître), 2 vols., 1958.

5. See J.-P. Richard, "Géographie magique de Nerval," in *Poésie et Profondeur*, Seuil, 1955, pp. 20-22.

6. "Gérard de Nerval," in *Contre Sainte-Beuve*, Gallimard, 1954, p. 165.

7. "Nerval," in *Les Métamorphoses du cercle*, Plon, 1961, p. 248.

8. The obsession with barriers, limits, and the "curse of the crust," has been excellently discussed by Jean-Pierre Richard in "Géographie magique de Nerval," in *Poésie et Profondeur*, Seuil, 1955.

8

1. *Correspondance générale*, Louis Conard, 1947, iii, 39-40.

2. The numbers in parentheses refer to the pages of *Œuvres complètes*, Bibliothèque de la Pléiade, 1963.

3. For a discussion of the network of passive and intentional images in Baudelaire, see Victor Brombert, "The Will to Ecstasy: The Example of Baudelaire's 'La Chevelure,' " in *Yale French Studies*, no. 50, 1974, pp. 55-63.

4. Gaston Bachelard, *La Poétique de l'espace*, Presses Universitaires de France, 1957, pp. 178-179.

5. *Corresp.*, i, 365.

6. *Ibid.*, v, 303.

7. *Ibid.*, i, 289.

8. *Ibid.*, ii, 6, 105; iii, 282.

9. Charles Mauron, *Le Dernier Baudelaire*, J. Corti, 1966, p. 28.

10. *Edgar Poe—Sa vie et ses œuvres*, Gallimard, 1928, p. 17.

11. Jung, *Métamorphoses et Symboles de la libido*, Editions Montaigne, 1931, p. 290.

12. According to Jung (*Un mythe moderne*, Gallimard, 1961, p. 117), the spider in the brain suggests madness or fear of madness.

13. *Corresp.*, III, 30.

14. Jean-Paul Sartre, "Introduction" to Baudelaire's *Ecrits intimes*.

9

1. "Autour des Fortifications," *O.C.*, I, 111. (The initials *O.C.* refer to the *Œuvres Complètes* in the edition G. Crès and Co., 118 vols. 1928-1934.) *Croquis parisiens, O.C.*, VIII, 105. *Le Quartier Saint-Séverin, O.C.*, XI, 30-32.

2. *En Route, O.C.*, XIII, 87.

3. *L'Art moderne, O.C.*, VI, 130. Italics mine.

4. *En Rade, O.C.*, IX, 125.

5. Quoted by Pie Duployé, *Huysmans*, Desclée de Brouwer, 1968, p. 119.

6. *Lettres inédites à Emile Zola*, Droz-Giard, Genève, Lille, 1953, p. 116.

7. *La Cathédrale, O.C.*, I, 122.

8. *L'Art moderne, O.C.*, VI, 117. *A Rebours, O.C.*, 37, 40. "Sac au dos" in *Les Soirées de Médan*, 1880, p. 249.

9. *La Cathédrale, O.C.*, XIV, 140. *A Vau-l'Eau, O.C.*, V, 33. *En Rade, O.C.*, IX, 245. *Là-Bas, O.C.*, XII, i, 149; ii, 8.

10. *A Vau-l'Eau, O.C.*, V, 18.

11. *Lettres inédites à Emile Zola*, pp. 114-115, 102. This horror of the sun is associated with contempt for southern races. See *La Cathédrale, O.C.*, XIV, ii, 68.

12. *Là-Bas, O.C.*, XII, i, 150.

13. *Là-Haut*, Casterman, 1965, p. 121. This text, discovered by A. Artinian, is a first draft of *En Route*.

14. The French is worth quoting: "*Haute en chair, habile, elle effondrait les moëlles, granulait les poumons, démolissait, en quelques tours de baisers, les reins.*" And again: "*. . . il subit énervé jusqu'à crier, le laborieux supplice des échinantes dragues.*" *Là-Bas, O.C.*, XII, i, 151.

15. *Certains, O.C.*, X, 43. Pierre Cogny, *J.-K. Huysmans à la recherche de l'unité*, Nizet, 1953, p. 55. Cogny develops the idea, detecting the complex of impotence: "Very often his reactions are those of a voyeur or of one of these little old men with shining eyes who prowl backstage in music-halls to brush against the dancers, happy to find a cheap illusion of a fleetingly rediscovered sexual vigor."

16. *Croquis parisiens*, O.C., viii, 41.

17. *Là-Bas*, O.C., xii, xii, 19.

18. Letter of November 21, 1900, quoted by Pierre Cogny, *op. cit.*, p. 230.

19. *Certains*, O.C., x, 70.

20. *Là-Haut*, Casterman, 1965, p. 75. Letter to G. Boucher, dated September 15, 1891, quoted by Pierre Cogny, *op. cit.*, p. 149.

21. *Du Côté de chez Swann*, Gallimard, 1929, i, 123; *Les Plaisirs et les jours*, Gallimard, 1924, p. 13.

22. *En Rade*, O.C., ix, 118.

23. *Là-Haut*, Casterman, 1965, p. 210.

24. *La Cathédrale*, O.C., xiv, ii, 112, 276.

25. *Ibid.*, i, 147.

26. *Ibid.*, ii, 129.

27. This is in fact a double, or rather parallel, intercession. It is hardly a coincidence that the landscape of the lesbian *chercheuses d'infini* in Baudelaire's "Femmes damnées" is explicitly associated with the figure of Saint Anthony.

28. Baudelaire, O.C., Pléiade, 1970, pp. 1182-1185, 509.

29. *L'Art moderne*, O.C., pp. 94-95, 242.

30. *En Rade*, O.C., ix, 174-175.

31. *En Route*, O.C., xiii, ii, 223.

32. *Les Sœurs Vatard*, O.C., iii, 323. *Le Drageoir aux épices*, O.C., i, 78-79. *Là-Bas*, O.C., xii, ii, 118.

33. *Là-Bas*, O.C., xii, ii, 144.

34. Letter to J. Boucher dated August 19, 1891. *Là-Haut*, Casterman, 244. *A Rebours*, O.C., vii, 99-100 (italics mine), 134.

35. *A Rebours*, O.C., vii, 99.

36. Letter dated July 8, 1898, quoted by Pierre Cogny, *J.-K. Huysmans à la recherche de l'unité*, Nizet, 1953, p. 211.

37. *L'Oblat*, O.C., xvii, i, 14; ii, 20.

38. Letter to Hannon quoted by Pierre Cogny, *op. cit.*, p. 73. *Lettres inédites à Emile Zola*, Droz-Giard, Genève, Lille, 1953, p. 96. In both quotations italics are mine.

39. *En Route*, O.C., xiii, 31.

40. *A Rebours*, O.C., vii, 330, 120.

41. Letter of February-March 1879, *Correspondance*, Conard, 9 vols., 1926-1933, viii, 225. Quoted by Michael Issacharoff, *J.-K. Huysmans devant la critique en France (1874-1960)*, Klincksieck, 1970, p. 36.

42. Maxime Gaucher, in *Revue Politique et Littéraire*, quoted in the edition of *Les Sœurs Vatard*, O.C., iii, 338.

10

1. Jean-Paul Sartre, *Situations II*, Gallimard, 1948, p. 245.

2. Literally: the "cell of spits."

3. Balzac, *La Peau de chagrin*, Classiques Garnier, 1955, pp. 97-98, 102.

4. Serge Doubrovsky, *La Place de la madeleine*, Mercure de France, 1974, pp. 72-73. Paul de Man, "Proust et l'allégorie de la lecture," in *Mouvements premiers. Etudes critiques offertes à Georges Poulet*, J. Corti, 1972, pp. 233, 243.

5. Chekhov, "Ward No. 6," in *The Portable Russian Reader*, New York, The Viking Press, 1947, p. 300.

6. Thomas Mann, *Death in Venice*, New York, Vintage Books, 1959, p. 24.

7. Malraux, *La Condition humaine*, Livre de Poche, 1962, pp. 246, 233; *Antimémoires*, Gallimard, 1967, pp. 39-40, 42.

8. *Antimémoires*, Gallimard, 1967, p. 213.

9. Victor Serge, *Les Hommes dans la prison*, in *Les Révolutionnaires*, Seuil, 1967, pp. 9, 11, 121.

10. *Ibid.*, pp. 70, 79, 33, 87.

11. Zamiatin, *We*, Dutton, New York, 1959, p. 34.

12. André Biély, *Pétersbourg*, Editions L'Age d'Homme, Lausanne, 1967 (translation by Georges Nivat and Jacques Catteau), pp. 24-25, 110, 113, 180, 299-300. Michel Foucault speaks of the "carceral city," of the "great carceral continuum." (*Surveiller et punir*, Gallimard, 1975, pp. 304, 314.)

13. Balzac, *Le Père Goriot*, Garnier, 1960, p. 7; Dickens, *Little Dorrit*, Penguin Books, 1967, pp. 67, 70; Melville, *Moby Dick*, Rinehart and Co., New York, 1957, pp. 1-2.

14. Walter Jens, *Le Monde des Accusés* (traduction de *Nein. Die Welt der Angeklagten*), Plon, 1950. See in particular pp. 35-37, 75, 87, 130-133.

15. Jean Cayrol, *Lazare parmi nous*, A la Baconnière, Neuchâtel, et Seuil, 1950, p. 69.

16. Michel Borvicz, *Ecrits des condamnés à mort sous l'Occupation allemande (1939-1945)*, Presses Universitaires de France, 1954, pp. 113, 205, 261.

17. David Rousset, *L'Univers concentrationnaire*, Editions du Pavois, 1946, p. 30. According to Solzhenitsyn, prison demands an ennobling moral effort. "But in camp, it would appear, you do not have that path." (*The Gulag Archipelago*, II, New York, Harper & Row, 1974, p. 619.)

18. Victor Serge, *op. cit.*, pp. 20, 70, 33, 87, 89, 54, 115.
19. David Rousset, *op. cit.*, pp. 13, 38, 63, 64-65, 85, 107, 185.
Jean Cayrol, *op. cit.*, pp. 17-18, 32, 40, 45, 50-51.
20. Camus, *La Peste*, Livre de Poche, p. 171.
21. Victor Serge, *op. cit.*, pp. 16, 113, 54.
22. Jean-Paul Sartre, *Situations II*, Gallimard, 1948, pp. 20-21.
23. Camus, *L'Exil et le Royaume*, Gallimard, 1957, p. 183; *La Peste*, Livre de Poche, p. 139.

11

1. *Situations II*, pp. 112, 313.
2. Jacques Guicharnaud very aptly observes this tendency on the part of Sartre's characters to reject the tyranny of a scenario written in advance (*Modern French Theater*, Yale University Press, New Haven, 1961, p. 142).
3. "Question de méthode," in *Critique de la raison dialectique*, Gallimard, 1960, pp. 63, 71.
4. *Situations II*, pp. 245, 153-154.
5. "Qu'est-ce que la littérature?" in *Situations II*, Gallimard, 1948, pp. 246, 248, 250.
6. *Situations II*, p. 112.
7. *Ibid.*, p. 250.
8. *L'Age de raison*, Gallimard, 1945, p. 118; *La Mort dans l'âme*, Gallimard, 1949, p. 245.
9. *L'Etre et le Néant*, Gallimard, 1943, p. 277.
10. *L'Age de raison*, Gallimard, 1945, p. 53. Italics mine.
11. *Ibid.*, p. 176.
12. *Ibid.*, pp. 43-44.
13. The notion of consciousness, in Sartre's work, almost automatically conjures up the image of the wall: ". . . another consciousness, a little frightened light that would fly about, knock against walls, unable to escape." (*Ibid.*, p. 51.)
14. *Ibid.*, pp. 15, 23, 272.
15. *Situations II*, pp. 155, 277.
16. *L'Etre et le Néant*, p. 639.
17. *Situations II*, pp. 311-312.
18. *Ibid.*, p. 313.
19. *Ibid.*, pp. 21-22; Malraux, "Préface" to *Le Temps du mépris*, Gallimard, 1935, pp. 10-11.
20. *Critique de la raison dialectique*, Gallimard, 1960, pp. 24-25.

12

1. Simone de Beauvoir, *Le Sang des autres*, Marguerat, 1946, pp. 19, 37, 90, 117, 158, 179, 242, 328–329.

2. Malraux, *La Condition humaine*, Livre de Poche, pp. 52, 150, 197; *L'Espoir*, Gallimard, 1937, p. 165.

3. Jean Starobinski, preface to Kafka's *La Colonie pénitentiaire*, Egloff, 1945, pp. 33, 24.

4. Kafka, "Brief an den Vater," in *Hochzeitsvorbereitungen auf dem Lande*, Schocken, New York, 1953, p. 217.

5. Kafka, "Er," in *Beschreibung eines Kampfes*, Schocken Books, New York, 1946, p. 279; *Journal intime*, introduction and translation by Pierre Klossowski, Grasset, 1945, pp. 251, 195.

6. Vyacheslav Ivanov, *Freedom and the Tragic Life*, Harvill Press, London, 1952, pp. 21, 44, 61, 78, 165.

7. Nathalie Sarraute, *Le Planétarium*, Gallimard, 1959, pp. 87, 187, 276, 287.

8. Jean Genet, *Journal d'un voleur*, Gallimard, 1949, pp. 91, 93, 272. *Œuvres complètes*, Gallimard, 1961, pp. 49, 114, 249.

9. Samuel Beckett, *L'Innommable*, Editions de Minuit, 1953, pp. 250-253. (*Three Novels by Samuel Beckett*, Grove Press, 1955, p. 410.)

10. *The First Circle*, Harper & Row, 1968, p. 250.

11. Jean-Paul Sartre, *Les Mots*, Gallimard, 1964, p. 152.

12. Camus, *La Chute*, Livre de Poche, 1956, pp. 119, 142, 143, 147.

13. Jean Cayrol, *op. cit.*, p. 28. Italics mine.

Bibliography

The following bibliography is limited to the works cited in the text.

Alfieri, *Opere*, Milano, U. Mursia, 1965.

Andreyev, Leonid, *The Seven Who Were Hanged*, New York, Illustrated Editions Company, 1941.

——*Thought*, in *The Portable Russian Reader*, ed. Bernard Guilbert Guernay, New York, The Viking Press, 1947, pp. 339-398.

Andryane (Alexandre), *Mémoires d'un prisonnier d'Etat au Spielberg*, Ladvocat, 1837-1838, 4 vol.

Anecdote Rare et piquante sur la Bastille, Trouvée parmi les chiffons de la rue Saint-Antoine, avec le titre: Respectez les trous, La Grange, 1789.

Apologie de la Bastille, Pour servir de réponse aux Mémoires de M. Linguet sur la Bastille . . . par un homme en pleine campagne, Kehl and Lausanne, François Lacombe, 1784.

Archives de la Bastille, A. Durand and Pedone-Lauriel, 1866.

Ariosto (Ludovico), *L'Orlando furioso*, Prato, Nella Stamperia di Luigi Vannini, 1816, 10 vol.

Arnould (A.) and Alboize du Pujol, *Histoire de la Bastille*, Administration de Librairie, 1844, 4 vol.

Arx Parisiensis expugnata et deleta. Carmen, par A. H., 1790.

Augustin (saint), *De Vera religione (De la Véritable religion)*, A. de La Roche, 1725.

Bachelard (Gaston), *La Poétique de l'espace*, Presses Universitaires de France, 1957.

——*La Terre et les rêveries du repos*, J. Corti, 1948.

Balzac (Honoré de), *La Peau de chagrin*, Classiques Garnier, 1955.

—— *Le Père Goriot*, Classiques Garnier, 1960.

La Bastille au Diable, chez Laurens, junior, 1790.

La Bastille Dévoilée ou Recueil de pièces authentiques pour servir à son histoire, Desenne, 1789, 3 vol.

Baudelaire (Charles), *Correspondance générale*, Louis Conard, 1947 (in *Œuvres complètes*, vol. 13-17).

——*Edgar Poë—Sa vie et ses œuvres*, Gallimard, 1928.

——*Œuvres complètes*, Bibliothèque de la Pléiade, 1963.

Baudoin (Charles), *Psychanalyse de Victor Hugo*, Editions du Mont-Blanc, Geneva, 1943 (A. Colin, 1972).

Beauvoir (Simone de), *Le Sang des autres*, Marguerat, 1946.

Beccaria (Cesare), *Dei Delitti e delle pene*, Firenze, Felice Le Monnier, 1950.

Beckett (Samuel), *L'Innommable*, Editions de Minuit, 1953.

Béguin (Albert), *L'Ame romantique et le rêve*, J. Corti, 1939.

——«Les Poètes et la prison», in *Création et Destinée*, A la Baconnière, Neuchâtel, 1973.

Bérulle (cardinal de), *Œuvres complètes*, J.P. Migne, 1856.

Biély (André), *Pétersbourg*, Lausanne, Editions l'Age d'Homme, 1967.

Blanc (Louis), *Histoire de la Révolution Française*, Pagnerre, Furne et Cie, 1869-1870, 12 vol.

Borel (Pétrus), *Champavert*, Editions La Force Française, 1922.

——*Madame Putiphar*, Léon Willem, 1877, 2 vol.

Borvicz (Michel), *Ecrits des condamnés à mort sous l'Occupation allemande (1939-1945)*, Presses Universitaires de France, 1954.

Bossuet (Bénigne), *Sermons choisis*, Hachette, 1929.

Briussov (Valery), *The Republic of the Southern Cross and other stories*, London, Constable Russian Library, 1918.

Brombert (Victor), «Stendhal lecteur de Rousseau», *Revue des Sciences Humaines*, October-December 1958, pp. 463-482.

——"The Will to Ecstasy: The Example of Baudelaire's 'La Chevelure,' " *Yale French Studies*, 50, 1974, pp. 55-63.

Brunschvicg (Léon), *Le Génie de Pascal*, Hachette, 1924.

Butor (Michel), *Répertoire II*, Editions de Minuit, 1964.

Byron (George Gordon, Lord), *The Poetical Works*, New York and London, Oxford University Press, 1946.

Le Cachot de Beauvais, A Aix, chez Gibelin-David et Emeric-David, L'An second de la République française.

Camus (Albert), *La Chute*, Gallimard, 1956.

——*L'Etranger*, Livre de Poche, 1957.

——*L'Exil et le Royaume*, Gallimard, 1957.

——*La Peste*, Gallimard, 1947.

Casanova (Giacomo), *Mémoires*, Livre de Poche, 4 vol.

Cau (Jean), *La Pitié de Dieu*, Gallimard, 1961.

Cayrol (Jean), *Lazare parmi nous*, A la Baconnière, Neuchâtel, et Seuil, 1950.

Cellini (Benvenuto), *Vita*, Rizzoli, 1954.

Charlier (Gustave), «Comment fut écrit "Le Dernier Jour d'un condamné"», *Revue d'Histoire Littéraire de la France*, 22, 1915, pp. 321-360.

Chekhov, Anton, "Ward No. 6," in *The Portable Russian Reader*, ed. Bernard Guilbert Guerney, New York, The Viking Press, 1947, pp. 244-320.

Chénier (André), *Œuvres complètes*, Bibliothèque de la Pléiade, 1950.

Chénier (Marie-Joseph), *Fénelon, ou les Religieuses de Cambrai*, Paris, Moutard, 1793.

Cogny (Pierre), *J.-K. Huysmans à la recherche de l'unité*, Nizet, 1953.

Corbière (Tristan), *Les Amours jaunes*, Gallimard, 1973.

Courcelle (Pierre), «Tradition Platonicienne et traditions chrétiennes du corps-prison», *Revue des Etudes Latines*, 43, 1965, t. XLIII, pp. 406-443.

Defoe (Daniel), *Robinson Crusoe*, New York, Signet Classics, 1961.

de Man (Paul), «Proust et l'allégorie de la lecture», in *Mouvements premiers. Etudes critiques offertes à Georges Poulet*, José Corti, 1972.

Desmoulins (Camille), *La France libre*, s.l., 1789.

————*Révolutions de France et de Brabant*, P. Garnery, Paris, 1791.

Dialogue entre le Donjon de Vincennes et la Bastille, l.l.n.d.

Dickens (Charles), *Little Dorrit*, Penguin Books, 1967.

Diderot (Denis), *Supplément au Voyage de Bougainville*, ed. Herbert Dieckmann, Geneva, Librairie Droz, 1955.

Didier (Béatrice), «"Madame Putiphar", roman sadien?», introduction to *Madame Putiphar* by Pétrus Borel, Regine Deforges, 1972.

Die so genannte Hölle der Lebendigen das ist die Weltberuffne Bastille zu Paris, 1719.

Dostoyevsky, Fyodor, *The Brothers Karamazov*, Signet Classics, 1957.

————*The House of the Dead*, New York, Grove Press.

————*Krotkaia*, translation by F. Halpérine, Paris, 1866.

————*Notes from Underground*, Dutton, 1960.

————*The Possessed,* Signet, 1962.

Doubrovsky (Serge), *La Place de la madeleine*, Mercure de France, 1974.

Dumas (Alexandre), *Ange Pitou*, Collection Nelson, 1923.

————*Le Comte de Monte-Cristo*, Livre de Poche, 1973.

————*La Tulipe noire*, Calmann Lévy, 1892.

Du Noyer (Mme), *Lettres de deux Dames au Sujet de l'abbé de Bucquoy*, R. Pincebourde, 1866.

Duployé (Pie), *Huysmans*, Desclée de Brouwer, 1968.

Durand (Gilbert), *Le Décor mythique de la Chartreuse de Parme*, José Corti, 1961.

Durand (Gilbert), *Les Structures anthropologiques de l'imaginaire*, Presses Universitaires de France, 1960.

Dussaulx (J.), *Observations sur l'Histoire de la Bastille publiée par Monsieur Linguet*, London, 1783.

Estève (Maurice), «Le "théâtre monacal" sous la Révolution», in *Etudes de Littérature préromantique*, Champion, 1923.

Faucher (Léon), *De la Réforme des Prisons*, Angé, 1838.

Felman (Shoshana), *La «Folie» dans l'œuvre romanesque de Stendhal*, José Corti, 1971.

Flaubert (Gustave), *Correspondance*, Conard, 1926-1933, 9 vol.

———*Novembre*, in *Œuvres complètes*, L. Conard, 1910, 18 vol.

Foucault (Michel), *Histoire de la Folie à l'âge classique*, Plon, 1961.

———«Les intellectuels et le pouvoir», entretien Michel Foucault-Gilles Deleuze, *L'Arc*, 49, 1972.

———*Surveiller et punir. Naissance de la prison*, Gallimard, 1975.

La France régénérée ou les traîtres punis, s.l.n.d.

Freud (Sigmund), *A General Introduction to Psychoanalysis*, Garden City Publishing Company, 1943.

Funck-Brentano (Frantz), *Légendes et Archives de la Bastille*, Hachette, 1902.

———*Les Lettres de cachet*, Hachette, 1926.

Geffroy (Gustave), *L'Enfermé*, Fasquelle, 1919.

Genet (Jean), *Journal d'un voleur*, Gallimard, 1949.

———*Œuvres complètes*, Gallimard, 1951.

Genette (Gérard), «Stendhal» in *Figures II*, Seuil, 1969, pp. 155-193.

Gerstenberg (Heinrich Wilhelm von), *Ugolino*, Mainz, 1789.

Gide (André), *Les Faux-Monnayeurs*, Gallimard, 1925.

Gilman (Stephen), *The Tower as Emblem*, Vittorio Klosterman, Frankfurt, 1967.

Le G.I.P. enquête dans une Prison Modèle: Fleury Mérogis, 1971.

Godechot (Jacques), *La Prise de la Bastille*, Gallimard, 1965.

Gohin (Yves), «Les réalités du crime et de la justice pour Victor Hugo avant 1829», in Victor Hugo, *Œuvres complètes*, Le Club Français du Livre, 1967, III, pp. i-xxvi.

Goldman (Lucien), *Le Dieu caché*, Gallimard, 1955.

Guilloux (Louis), *Le Sang noir*, Gallimard, 1935.

Hamont (Emile), *Prise de la Bastille, Poème National par le Peuple, Le 14 juillet 1789*, Challamel Aîné, 1881.

Histoire du sieur abbé-comte de Bucquoy, singulièrement son évasion du For-L'Evêque et de la Bastille, Paris, R. Pincebourde, 1866.

Hoffmann (E.T.A.), *Die Elixiere des Teufels*, Walter de Gruyter and Co., Berlin, 1958.

——*Der Goldene Topf*, in *Gesammelte Schriften*, Berlin, Georg Reimer, 1873.

Hugo (Victor), *Carnets intimes*, Gallimard, 1953.

——*Dieu*, critical editions by René Journet and Guy Robert (*Le Seuil du gouffre*, Nizet, 1961 et *L'Océan d'en haut*, Nizet, 1960).

——*Les Misérables*, Editions Garnier, 1957, 2 vol.

——*Œuvres complètes*, Le Club Français du Livre, 1967-1970, 18 vol.

Huysmans (J.-K.), *Là-Haut*, Casterman, 1965.

——*Lettres inédites à Emile Zola*, Droz-Giard, Genève et Lille, 1953.

——*Œuvres complètes*, G. Crès et Cie, 1928-1934, 18 vol.

—— «Sac au dos», in *Les Soirées de Médan*, 1880.

L'Imitation de Jésus-Christ, F. Alcan, 1906.

Issacharoff (Michael), *J. K. Huysmans devant la critique en France (1874-1960)*, Klincksieck, 1970.

Jacob (Paul, L., dit «Le Bibliophile»), «Quelques recherches sur l'Emploi du temps dans les Prisons d'Etat», preface to Saintine's *Picciola*, Boston, Otis, Broaders et Cie, 1845.

Janin (Jules), *L'Ane mort et la Femme guillotinée*, Ernest Bourdin, 1842 (illustrations by Tony Johannot).

Jens (Walter), *Le Monde des Accusés* (translation of *Nein. Die Welt der Angeklagten*), Plon, 1950.

Jung (Carl Gustav), *Métamorphoses et Symboles de la libido*, Editions Montaigne, 1931.

——*Un Mythe moderne. Des «signes du ciel»*, Gallimard, 1961.

Kafka (Franz), *Beschreibung eines Kampfes*, New York, Von Schocken Books, 1946.

——*The Complete Stories*, New York, Schocken Books, 1971.

——*Hochzeitsvorbereitungen auf dem Lande*, S. Fischer Verlage, New York, Von Schocken Books, 1953.

——*The Diaries*, New York, Schocken Books, 1948-1949.

Keller (Luzius), *Piranèse et les Romantiques français*, José Corti, 1966.

Lachabeaussière, *Les Huit Mois d'un détenu aux Madelonnetes* (*sic*), s.l.n.d.

Laporte (Roger), «Kafka: Le dehors et le dedans», *Critique*, May 1967, pp. 407-419.

Latude (Henri Masers de), *Le Despotisme dévoilé ou Mémoires de Henri*

Masers de Latude, in *Mémoires de Linguet et de Latude suivis de Documents divers sur la Bastille et de fragments concernant la captivité du Baron de Trenck*, Firmin Didot, 1866.

————*Histoire d'une détention de trente-neuf ans dans les prisons d'état*, Amsterdam, 1787.

————*Mémoires de Henri Masers de Latude, Ancien Ingénieur*, Nouvelle Edition, revue, corrigée et augmentée par le citoyen Thierry, 2 vol., De l'Imprimerie de la Veuve Lejay, Desenne et Denné, 1793.

Leauté (Jacques), *Les Prisons*, Presses Universitaires de France, 1968.

Le Guern (Michel), *L'Image dans l'œuvre de Pascal*, A. Colin, 1969.

Le Langage des Murs ou les Cachots de la Bastille dévoilant leurs secrets, Lefevre, 1789.

Le Moyne (Pierre), *Devises héroïques et morales*, A. Courbé, 1649.

Leopardi (Giacomo), «Dialogo di Torquato Tasso e del suo genio familiare», in *Le Poesie e le Prose*, Arnaldo Mondadori, 1949, 1, pp. 874-881.

Le Petit (Claude), *Les Œuvres libertines*, Paris, Imprimerie de Capiomont, 1918.

Lettre d'un ancien prisonnier de la Bastille, 1790.

Levin (Harry), «La Citadelle de Parme», *Revue de Littérature Comparée*, 1938, pp. 346-350.

Lévy (Maurice), *Le Roman «Gothique» anglais (1764-1824)*, Toulouse, Imprimerie M. Espic, 1968.

Lewin (Bertram D.), *The Psychoanalysis of Elation*, London, The Hogarth Press, 1951.

Lewis (Mathew G.), *The Monk*, New York, Grove Press, 1952.

Linguet, *Mémoires sur la Bastille et sur la détention de M. Linguet, écrits par lui-même*, London, Thomas Spilsbury, 1783.

London (Jack), *The Star Rover*, New York, The Macmillan Co., 1917.

Lukács (Georg), *Existentialisme ou marxisme*, Nagel, 1948.

Malraux (André), *Antimémoires*, Gallimard, 1967.

————*La Condition humaine*, Gallimard, 1933.

————*L'Espoir*, Gallimard, 1937.

————*Le Temps du mépris*, Gallimard, 1935.

Mann (Thomas), *Death in Venice*, New York, Vintage Books, 1959.

————*Tonio Kröger*, S. Fischer, Berlin, 1923.

Maturin (Charles Robert), *Melmoth the Wanderer*, Boston, Wells and Lilly, 1821, 4 vol.

Mauron (Charles), *Le Dernier Baudelaire*, José Corti, 1966.

Melville (Herman), *Moby Dick*, New York, Rinehart and Co., 1947.

Mémoires Historiques et Authentiques sur la Bastille, London, 1789, 2 vol.

Mémoires de Linguet et de Latude suivis de Documents divers sur la Bastille et de fragments concernant la captivité du Baron de Trenck, Firmin Didot, 1866.

Michelet (Jules), *Histoire de la Révolution Française*, in *Œuvres Complètes*, E. Flammarion, 1893-1899.

Milton (John), *Paradise Lost*, New York, The Odyssey Press, 1935.

Mirabeau (Honoré-Gabriel, comte de), *Des Lettres de Cachet et des Prisons d'Etat*, Hamburg, 1782.

Mistler (Jean), *Le 14 juillet*, Hachette, 1963.

Mombello (Gianni), «Breve nota su "Mes Prisons" de Verlaine», *Studi Francesi*, 17, May-August 1962, pp. 292-293.

Montaigne, *Essais*, Classiques Garnier, 1942, 3 vol.

Monvel (Jacques Marie Boutet de), *Les Victimes cloîtrées*.

More (saint Thomas), *A Dialogue of Comfort Against Tribulations*, ed. Leland Miles, Bloomington, Indiana University Press, 1965.

Nerval (Gérard de), *Œuvres*, Bibliothèque de la Pléiade, 1956.

————*Œuvres*, Classiques Garnier, 1958, 2 vol.

Les Oubliettes retrouvées dans les souterrains de la Bastille, Grangé, s.d.

Particularités concernant la Bastille, Paris, Volland, s.d.

Pascal, *Pensées et Opuscules*, ed. Brunschvicg, Hachette, 1909.

Pellico (Silvio), *Le Mie Prigioni*, Ulrico Hoepli, 1932.

Plato, *Works*, ed. B. Jowett, New York, Tudor Publishing Company, s.d.

Poulet (Georges), *La Distance intérieure*, Plon, 1952.

————*Les Métamorphoses du cercle*, Plon, 1961.

————«Piranèse et les poètes romantiques français», *Nouvelle Revue Française*, 160 et 161, April, May 1966, pp. 660-671, 849-862.

La Prise de la Bastille, Hiérodrame tiré des Livres saints suivi du cantique en Actions de grâces, *Te Deum Laudamus*, par M. Desaugiers.

Proust (Marcel), *A la Recherche du Temps perdu*, Bibliothèque de la Pléiade, 1954.

————*Contre Sainte-Beuve*, Gallimard, 1954.

————*Du Côté de chez Swann*, Gallimard, 1929.

————*Les Plaisirs et les jours*, Gallimard, 1924.

Ravaisson (François), *Introduction aux Archives de la Bastille*, A. Durand and Pedone-Lauriel, 1866.

Récit Historique de qui s'est passé dans la Ville de Paris, depuis le com-

mencement de Juillet, jusqu'au 13, 14, 15 et 16 du même mois de l'an-née 1789, de l'Imprimerie de Valleyre, s.d.

Récit des malheurs, peines et souffrances, qu'éprouvaient les prisonniers en-fermés à la Bastille. Par un d'eux détenu pendant 50 ans dans cette prison, Paris, chez Cailleau fils, s.d.

Recueil fidèle de plusieurs manuscrits trouvés à la Bastille, Paris, Girardin, 1789.

Remarques et anecdotes sur le château de la Bastille, Goujon, 1789.

Renneville (Constantin de), *L'Inquisition Françoise ou l'Histoire de la Bastille*, Amsterdam, Balthazar Lakeman, 1724, 5 vol.

Richard (Jean-Pierre), *Littérature et Sensation*, Seuil, 1954.

————*Poésie et Profondeur*, Seuil, 1955.

Riffaterre (Michael), « La poésie métaphysique de Victor Hugo. Style, symboles et thèmes de *Dieu* », *Romanic Review*, December 1960, pp. 268-276.

Robbe-Grillet (Alain), « Une voie pour le roman futur », *Nouvelle Nouvelle Revue Française*, July 1956, pp. 77-84.

Robert (Clémence), *Les Martyrs vengés*, Calmann-Lévy, 1890.

Rosa (Guy), Présentation des « Feuilles paginées », in Victor Hugo, *Œuvres complètes*, Le Club Français du Livre, 1967, III, pp. 1151-1162.

Rost (Nico), *Goethe in Dachau*, Munich, 1948.

Rousseau (Jean-Jacques), *Les Rêveries du promeneur solitaire*, Classiques Garnier, 1960.

Rousset (David), *L'Univers concentrationnaire*, Editions du Pavois, 1946.

Sade (marquis de), *La Nouvelle Justine ou les Malheurs de la vertu*, Au Cercle du Livre Précieux, 1963.

Saint-Cyran, *Lettres Chrestiennes et Spirituelles*, Paris, 1645-1647.

Saintine (Xavier Boniface), *Picciola*, J. Hetzel, s.d.

San Pedro (Diego de), *Cárcel de amor*, Madrid, Castalia, 1972.

Sardou (Victorien), Preface to *Légendes et Archives de la Bastille*, Hachette, 1902.

Sarraute (Nathalie), *L'Ere du Soupçon*, Gallimard, 1956.

————*Le Planétarium*, Gallimard, 1959.

Sartre (Jean-Paul), *L'Age de raison*, Gallimard, 1945.

————*Critique de la raison dialectique*, Gallimard, 1960.

————*Le Diable et le bon Dieu*, Gallimard, 1951.

————*L'Etre et le Néant*, Gallimard, 1943.

————*Les Mains sales*, Gallimard, 1948.

————*La Mort dans l'âme*, Gallimard, 1949.

————*Les Mots*, Gallimard, 1964.

————*Le Mur*, Gallimard, 1939.

————«Présentation des *Temps Modernes*», in *Situations II*, Gallimard, 1948, pp. 9-30.

————*Les Séquestrés d'Altona*, Gallimard, 1960.

————*Saint-Genet: comédien et martyr*, Gallimard, 1952.

————*Situations II*, Gallimard, 1948.

————*Théâtre*, Gallimard, 1947.

Savage (Catherine), «Cette prison nommée la vie: Vigny's Prison Metaphor», *Studies in Romanticism*, IX, 1970, pp. 99-113.

Savey-Casard (P.), *Le Crime et la Peine dans l'œuvre de Victor Hugo*, Presses Universitaires de France, 1956.

Schiller, *Werke*, Leipzig, 1895, 12 vol.

Senancour (Etienne Jean-Baptiste de), *Oberman*, 10/18, 1965.

Serge (Victor), *Les Hommes dans la Prison*, in *Les Révolutionnaires*, Seuil, 1967.

Shakespeare (William), *The Tragedy of King Lear*, Yale University Press, New Haven, 1947.

Solzhenitsyn, Alexander, *The First Circle*, New York, Harper & Row, 1968.

————*The Gulag Archipelago*, II, New York, Harper & Row, 1974.

Starkie (Enid), *Petrus Borel—The Lycanthrope*, London, Faber and Faber, 1954.

Starobinski (Jean), *L'Invention de la liberté*, Skira, 1964.

————*L'Œil vivant*, Gallimard, 1961.

————Preface to *La Colonie pénitentiaire* de Franz Kafka, Egloff, 1945.

Steinmetz (Jean-Luc), «Les Malheurs du récit», Postscript to *Madame Putiphar* by Pétrus Borel, Regine Deforges, 1972.

Stendhal, *La Chartreuse de Parme*, Classiques Garnier, 1942.

————*Mélanges de Littérature*, Le Divan, 1933.

————*Œuvres complètes*, Le Divan, 1927-1937, 79 vol.

————*Œuvres intimes*, Bibliothèque de la Pléiade, 1966.

————*Romans*, Bibliothèque de la Pléiade, 1968, 1972.

Strowski (Fortunat), *Pascal et son temps*, Plon-Nourrit, 1907.

Tasso (Torquato), *Poesie*, Rizzoli, Milano-Rome, 1934.

Tristan L'Hermite, *Les Amours et autres poèmes choisis*, Classiques Garnier, 1925.

Verlaine (Paul), *Œuvres poétiques complètes*, Bibliothèque de la Pléiade, 1965.

Verne (Jules), *Voyage au centre de la terre*, Livre de Poche, 1966.

Vidocq (Eugène François), *Mémoires*, Les Amis du Club du Livre, 1959.

Vigny (Alfred de), *Œuvres complètes*, Bibliothèque de la Pléiade, 1948, 2 vol.

Villiers de L'Isle-Adam (Auguste), *Axël*, Les Maîtres du Livre, 1912.

Virolle (R.), «Vie et survie du roman noir», in *Manuel Littéraire de la France*, Editions sociales, 1972.

Voltaire, *Lettres philosophiques*, Classiques Garnier, 1962.

————*Questions sur l'Encyclopédie*, in *Œuvres complètes*, Kehl, Imprimerie de la Société littéraire Typographique, 1785-1789, vol. 46.

Walpole (Horace), *The Castle of Otranto*, New York, Dover Publications, 1966.

Weil (Simone), *La Pesanteur et la grâce*, Plon, 1948.

Wordsworth (William), *The Poetical Works*, New York, Oxford University Press, 1933.

Yourcenar (Marguerite), «Les prisons imaginaires de Piranèse», *Nouvelle Revue Française*, 97, January 1961, pp. 63-78.

Zimmerman (J. G.), *Solitude*, London, 1799.

Index of Proper Names

LIBRARY OF CONGRESS CATALOGING IN PUBLICATION DATA

Brombert, Victor H.
  The romantic prison.

  Translation of La prison romantique.
  Bibliography: p.
  Includes index.
  1. French literature—History and criticism.
2. Prisons in literature.   I.   Title.
PQ145.4.P7B713   840'.9'32   77-85532
ISBN 0-691-06352-4